Praise for Knitting For Dummies

"*Knitting For Dummies* is an excellent book for new knitters or those who want to know more about the craft. As a huge fan of Pam Allen's work, I was delighted to see how she has shared both her design skill and technical knowledge."

> — Debbie Bliss, knitwear designer and author of
> *Debbie Bliss Knitting Workbook, Family Knits: Over
> 25 Versatile Designs for Babies, Children, and Adults,*
> and *Great Knits for Kids: Classic Designs for Infants to
> Ten-Year Olds*

"Pam Allen is one of this country's most gifted and generous knitwear designers and knitting teachers. Her skill, enthusiasm, and many years of experience come together in this comprehensive book of beginning and intermediate knitting techniques. If we're lucky, this will be the first of many knitting books from Allen."

> — Melanie Falick, Editor-in-Chief, *Interweave Knits*,
> author of *Knitting in America* and *Kids Knitting*,
> co-author of *Knitting for Baby*

"The next best thing to having Pam Allen as your personal knitting teacher is having *Knitting For Dummies* by your side like a knowledgeable friend to guide you through the thick and thin of learning to knit. In this wonderful banquet of knitting know-how, Allen patiently smoothes the way in the learning process with her knitting tips, taking pains to describe the architecture of knitted fabric at every turn and encouraging a real understanding of every step. This book gives the beginning knitter the competence and confidence to tackle even intermediate level projects with aplomb."

> — Kathleen Power Johnson, knitting instructor, designer,
> and author

"Pam Allen's *Knitting For Dummies* is a wonderful resource for knitters just learning the craft. It will grow with you as your skills progress and become a book you will refer to time and again. The clear instructions and illustrations will help you through numerous projects for years to come."

> — Kristin Nicholas, knitwear designer, author of *Knitting
> the New Classics* and *Knitting Today's Classics*,
> co-author of *Knitting for Baby*

Knitting
FOR
DUMMIES®

Knitting FOR DUMMIES®

by Pam Allen

Foreword by Trisha Malcolm

Wiley Publishing, Inc.

Knitting For Dummies®

Published by
Wiley Publishing, Inc.
909 Third Avenue
New York, NY 10022
www.wiley.com

Copyright © 2002 by Wiley Publishing, Inc., Indianapolis, Indiana

Published simultaneously in Canada

No part of this publication may be reproduced, stored in a retrieval system, or transmitted in any form or by any means, electronic, mechanical, photocopying, recording, scanning, or otherwise, except as permitted under Sections 107 or 108 of the 1976 United States Copyright Act, without either the prior written permission of the Publisher, or authorization through payment of the appropriate per-copy fee to the Copyright Clearance Center, 222 Rosewood Drive, Danvers, MA 01923, 978-750-8400, fax 978-646-8700. Requests to the Publisher for permission should be addressed to the Legal Department, Wiley Publishing, Inc., 10475 Crosspoint Blvd., Indianapolis, IN 46256, 317-572-3447, fax 317-572-4447, or e-mail permcoordinator@wiley.com

For general information on our other products and services or to obtain technical support, please contact our Customer Care Department within the U.S. at 800-762-2974, outside the U.S. at 317-572-3993, or fax 317-572-4002.

Wiley also publishes its books in a variety of electronic formats. Some content that appears in print may not be available in electronic books.

Library of Congress Cataloging-in-Publication Data:

Library of Congress Control Number: 2001093846

ISBN: 0-7645-5395-X

Manufactured in the United States of America

15 14 13 12 11

1B/TR/QU/QT/IN

About the Author

Like every beginning knitter, **Pam Allen** made her share of wobbly edged scarves in garter stitch before committing herself to learning everything she could about making stitches with two needles and a ball of yarn. In the 15 years she has been designing hand-knit sweaters for magazines and yarn companies and creating "swatches" and knitwear ideas for ready-to-wear, she has tried nearly every knitting, finishing, and embellishment technique she could find or come up with.

Her knitwear designs have been published in *Family Circle*, *Woman's Day*, *Vogue Knitting*, *Interweave Knits*, *Knitters*, and *McCall's* among others. Her work has also been featured in the books *Knitting in America* and *Vogue Knitting Contemporary Collection* and shown in the Maryland exhibit *Breaking Patterns: Contemporary Hand Knitting in the United States*. In addition to designing, Pam gives workshops on a variety of knitting techniques for knitting guilds, yarn shops, and knitting "conventions."

She lives and continues to explore knitting and its possibilities in Camden, Maine, with her son and daughter and more cats than she needs.

Dedication

To Paul S. Allen and Marilee McRill Allen — *more than tongue can tell*

Author's Acknowledgments

I most want to thank my editor, Marcia Johnson, for her meticulous care in editing this book. With the reader ever in mind, she has helped to make the information in this book thoroughly accessible to the beginning knitter. Her thoughtful queries and suggestions have made this a far better book than it would otherwise have been. I want to thank her, too, for her unfailing sense of humor — even when working overtime to juggle the unending number of details that go into a book like this — and for her willingness to read and work on the text with needles and yarn in hand.

I'd also like to thank copy editor Tina Sims and editorial manager Pam Mourouzis for their excellent comments and suggestions and especially Jean Lampe for her detailed and thorough technical editing. My gratitude as well to Cheryl Fall for her clean illustrations and to Clint Lahnen and others on the production staff at Wiley for going out of their way to help on the art component of this book.

Thanks to my friends Misty Van Kennen and Faith Getchell, who gladly and expertly knitted the striped socks and garter stitch projects in this book. And thanks to friends and neighbors Wendy Crossman and Sandy Bodemer for their willingness to let me teach them knitting basics — invaluable in testing the instructions in the first chapter of this book — and to Meema Spodola for trying out the color chapter and offering invaluable suggestions on it.

Thanks to Margery Winter at Berroco and Diane Friedman at Tahki-Stacy Charles for answering my questions on yarns and fibers.

Thanks to Joan Somerville at Cascade Yarns, Linda Lacher at Classic Elite, Rae Yurek at Harrisville Yarns, and Nora Gaughan at JCA for generously contributing yarn for the projects in this book.

Thanks to the friendly and supportive women who work in my local yarn shops, Unique One and Stitchery Square. Especially to Beth Collins at Unique One for graciously letting me cart off a collection of lovely novelty yarns to photograph, and to Brenda Laukka for keeping the shop open so late in the evening.

Thanks to Sally Regan, Holly Torsey, and Priscilla Wood at the Rockport Public Library and to Dotty Moralis at the Camden Public Library for their help in obtaining books for me and for letting me renew them — and renew them and renew them.

I am enormously grateful to Sabrina Seelig for her good eye and fine photographs in the color insert and to Julie Cocoran for her equally lovely photographs and for being available at the last minute to shoot the final projects. My gratitude to Caitlin FitzGerald for her willingness to get up earlier than usual — smiling — to model the sweaters in this book and to Alexi Xenakis for his helpful suggestions on photographing knitted fabric. Thanks to Laurie Adams for letting us take pictures in her incomparable garden and to Laura at the Ortolan Café for opening up before hours to let us take pictures in the patio.

Finally, I'm grateful to Dora Lievow, Dyan Dyer, Angela Loavenbruck, Jodi Carpenter, Frank and Cyrene Slegona, and my pal Tasheba Davis for their friendship and support over the years, for their full appreciation of the number of hours it takes to make the thousands of stitches in a single sweater, and for never losing patience or taking it personally when I have had to cancel dates and hibernate to meet a deadline.

And, of course, my heartfelt gratitude to my children, Caitlin and Ryan FitzGerald, who for years have gracefully put up with the clutter, learned to prefer spaghetti sauce out of a jar to homemade, and were almost always willing to wait until I finished the row.

Finally, I'm indebted to all knitters past and present who have experimented with yarn and needles, researched the history and regional techniques of knitting, recorded patterns, and written books and articles on their findings. They have greatly enriched our world by making us conscious of our knitting heritage, giving us knowledge to grow with and build upon.

Publisher's Acknowledgments

We're proud of this book; please send us your comments through our online registration form located at www.dummies.com/register.

Some of the people who helped bring this book to market include the following:

Acquisitions, Editorial, and Media Development

Project Editor: Marcia L. Johnson

Managing Editor: Tracy Boggier

Copy Editor: Tina Sims

Technical Editor: Jean Lampe

Editorial Managers: Christine Meloy Beck, Pamela Mourouzis

Editorial Assistant: Carol Strickland

Special Help: Chrissy Guthrie

Cover Photos: © Bob Daemmrich/Stock, Boston Inc./PictureQuest

Production

Project Coordinator: Nancee Reeves

Layout and Graphics: Jackie Nicholas, Jeremey Unger

Proofreaders: Laura Albert, Carl Pierce, Marianne Santy, TECHBOOKS Production Services

Indexer: TECHBOOKS Production Services

Special Art: Cheryl Fall, illustrator; Sabrina Seelig, color photography

---

Publishing and Editorial for Consumer Dummies

    Diane Graves Steele, Vice President and Publisher, Consumer Dummies

    Joyce Pepple, Acquisitions Director, Consumer Dummies

    Kristin A. Cocks, Product Development Director, Consumer Dummies

    Michael Spring, Vice President and Publisher, Travel

    Brice Gosnell, Publishing Director, Travel

    Suzanne Jannetta, Editorial Director, Travel

Publishing for Technology Dummies

    Richard Swadley, Vice President and Executive Group Publisher

    Andy Cummings, Vice President and Publisher

Composition Services

    Gerry Fahey, Vice President of Production Services

    Debbie Stailey, Director of Composition Services

Contents at a Glance

Cartoons at a Glance

By Rich Tennant

The 5th Wave By Rich Tennant

"So how old were you when you realized that metallic yarn didn't come from steel wool?"

page 319

The 5th Wave By Rich Tennant

"You're right – I probably will be the only one on the dirt track circuit to own a carburetor cozy."

page 7

The 5th Wave By Rich Tennant

"She started knitting oven mitts and toaster cozies. Then one day she saw 'Snowball' shivering next to her drinking bowl and, well, her tail's still wagging in there, so I don't see the harm."

page 219

The 5th Wave By Rich Tennant

In his later years, Capt. Hook gave up on chasing Peter Pan and took up knitting.

page 107

The 5th Wave By Rich Tennant

SCOTTISH TOURS

"Looks like our trip into the town of Argyll will be delayed while we let one of the local farmers pass with his sheep."

page 189

Cartoon Information:
Fax: 978-546-7747
E-Mail: richtennant@the5thwave.com
World Wide Web: www.the5thwave.com

Table of Contents

Part III: Color Me Knitting: Working with More than One Color 189

Foreword

"You knit! How cool!" is the usual response I get after I tell people what I do for a living. In our small knitting world, most of the people I meet — editors, designers, store owners, yarn spinners, and distributors — are avid knitters and have been for most of their lives. But when the day is done and I rejoin the world at large, there are the inevitable social situations in which I find myself being asked about my occupation. "I've always wanted to learn to knit," is the response that usually follows, with either "It looks so complicated; I'm not sure I could do it" or "Where can I learn?" I reassure them that *anyone* can learn to knit and that there are classes, Web sites, and lots of willing teachers who would be honored to introduce them to the secret workings of their life's passion.

Until now, what I haven't told anyone is that there is the perfect book that will lead them step-by-revealing-step through every aspect of this amazing craft, and it is written with them, who think they're unable to knit, in mind. *Knitting For Dummies* is for *every* new knitter and is filled with all the information they will need to equip themselves for their new endeavor. From gathering their materials to making the first awkward knots and stitches to completing a simple project, this book will hold their hands as they make their way to knitting nirvana.

Soon they'll be like the rest of us — our homes and offices stashed to the gills with sumptuous yarns in every color and fiber combination possible and with needles in every size and style imaginable, from basic plastics to circular metals and hand-carved woods. They will start collecting magazines and patterns for future projects, not one of which they can ever part with, even if they will never have time to make them. And then there are the beautiful totes they will buy to carry their knitting with them wherever they go. . . .

It takes a special author to break the mysteries of knitting into bite-sized chunks that can easily be digested, even by "Dummies." Pam Allen brings to this book many years of knitting mastery, a successful career as a hand-knit designer, and a following of dedicated students she has taught and inspired. Pam knows intuitively how to dish up all this information to entice even the newest of knitters. From their first taste to the joy of completing the whole course, she will feed them until they too are feasting just like the rest of us!

— Trisha Malcolm, Editor-in-Chief, *Vogue Knitting International* Magazine

Introduction

• •

Not long ago, a major New York City department store ran a humorous ad disparaging knitting as an activity for grandmothers. Imagine their surprise when ardent members of New York's Big Apple Knitting Guild took up their yarn and needles and staged a knit-in. To demonstrate that knitting isn't an activity limited to the rocking chair set but rather is an alive and timely art, a group of knitters of every age and gender gathered in the store to spend the afternoon knitting. Designer and knitter par excellence Lily Chin designed, knit, and wore a shimmering slit-to-the-thigh floor length gown — demonstrating that more than button-to-the-throat cardigans and stiff socks can come off the needles.

Sure, grandmothers knit, but so do movie stars, football players, doctors, and lawyers. They know what our grandmothers do: Knitting does more than just provide you with warm and cozy things to wear. Knitting stirs creativity, gives you an ongoing sense of purpose, teaches patience, and soothes the soul. Don't believe me? Try it!

Now is a great time to learn to knit. Never before have you had so many lovely and imaginative yarns from which to choose and so many stylish and sophisticated patterns to work with. Traditional knitting is still going strong. Beautifully illustrated books and magazine articles that explore and document knitting techniques and designs from all parts of the world are regularly published. You can find knitting workshops, conferences, cruises, and camps to sign up for, and everywhere plenty of fellow knitters are happy to share their love of knitting with you.

This book is designed as a hands-on book, as well as a reference book. Throughout *Knitting For Dummies*, you find lots of opportunities to practice and perfect your skills. Every chapter explaining a specific knitting technique includes a Knitting Notebook of sample patterns to show you some of the different ways it can be used and a section of Practice Projects that gives step-by-step instructions for simple and attractive knitted accessories nearly all of which are featured on the pages of the color insert. Most projects end with a list of project variations — ways to expand on your understanding of how to craft and design projects on your own.

How to Use This Book

If you're an absolute beginner, start at the beginning and read and practice your way through Part I — the basics. This section will ground you in the moves you'll need to know in order to progress to more complicated kinds of knitting. I've tried to anticipate your questions and where you might run into problems. By the time you've read (and knitted) through Part I, you'll be up and clicking and well on your way to being an accomplished knitter.

If you already know how to knit and purl, you'll find plenty in Parts II and III to build your skills and confidence. If you're interested in knitting techniques, work through the chapters of Part II consecutively to learn more about cables, lace, and color knitting, or jump into the chapter that discusses what you're most interested in.

Maybe you've had your eye on a pattern for a complicated-looking Aran sweater (those poetic combinations of twists and turns) but you've never worked a cable, or maybe you've seen a sweater with a knitted lace border but haven't a clue how to read the chart for it. You'll find out how to do these things and more. And all the way through, I give you loads of pictures and special extras to guide you along and make your learning process as easy as possible.

How This Book Is Organized

This book is divided into five parts. Each one focuses on a separate aspect of knitting, but together they lay the foundation for successful knitting experiences at all levels.

Part I: Knitting Primer

Part I introduces you to the whys and wherefores of knitting — what it is and how to do it. It shows you the fundamental moves, including how to cast on, knit, purl, and bind off. It introduces you to the variety of ways that knit and purl stitches can be combined to make different stitch patterns. It gives advice on troubleshooting the most common mistakes. It tells you about the materials and tools you'll need to get up and running right now and what you'll want to have after you're launched. Finally, it introduces gauge and the simple math you need to know to go from knitting practice fabric to knitting a finished project. By the time you reach the projects in Chapter 6 at the end of Part I, you'll be ready to make any of the scarves, hats, bags, and pillows shown there.

Part II: Manipulating Stitches

In Part II, you expand on your new skills. You find out how to manipulate stitches for different effects. You discover how to shape your work with increases and decreases — adding stitches and getting rid of them. I also take you step by step through crafting cables and knitting lace patterns.

Part III: Color Me Knitting

Part III introduces you to the pleasures and possibilities in knitting with more than one color. Start by seeing how stripes and simple slip-stitch patterns can get you going. Then find out how to work more complex color patterns using more than one color per row. You learn how to make colorful repeating patterns using the Fair Isle technique and how to "paint" with yarn using the intarsia method.

Part IV: Making Garments

Part IV puts it all together — how to take your knitting skills and apply them to making garments. It tells you how to make sense of a commercial knitting pattern, and follow a pattern step by step to a finished sweater or project. You uncover the secrets of *finishing*, or turning your frumpled knitted pieces into a smooth and tidy project. You find explicit instructions for working defining details such as neckbands, cardigan bands, and buttonholes. This part also introduces you to the whys and hows of knitting in the round. If you want to practice your sweater-making skills, in the final chapter, you can get detailed, step-by-step instructions for three beginning sweaters.

Part V: The Part of Tens

In Part V, you see how to unkink when you've been sitting and knitting too long. You also find a helpful list of my favorite knitting books.

Appendixes

In the appendix section, you find lists and contact information for knitting magazines, knitting supply sources, yarn suppliers, and Web sites. I also include a brief discussion on color to shed some light on the question of why certain colors look good together (and why some don't) and to help you hone your own color sense. Finally, because I feel so strongly that by working samplers you gain a true understanding of the stitches and techniques, I've added two more sampler projects for you. Enjoy!

Swatching

Swatching (making a sample of knitted fabric) is to the knitter what scales and exercises are to the pianist and what rough sketches and doodles are to the painter. A swatch is a sample of knitting. It can be big (50 stitches and 50 rows) or small (20 stitches and 20 rows). Most of the time, knitters make a swatch to measure gauge (to see how many stitches and rows there are to an inch). But dedicated knitters also work up swatches to learn, to practice, to experiment, and to invent.

Here are some things your swatch can tell you:

- Whether your yarn and needles work up to the necessary gauge
- Whether your yarn shows off your stitch pattern or obscures it
- Whether your chosen color combination works or needs tweaking
- Whether you understand a new technique

If the swatches answer the questions you started with, they'll pose even more questions as you become a more advanced knitter.

I urge you as you go through or skip around this book to keep your yarn and needles handy as you read and try out the patterns stitches and techniques given. In some cases, I even provide specific instructions in the project sections for making a sampler of a particular technique.

The samples you make will keep you limber, stretch your knowledge, and be your own best teacher.

Putting It into Practice

Each part provides projects to allow you to practice the basic skills and discover something about how hats, bags, and stitches are put together. By the time you reach Part II, you may want to try your hand at applying some of the techniques, such as making cables or lace, in a sweater. As soon as you're confident in your basic knit and purl skills, consider finding a basic sweater pattern. Once you've worked it up and are happy with its fit and style, use it as a base for the fabric design ideas in Part II. Armed with a sweater pattern whose mechanics and shape are familiar to you, you can add your own cables, lace panels, and color patterns — in short, become your own designer.

Icons Used in This Book

Throughout this book, you find icons highlighting important information.

This icon lets you in on some secrets most knitters learn from one another. It also indicates special ways to make your project just a little bit better. You can get by without applying this info, but if you do, your project will be that much nicer.

If you see this icon, I'm pointing out hazards on the knitting path. Pay attention to these if you don't want to find yourself in tangles.

This symbol indicates information on the structure of knitting. It's information that you don't absolutely have to have to knit but that will facilitate mastery.

This icon alerts you to something you probably already know and that you'll need to remember and apply to what you're doing at this point in the text.

Teaching Yourself to Knit from a Book

Everyone learns a new skill in a different way. If you're not sure that you can teach yourself to knit from a book, you can do a few things to make the process easier and help to ensure success.

- First, study the illustrations carefully and compare them with what your own hands, needles, and yarn are doing.

- Use your right hand (not your left) if a right hand is pictured.

- Notice the path of the yarn in the illustration and see whether yours is doing the same thing. For example, does the yarn cross from right to left, or over or under the needle?

- If necessary, keep a pad of self-stick notes nearby and use them on these pages to help you focus on the illustration or text you're trying to understand.

- Have a friend read the instructions aloud to you while you look at the pictures and your hands.

✔ If you get stuck, gather your materials and head to your local knitting shop. Most store personnel are happy to get a new knitter up and running. While you're there, ask whether the store sponsors a knitting group or knows of any. You can learn loads from other knitters. Or sign up for a knitting list on the Web, and you won't have to leave home. Whatever you do, don't give up. The rewards of being a knitter are worth the effort of learning how to be one.

Part I
Knitting Primer

The 5th Wave   By Rich Tennant

"You're right - I probably will be the only one on the dirt track circuit to own a carburetor cozy."

In this part . . .

This is where you find out what you need to get clicking. In this part, you find out about the four basic knitting moves — casting on, knitting, purling, and binding off. You also discover how you can use the building blocks of knitting — knit and purl stitches — to create hundreds of stitch patterns. Noticing glitches in your knitting? Not to worry. I explain how to recognize the common mistakes and how to correct them.

Next, you get an idea of the yarns and other tools of the trade that you can expect to see in your local knitting shop. You find out about friendly math and how to use it when you're knitting a project. And finally, before you move on to Part II, you have a chance to put it all together in some starter projects. Before you know it, you'll be turning out hats, scarves, and bags in all your favorite colors. So check the next page and get started.

Chapter 1

Two Needles and a Ball of Yarn

In This Chapter

▶ Exploring the many reasons to knit

▶ Learning how to cast on, knit, purl, and bind off

▶ Recognizing the difference between English and Continental styles of knitting

Knitting is a relatively simple process requiring a minimal set of tools — two needles and a ball of yarn. Its basic structure of interlocking loops couldn't be less complicated. Yet the possibilities for design and pattern innovation seem endless. Knitting has more than cozy socks and colorful sweaters to offer. Knitting is also an excellent way to mitigate some of the stresses and frustrations of day-to-day life.

This chapter introduces you to knitting — what it is and how to do it. You learn the four elemental moves of knitting: casting on, knitting, purling, and binding off. Practice these, and by the end of the chapter, you'll be ready to launch a project. With the skills you learn in this chapter and the ones introduced in the chapters that follow, you can explore with confidence the myriad things you can do with two needles and a ball of yarn.

Knitting up Good Karma

The repetitive movements of needles and yarn truly knit up the raveled sleeve of care. Have you ever noticed a knitter's face while working away on the needles? Did you see the expression of relaxed alertness? It's the look we'd all be wearing if our alpha waves were lined up properly. The rhythmic movements of knitting, together with the mental focus needed for building a fabric stitch by stitch, make for a kind of meditation. It's real. Ask anyone who knits.

Turning colorful skeins of yarn into exciting knitted hats and sweaters gives you a feeling of competence and accomplishment. If you knit a little while waiting for your computer to change screens, red lights to turn green, and commercials to end, you'll never have to worry about wasting time again.

Knitting is portable, too, so you can work on your karma wherever you find yourself. You can knit in the living room while you're watching TV or in the kitchen waiting for the pasta to cook. You can knit while waiting to catch a plane or sitting on a park bench watching your children play. You can take your knitting with you, whether it's a challenging project that requires quiet concentration (and possibly your glasses) or something simple that you can tote along and pull out at the odd moment for a quick row or two.

If you carry your knitting wherever you go, you always bring along a little well-being with you. In a world giving way to things global and anonymous, a knitting project at hand reminds you of the comforts and familiarity of things small, local, and individual.

Calling on Your Creativity

Knitting is a process of combining yarn, needles, pattern, and color. Even if all you do is follow a sweater pattern by using the exact yarn and needles it calls for, each stitch is of your own making, and no two sweaters from the same pattern worked by different knitters are ever exactly the same.

Chances are, after your first project or two, you'll be venturing with pleasure into the wonderland of new combinations of yarn, pattern stitch, color, and embellishment. You'll be wondering how you'll ever find the time to make all the things you have ideas for.

Creativity is less about being born with a friendly muse and more about putting time and effort into developing know-how. Granted, moments of inspiration *can* wake you up at 4:00 in the morning, but rarely do they happen unless you first lay the groundwork. Work all day on finding the right color combination for a project, and the solution will come at an unlikely moment. By learning, practicing, and mastering your art and craft, you become creative.

Mastering the Basics

A pair of needles, some yarn, and a little uninterrupted time are all you need to learn to knit. Practice each of the four basic moves — casting on, knitting, purling, and binding off — and you'll soon be amazed at your nimble fingers.

In order to practice, you need a ball of medium-weight yarn and a pair of size 8 or 9 needles. You don't have to buy the best-quality yarn, but if at all possible, choose wool, the knitter's best friend. Wool is elastic, making it easy to get your needles in and out of the stitches. (See more on yarn and needles in

Chapter 2.) Cotton doesn't give enough to make it a good choice for your first forays into knitting, and 100 percent acrylics can give you sweaty palms. Whatever yarn you choose, pick a light or bright color yarn, which makes it easier to see the stitches.

Knitting needles come in a variety of materials. Plastic or wood needles are a good choice for beginners because they aren't slick, so you won't have to worry about your stitches sliding off when you're not looking (or when you are).

Casting on

Creating the first row of stitches is called *casting on*. There are various ways to cast on, and different knitters have their favorites. The two-strand method given in this section is a great all-around cast-on for your starting repertoire. It's elastic, attractive, and easy to knit from.

Making a slip knot (the first stitch)

The first stitch on your needle will be a slip knot. Here's how to make it.

1. **Measure off approximately 30 inches from the end of the yarn (a little more than 1 inch for each stitch to be cast on) and make a pretzel-shaped loop.**

2. **With your knitting needle, reach into the loop, as pictured in Figure 1-1a, and with your hands gently pull on both ends of yarn until the stitch is firmly on the needle but can still slide easily back and forth, as shown in Figure 1-1b.**

Figure 1-1:
Getting the
first stitch
on your
needle.

A. Insert the needle into the pretzel.   B. Tighten up the slip-knot stitch.

 The first few times you make a slip knot, arrange your starting pretzel on a flat surface or table. It will be easier to see what you're doing. Once you get the hang of it, you'll be able to make a slip knot anywhere. Practice making the slip knot stitch several times until you feel comfortable with it.

Completing the cast-on row

Notice the two strands hanging down from your slip-knot stitch — the short or tail end and the ball end of your yarn. You'll use both strands for the cast-on — that's why it's called the two-strand cast-on.

1. **Holding the needle in your right hand, with the tip pointing away from you, take the short end of yarn over your left thumb, as illustrated in Figure 1-2a.**

2. **Keeping a little tension on the short end by holding it gently against your palm with the fingertips of your left hand, insert the tip of the needle into the thumb loop, as shown in Figure 1-2b.**

3. **With your right hand, bring the ball end of your yarn under the needle to the left then back over the needle to the right, as shown in Figure 1-3a.**

4. **Keeping a little tension on the ball yarn, use your left thumb to guide the thumb loop up and over the tip of the needle and at the same time bring the tip of the needle through the thumb loop. See this step in Figure 1-3b.**

5. **Take your thumb out of the loop and pull gently on the short strand to snug up the stitch.**

   If it's still sloppy, pull a little on the long strand. The stitches should be firm but slide easily along the needle, as shown in Figure 1-4.

Continue Steps 1 through 5 until you have 28 stitches on your needle, including your first slip-knot stitch.

Figure 1-2:
Getting into position to cast on your first stitch.

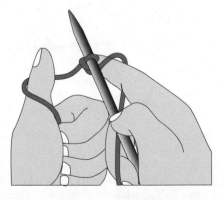

A. Hold the short end of the yarn around your left thumb.

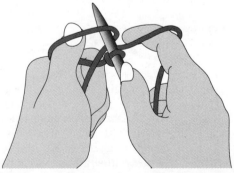

B. Insert the needle in the thumb loop.

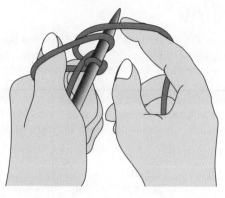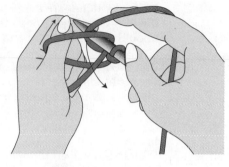

Figure 1-3:
Picking up
the yarn for
your first
cast-on
stitch.

A. Wrap the yarn around the needle.

B. Bring the tip of the needle
through the loop toward you.

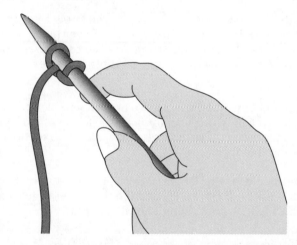

Figure 1-4:
Finished
cast-on
stitch.

Phew! Feeling a little tense? Take a breather. Shake your hands and wriggle
your shoulders. You've accomplished a lot. Did you notice that the last few
stitches you cast on felt a little easier than the first few? Although these
motions may feel awkward at first and you have to pay attention to each
movement, with time and practice, you'll no longer have to think about what
your hands are doing. You'll be surprised how quickly your hands will learn
the movements and make them smoothly and effortlessly while you think
about something entirely unknitterish. For additional cast-on techniques,
see Chapter 8.

Now you're knitting

Knitted stitches are made by using a continuous strand of yarn and two needles to pull new loops through old loops. That's it. But how a knitter goes about holding the yarn and needles to make these new loops varies.

The merits and weakness of holding the yarn in the right hand *(wrapping)* versus holding the yarn in the left hand *(picing,* pronounced "picking") is always a lively, if not hot, topic of conversation when knitters of different persuasions get together.

Is there a best way? Yes. The best way is whatever feels right to you. Knitting is an individual art. Sooner or later, everyone who knits develops her own style of knitting. The good news is that no matter which method you use, you'll get the same result — loops pulled through loops to make knitted fabric. The most important thing is that knitting should feel comfortable to you and your stitches should look even.

How should you decide which method to use? If you know a knitter who would sign on to be your knitting mentor (and I've never met a fellow knitter who didn't love to show off her techniques), do what that person does. If you're learning on your own, start with one method. If it gives you trouble, try the other.

In the best of all possible worlds, you'll learn both. If you plan to knit color patterns, being able to knit with one color in the right hand and the other color in the left hand makes things quicker and easier. The sections that follow introduce you to both styles.

From now on, the needle in your left hand carrying the stitches to be worked will be called the left-hand (LH) needle, and the needle on which you're making new stitches will be your right-hand (RH) needle.

Knitting with the yarn in your right hand (English style)

If you've chosen to knit with the yarn in your right hand, known as the English style, here's how to proceed. When you have finished casting on, hold the needle with the cast-on stitches in your left hand, pointing to the right. Make sure that the first stitch is no more than 1 inch from the tip of the needle.

1. **Insert the tip of the empty (RH) needle into the first stitch on the LH needle from left to right and front to back, forming a T with the tips of the needles.**

   The RH needle will be behind the LH needle, as shown in Figure 1-5.

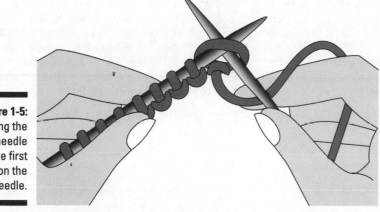

Figure 1-5:
Inserting the
RH needle
into the first
stitch on the
LH needle.

2. **With your right hand, hold the ball yarn 2 or 3 inches from your needles and bring the yarn to the back on the *left side* of the RH needle, and then over the RH needle to the right and down between the needles (Fig. 1-6a).**

   You can try to maneuver the yarn with your right forefinger, as shown in Figure 1-6a, or just hold it between your thumb and forefinger for now.

3. **Keeping a slight tension on the wrapped yarn, bring the tip of the RH needle with its wrap of yarn through the loop on the LH needle to the front.**

   The RH needle is now in front of the LH needle, as shown in Figure 1-6b. Keep the tip of the left forefinger on the point of the RH needle to help guide the needle through the old stitch and prevent losing the wrap of yarn.

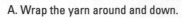
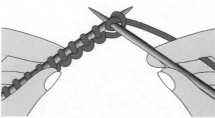

Figure 1-6:
Completing
a knit stitch.

A. Wrap the yarn around and down.   B. Bring the loop through.

When you bring the new loop through the old, bring the RH needle up far enough that the new stitch forms on the large part of the needle, not just on the tip. If you work too close to the tips, you will form new stitches on the narrow part of your needles, and your stitches will be too tight to knit with ease. Tight stitches have brought many a new knitter to a frustrated halt. By the same token, don't knit too far from the tips. Keep the stitches on the LH needle close enough to the tip so that you don't struggle and stretch to pull off the old stitch.

4. **Slide the RH needle to the right till the old loop on the LH needle drops off.**

   You now have a new stitch/loop on the RH needle — the old stitch hangs below it. Does it look like Figure 1-7?

   Congratulations! You've just made your first knitted stitch!

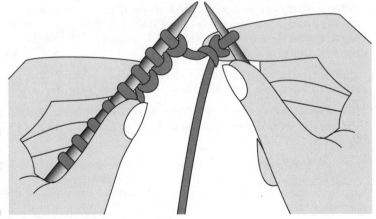

Figure 1-7:
Your first
knitted
stitch!

As you repeat these steps, you may want to recite the following knitting mantra to yourself: "Needle in, yarn around, new loop through, old loop off."

Continue until you have knitted all the stitches from your LH needle. Your LH needle is now empty, and your RH needle is full of beautiful, new stitches. Now switch hands: Turn your RH needle and hold it in your left hand, pointing right. Your RH needle has now become your LH needle. And your old, empty LH needle has become your new, empty RH needle ready to take on a new row of stitches.

Repeat the sequence of the preceding steps for several more rows (or all afternoon) until you're comfortable with the movements. Aim to make these steps one continuous movement, to make even stitches, and to stay relaxed!

Note that when you've finished making a knit stitch, the yarn is coming out the *back* on the side of the needle facing away from you. Be sure that the yarn hasn't ended up in front of your work or over the needle before you start your next stitch.

When you turn your work from right facing to wrong side facing or vice versa, it's called *turning your work*. When knitting instructions tell you to turn, simply pivot your needle so that the opposite side is facing and you're ready to work again.

When you turn your work, the yarn strand coming out of the first stitch to knit will *not* be in back. Instead, it will hang down in the front, as shown in Figure 1-8.

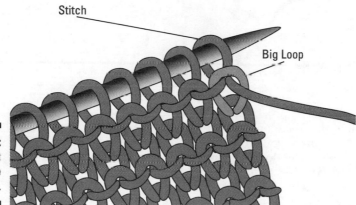

Stitch

Big Loop

Figure 1-8:
The first
stitch of the
next row.

Often the stitch just below the first stitch on your LH needle is larger than the rest and can obscure your view of where your needle should go. You may be tempted to pull the yarn strand over the needle to the back to tighten up the stitch. If you do this, it will look like you have 2 stitches on your needle instead of 1. Keep the strand in front and gently pull down on it, and the big stitch if necessary, to better see the opening you're supposed to go into.

Insert the point of the RH needle in the loop on the LH needle and not into the stitch below.

Once you feel comfortable making knit stitches, you can try weaving the yarn through the fingers of your right hand in one of the ways illustrated in Figure 1-9. Carrying the yarn this way puts a gentle tension on the strand, making it possible to work tidy stitches at a good clip.

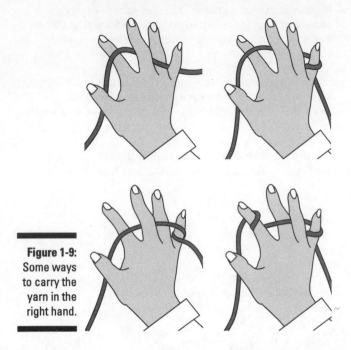

Figure 1-9: Some ways to carry the yarn in the right hand.

If you find that hunching over little loops on your needles and scrutinizing the illustrations make you tense, take time regularly to shake out your hands, take a deep breath, and do some stretches for a minute or two. (See Chapter 20 for suggested exercises to unkink your fingers.)

Knitting with the yarn in your left hand (Continental style)

If you choose to knit with the yarn in your left hand, known as the Continental style, follow these instructions. When you have finished casting on, hold the needle with the cast-on stitches in the left hand, pointing to the right. Make sure that the first stitch is no more than 1 inch from the tip of the needle. Wind the yarn around your left pinky and over your left forefinger, as shown in Figure 1-10.

You'll be holding both the yarn and the needle with the stitches in your left hand. Your left forefinger should be close to the tip of the LH needle, and the yarn between the needle and your forefinger should be a bit taut. The yarn strand will be *behind* your LH needle, as shown in Figure 1-11a.

1. **Insert the tip of the empty (RH) needle into the first stitch on the LH needle from left to right and front to back (RH needle is behind the LH needle), as shown in Figure 1-11b.**

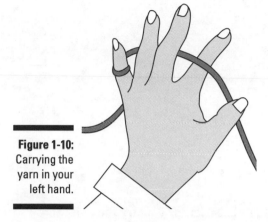

Figure 1-10:
Carrying the
yarn in your
left hand.

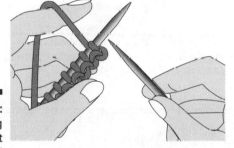

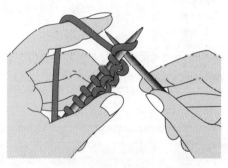

Figure 1-11:
Getting
ready to knit
Continental
style.

A. Getting ready to knit with
the yarn in the left hand.

B. Insert the RH needle into the first
stitch on the LH needle.

2. **Swivel the tip of the RH needle to the right and under the yarn strand, scooping up the yarn from your left forefinger.**

   You end up with the yarn wrapped around the needle, as shown in Figure 1-12a.

3. **Bring the tip of the RH needle with the strand of yarn through the loop on the LH needle, as shown in Figure 1-12b.**

4. **Slide the old loop off the LH needle and let it drop.**

As you practice, aim to make these four steps a smooth continuous action — in, around, through, off.

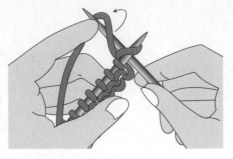

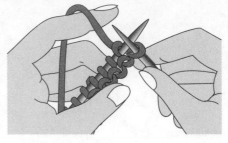

Figure 1-12:
Completing
a
Continental
knit stitch.

A. Swivel the RH needle to pick up the yarn strand.

B. Bring the new loop through.

To make Continental style knitting a little easier for you, try the following:

✔ Put the tip of your right forefinger on each new stitch made on the RH needle to secure it while you insert the RH needle into the next stitch on the LH needle.

✔ After you've inserted the RH needle into the next stitch to be knitted, slightly stretch the loop on the LH needle to the right, opening it out somewhat, before you scoop the strand of yarn.

For left-handed knitters

Knitting is a two-handed endeavor. Whether you use your right hand or your left hand to write or stir your coffee, you use them both to knit.

For better or worse, knitting patterns are written for right-handed knitters (those who work from the left needle to the right needle). If you can master either of the knitting methods presented in this chapter, you won't have to reinterpret patterns in order to work them in reverse. Chances are, like most right-handed knitters, sooner or later you'll work out a series of movements that feel natural and easy, and your stitches will be smooth and even.

If you find that, while trying the steps presented in this chapter, the initial awkward feeling isn't going away, then try to work in reverse — moving the stitches from the RH needle to the LH one.

Follow the instructions for either English or Continental style, substituting the word *right* for *left* and vice versa. To make the illustrations work for you, hold a mirror up to the side of the relevant illustration and mimic the hand and yarn positions in the mirror image.

If you find that working in reverse is the most comfortable method, be aware that some directions in knitting patterns, such as decreases, look different when worked in the opposite direction. This will be most problematic for lace patterns, but it's a small price to pay for comfortable knitting. If you go this route, hunt up a copy of *Left-Handed Knitting* by Regina Hurlbert (Van Nostrand Reinhold, 1977).

Whether you decide to master English or Continental style, practice until the movements feel comfortable and relaxed. When you feel like you're getting the hang of it, try an experiment. Close your eyes or look at the ceiling while you knit — let your fingers feel their way. Can you knit without looking yet? Eventually you'll be able to. If you make this your goal, you can get lots done at the movies!

If you're having trouble getting your knitting to "flow," try changing the way you carry the yarn in your hand. If you knit with the yarn in the right hand, try propping the knob of your RH needle under your armpit or on your hipbone to keep it stationary, and use the left hand to initiate the movements. Study how other knitters do things. Be willing to try it different ways until you find your knitting "home." Once you understand how the yarn travels around your needle to make new loops, you'll find the best way to hold your yarn and needles for comfort, speed, and even stitches.

Creating garter stitch by repeating knitted rows

Garter stitch is the most basic of all knitted fabrics. It's made by knitting every row. (After you learn to purl, you'll realize that you can also create garter stitch by purling every row. Neat, huh?) You can recognize garter stitch by the horizontal ridges formed by the tops of the knitted loops on every other row.

After you've knitted several rows, pull down slightly on your knitting. You should be able to see the individual loops and how they're connected. Look carefully at your knitting and compare what you've made to Figure 1-13. Can you identify the loops? Can you follow the path of your yarn?

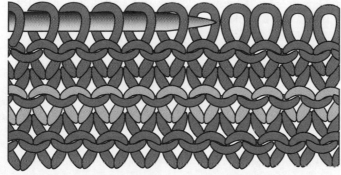

Figure 1-13: Garter stitch.

If you have trouble making out individual stitches and the path of the yarn, knit a row with a different color and then several rows in the original color. The row worked in a different color will stand out and be easy to follow.

Joining yarns

Balls of yarn are finite. When you're knitting away and you least expect it, you'll run out of yarn. Time to start the next ball of yarn, called "joining yarn."

When possible, start a new ball of yarn on an edge that will be enclosed in a seam. However, try not to start a new ball of yarn on an edge that will be exposed. You can knit the first stitch of the next row with both ends held together, drop the old strand, and carry on. Or knit the first few stitches with the new yarn only, stop, and tie the two ends together temporarily to secure them. Either way, leave the ends at least 3 inches long.

If you run out of yarn in the middle of a row, you can do the same thing. Tie a temporary knot with both yarns, leaving 3-inch ends, or knit the next stitch with both strands, drop the old one, and continue knitting from the new ball. (See Chapter 15 for how to finish off the ends.)

Garter stitch has a lot going for it in addition to being easy to create. It is reversible, lies flat, and has a pleasant rustic look. Unlike most knitted fabrics, garter stitch has a square gauge, meaning that there are usually twice as many rows in 1 inch as there are stitches. To count rows in garter stitch, count the ridges and multiply by 2 or count the ridges by twos. Flip to Chapter 5 for more about gauge.

Perfect purling

Purling is working a knit stitch backwards. Instead of going into the stitch from front to back, you enter it from back to front. Combining knit stitches with purl stitches enables you to make a wide variety of textured stitch patterns.

Purling with the yarn in your right hand (English style)

Purling, like knitting, can be done with the yarn held in the right hand or in the left hand. Use whatever method you've chosen for knitting. If you've chosen to hold the yarn in your left hand, skip over this section and go right to the section on purling Continental style. However, if English style works best for you, follow the steps that follow.

1. **Cast on 28 stitches.**

2. **Hold the needle with the cast-on stitches in your left hand pointing to the right. Insert the tip of the RH needle into the first loop on the LH needle from right to left, forming a T with the needle tips. In other words, the RH needle is in front of the LH needle, and the ball yarn is in front of your needles.**

   Check out Figure 1-14a. This is the reverse of what you do when you form a knit stitch.

3. **With your right hand, follow Figure 1-14b and wrap the yarn around the back of the needle from right to left and down.**

Figure 1-14:
Getting
ready to
purl English
style.

A. Insert the RH needle into the
first stitch on the LH needle.

B. Wrap the yarn around the needle.

4. **Keeping a slight tension on the wrap of yarn, bring the tip of the RH needle with its wrap of yarn down and through the loop on the LH needle to the *back* side of the LH needle, as shown in Figure 1-15a.**

5. **Slide the old loop off the tip of the LH needle.**

   A new loop/stitch is made on the RH needle. You can see how it should look in Figure 1-15b.

Figure 1-15:
Finishing
your purl
stitch.

A. Bring the new loop through the back.

B. New stitch made on the RH needle.

6. **Repeat Steps 1 through 5.**

Here's the purl mantra: "Needle in (from the right), yarn around and down, loop through to the back, old stitch off."

When you purl, the yarn strand comes out of the new stitches on the side of the knitting facing you. When you knit, the yarn comes out of the new stitches on the side facing away from you.

Continue to the end of the row. Repeat this row as many times as you need to feel comfortable with purling. Then take a look at what you've made. Looks just like your knitted swatch, doesn't it? Purling is simply the reverse of knitting.

Whether you knit all the rows or purl all the rows, you're working garter stitch (see the section "Creating garter stitch by repeating knitted rows" earlier in this chapter for more on garter stitch).

Purling with the yarn in your left hand (Continental style)

If you choose to knit Continental style, follow these steps for purling.

1. **Cast on 28 stitches.**

2. **Hold the needle with the stitches in the left hand, pointing to the right.**

   Make sure that the first stitch is no more than 1 inch from the tip of the LH needle.

3. **Wind the yarn around your left pinky and over your left forefinger.**

   You hold the yarn the same as when you knit in Continental style. Flip back to Figure 1-10 to review what this looks like.

   You'll be holding both the yarn and the needle with the stitches on it in your left hand. Your left forefinger should be close to the tip of the LH needle, and the yarn between the needle and your forefinger should be a bit taut. The yarn between your needle and forefinger will be in *front* of the needle.

4. **Insert the tip of the RH needle into the first loop on the LH needle from right to left.**

   The RH needle is in *front* of the LH needle, and the ball yarn is in *front* of your needles. Things should be arranged as shown in Figure 1-16a.

5. **Slightly swivel the right needle tip to the right while the pad of your left forefinger brings the yarn between the needles from right to left and down between the needles, as shown in Figure 1-16b.**

   The left forefinger keeps the yarn taut.

Figure 1-16: Getting into position to purl Continental style.

A. Insert RH needle into the first stitch on LH needle.

B. Bring yarn around and down between the needles

6. **Bring the tip of the right needle with its wrap of yarn through the stitch on the LH needle to the back away from you.**

   Check Figure 1-17a to see what this looks like.

7. **Slip the old stitch off the LH needle, tightening it with the left forefinger, as shown in Figure 1-17b.**

Figure 1-17:
Completing
a
Continental
purl stitch.

A. New loop through the back.

B. New stitch made on the RH needle.

KNITTING TIP If possible, finish working an entire row before putting down your knitting — it's too easy to pick up your knitting later and find you don't know which is the LH and which is the RH needle. If you have to stop in the middle of a row, check that you're knitting in the right direction when you pick up your work again. The yarn is always hanging down from the last stitch you made, and the last stitch you made should be on your RH needle — not on your LH needle. When you pick up your work, make sure that the yarn is coming out of the first stitch at the tip end of your RH needle.

Combining knit and purl rows to make stockinette stitch

Now that you can knit and purl, you can create a knitted fabric in stockinette stitch. Stockinette stitch (St st) is what you probably picture when you hear the word *knit*. When you alternate a knit row with a purl row you get stockinette stitch.

Here's how stockinette stitch would look written up as knitting instructions:

Row 1 (right side = RS): Knit.

Row 2 (wrong side = WS): Purl.

Repeat Rows 1 and 2 for desired length.

Stockinette fabric looks and behaves differently from garter stitch fabric (introduced earlier in this chapter). It has a right and a wrong side, though either side may be the *right* side depending on the intended design.

The smooth side is called *stockinette* or *knit*. Look closely at the smooth side (See Figure 1-18). From this side, the stitches/loops look like small Vs — you see only their lower part.

The bumpy side of stockinette stitch fabric is called *reverse stockinette* or *purl*. The bumps on this side are formed by the tops of the loops running horizontally and vertically. You can follow the strand of yarn making the stitches in Figure 1-19.

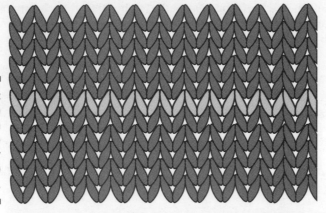

Figure 1-18: Stockinette stitch showing the knit (or smooth) side.

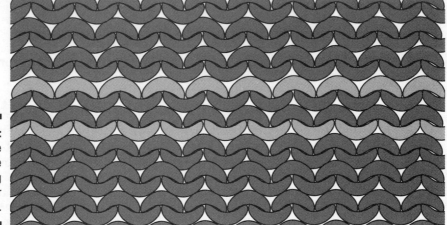

Figure 1-19: Reverse stockinette showing the purl (or bumpy) side.

If you're working in stockinette stitch and you lose track of whether you've knit the last row or purled it, not to worry. You can tell what to do next by looking at your knitting. Hold your needle ready to go in the left hand. What's facing you? If you're looking at the knit (smooth) side, you knit. If you're looking at the purl (bumpy) side, you purl.

Stockinette fabric curls on the edges. The top and bottom (horizontal) edges curl toward the front or smooth side. Sweater designers frequently use this rolling feature deliberately. The side (vertical) edges roll toward the reverse side.

If you knit a scarf in stockinette stitch, the side edges will roll toward the wrong side, and your scarf will resemble a tube. One way to counteract this tendency when you want a piece of stockinette to lie flat is to work the 3 or 4 stitches on the edge in garter stitch. These are called *selvedge stitches*.

Stockinette fabric also has more rows to the inch than it does stitches. The highlighted square in Figure 1-20 represents a typical stitch-to-row relationship — 5 stitches and 7 rows to 1 square inch.

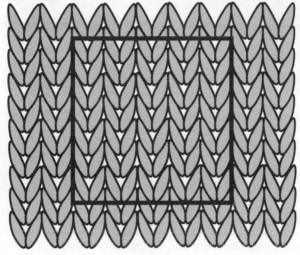

Figure 1-20: One square inch of stockinette stitch fabric.

To count rows in stockinette stitch, count the bumps from the wrong side. They're easier to see than Vs.

Get in the habit of looking closely at your knitting. Learn to identify individual stitches. Compare your work with the pictures in this book. If you take the time to do this, you will soon be a master of the craft.

Binding off

To finish your knitted piece, you have to *bind off,* or secure, the stitches in the last row worked so that they don't unravel. This is easy to do if you follow these basic steps:

1. **Knit the first 2 stitches from the LH needle. These become the first 2 stitches on your RH needle.**

2. **With your LH needle in front of your RH needle, insert the LH needle into the first stitch worked on the RH needle (the one on the right), as shown in Figure 1-21a.**

3. **Bring this loop over the second stitch and off the tip of the RH needle, as shown in Figure 1-21b.**

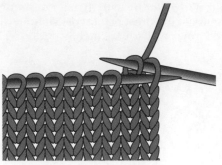 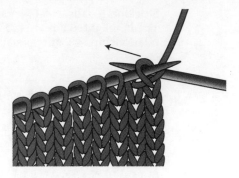

Figure 1-21:
Binding off
a stitch.

A. Insert LH needle into the stitch
on the right.

B. Bring the loop over the second stitch
and off the needle.

At this point, you have 1 stitch bound off and 1 stitch remaining on your
RH needle. Your work should look like Figure 1-22.

4. **Knit the next stitch on the LH needle. Now you have two stitches on
   your RH needle.**

5. **Repeat Steps 2 and 3 so that you again have 1 stitch remaining on
   your RH needle.**

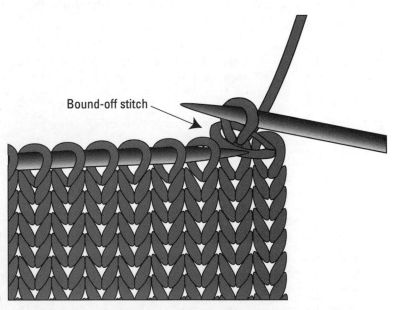

Bound-off stitch

Figure 1-22:
One stitch
bound off.

6. **Repeat steps 2 through 4 until you've worked all the stitches from the LH needle and have 1 stitch remaining on the RH needle. Cut the yarn a few inches from the needle and pull the tail through the last stitch to lock it.**

   Leave the tail 12 inches long or longer, and you'll have a built-in strand to sew up a seam.

When you have 2 stitches on the RH needle, you're ready to bind off 1 stitch (as shown in Figure 1-21). When you have 1 stitch on the RH needle (as shown in Figure 1-22), you need to work one more stitch before you can bind off again.

The loop below the last bind-off stitch is often (for some mysterious reason) big and baggy. To tighten it up, when you come to the last stitch (1 stitch on the RH needle and one stitch on the LH needle), slip the stitch on the RH needle back to the LH needle. Insert the tip of the RH needle into the left stitch on the LH needle and bring it over the stitch you slipped back and off the needle — binding off in the reverse direction. Cut the yarn and draw the tail through the remaining loop.

Unless otherwise told to do so, always bind off according to the stitch pattern given. If you would normally be working a purl row, purl the stitches instead of knitting them before binding off.

It's easy to bind off too tightly. Remember, knitting should be elastic, especially around neck edges if you want to be able to get a sweater on and off comfortably. To avoid a tight and inelastic bound-off edge, try working the bind-off row on a needle one or more sizes larger than what you've been using.

Stocking parts to knitting names

The names *garter stitch* and *stockinette stitch* date from the 1500s, when hand-knit stockings were a major industry in England. Garter stitch was used garterlike at the top of the stocking where it needed to expand for the thigh, and stockinette (or stocking stitch) was used for the fitted leg portion.

Chapter 2

Knits and Purls: The Bricks and Mortar of Knitting

In This Chapter

▶ Reading stitch patterns

▶ Combining knits and purls

▶ Understanding pattern instructions

▶ Starting a Knitting Notebook

*O*nce you know how to knit and purl, you can combine these stitches in a seemingly endless variety of textured stitch patterns, not to be confused with garment or project patterns. The stitch patterns in this chapter make a good starting repertoire. Some are simple and repetitive, and others are best charted and followed row by row.

The best way to understand how knit-and-purl patterns work is to knit them up yourself. Using a medium-weight, solid-color yarn, cast on a multiple of the stitches required for the pattern (but no less than 24) and knit up about 4 inches. Save your samples (swatches) in a knitting notebook for later reference or sew them together to create a patchwork scarf or afghan. (In the color insert, you can see a scarf made by sewing together the swatches shown throughout this book.)

If you want a tidy edge on your sample, knit the first and last stitch of every row regardless of the stitch pattern.

When you find a pattern you especially like, sample it by using the yarn and needle of your choice. Then you can take your favorite stitch pattern and apply it to one of the basic projects in Chapter 6.

Learning to Read Stitch Patterns

Stitch patterns are based on *repeats* — stitch repeats and row repeats. A given stitch sequence repeats horizontally across a row. A series of rows of given stitch sequences repeats vertically. Together they make up a stitch pattern that determines what your knitted fabric will look like: smooth or bumpy, cabled or striped. Stitch pattern instructions show you the stitches and rows that make up a single repeat. For example, seed stitch has a 2-stitch repeat (knit 1 stitch, purl 1 stitch — k1, p1) and a 2-row repeat (knit 1, purl 1 for one row; purl 1, knit 1 for the second row).

Stitch patterns begin by giving you a *multiple* of stitches that make a complete repeat of the pattern — sometimes requiring a few extra stitches to satisfy a specific stitch pattern. When you make a swatch of a pattern, always cast on a number of the multiple plus the extra stitches the pattern calls for. For example, if the pattern calls for a multiple of 12 stitches plus 6, you'll cast on 18 (12 + 6) stitches, or 30 (24 + 6) stitches, and so on — just as long as it's 6 stitches plus a multiple of 12.

Directions for stitch patterns can be given in two different ways: in written form and chart form. Written instructions tell you what to do with the stitches in each row as you come to them. A chart shows a picture of each stitch and how it's worked. Some people prefer written instructions, and others like to follow a graphed "picture" of the pattern. Nowadays, the trickier the pattern, the more likely it is to be charted out. Not true for vintage patterns, however. Being familiar with both ways of describing a pattern enables you to convert a chart into written instructions if you find it easier to work with words and, conversely, to convert into graph form a convoluted set of written instructions.

Following written stitch patterns

Written instructions give you row-by-row directions for a single repeat. They follow certain conventions and use lots of abbreviations. (Check the Cheat Sheet in the front of this book for a detailed list of abbreviations.) The key to understanding written instructions is paying attention to commas and asterisks.

What is written between commas is a single step. If you read the instructions "Slip 1 with yarn in front, k5," you would slip a stitch with the yarn on the front side of the work and *then* you would take the yarn to the back in order to knit 5. The instructions don't ask you to knit 5 stitches with the yarn in front. An asterisk (*) indicates that whatever follows gets repeated (rep) — usually the (*) indicates that what follows is the stitch repeat.

The following example shows a stitch pattern in written form:

> Row 1 (right side): *P2, k2; rep from *.
>
> Row 2 (wrong side): *K2, p2; rep from *.

Translation: On the first row (the *right* side is facing you on the first row in this pattern), you purl 2 stitches, knit 2 stitches, purl 2 stitches, knit 2 stitches, and so on, to the end of the row. (Your row would have to be a multiple of 4 stitches for these instructions to come out evenly.) On the next row (wrong side facing now), you begin by knitting 2 stitches, then purling 2 stitches, knitting 2 stitches, purling 2 stitches, and so on, repeating this sequence to the end of the row.

Reading charted stitch patterns

Charts use a square to represent each stitch and a symbol inside the square to indicate how to work the stitch. Though there is no universally used set of symbols, each pattern that uses a chart will give you a key to reading it. Always begin by finding the key to the chart. Generally, if the first row is a right-side row, charts start in the bottom right-hand corner and read to the left. The second row is read from left to right. (If the first row is a wrong-side row, the first row of the chart reads from left to right.)

The most important thing to remember about charts is that they represent the pattern of the knitted fabric as you're looking at it — the *right* side of the fabric. This means that on wrong side rows (from left to right) you must purl any stitch that has a knit symbol and knit any stitch that has a purl symbol. This isn't difficult once you get the hang of it. The pattern key will remind you. Of course, if you're knitting in the round, you can follow the chart without worrying about whether you have the wrong side or right side of the fabric facing. See Chapter 17 for more about knitting in the round.

The chart in Figure 2-1 shows the same pattern as in the previous section on following written stitches, but it presents this pattern in charted form.

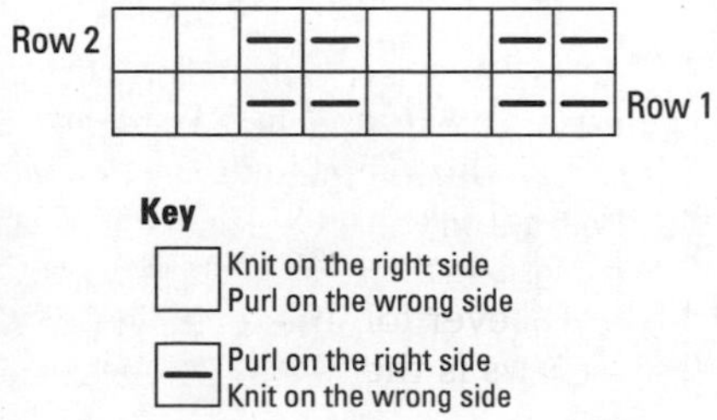

Figure 2-1: Presenting pattern instructions in chart form.

Row 2

Row 1

Key

Knit on the right side
Purl on the wrong side

Purl on the right side
Knit on the wrong side

Cool Things You Can Do with Knits and Purls

Although you can craft any number of patterns and textures by combing knits and purls in different ways, the easiest way to begin is to use them to create stripes (horizontal and vertical) and checkerboard patterns.

Creating stripes with texture

In stockinette stitch, you alternate a row of knit stitches with a row of purl stitches. By varying the sequence of knit rows and purl rows, you can create horizontal stripes (sometimes called by their ancient name *welts*). The two patterns in this section give different examples of this. In the first one, the stripes are created with rows of reverse stockinette stitch on a plain stockinette stitch background. In the second, the stripes are made with garter stitch ridges. Jump back to Chapter 1 if you need to review garter and stockinette stitches.

"Knit" can refer to how you make a stitch, but it can also describe the *appearance* of a stitch on the *right side* of the fabric. A knit stitch on the right side of the fabric is a smooth V-shaped stitch. If it was made with the right side facing, it was knitted, but if it was made from the wrong side, it was purled. The same thing applies to the word "purl." It can refer to how you make a stitch, and it can describe the appearance of a stitch from the right side of the fabric. A purl bump on the right side of the fabric is called a purl stitch even if it was made by knitting it on the wrong side.

Walking through knitting with Barbara Walker

Barbara Walker has given the knitting world many indispensable books, beginning with her series of stitch dictionaries: *A Treasury of Knitting Patterns, A Second Treasury of Knitting Patterns,* and *Charted Knitting Designs: A Third Treasury of Knitting Patterns* — all recently republished by Schoolhouse Press (see the appendix for contact information, or visit www.schoolhousepress.com). In addition to page after page of photographs of different knit and purl patterns, cables, rib variations, and laces — with row-by-row instructions for each one — these books offer lots of information about knitting in general.

As you increase your knitting skills and want to explore other aspects of knitting — like how to knit a sweater from the neck down instead of from the bottom up — look for these other books by Barbara Walker: *Knitting from the Top, Learn-to-Knit Afghan Book,* and *Mosaic Knitting* (all recently republished by Schoolhouse Press).

Descriptions of knit-and-purl patterns usually refer to how a stitch looks from the right side of the fabric — a smooth v or a bump — not how it was made.

Reverse stockinette stitch stripes

Reverse stockinette stitch (rev St st) is just one example of how to make textured stripes (see Figure 2-2). This stitch pattern uses rows of reverse stockinette on a plain stockinette background.

Figure 2-2:
Reverse
stockinette
stripes.

You can vary the width and spacing of the stripes by adding rows of purl and/or knit stitches. Try the following pattern for a basic Rev St st stripe:

Cast on any number of stitches.

Rows 1, 3, and 6: Knit.

Rows 2, 4, and 5: Purl.

Repeat Rows 1-6.

Garter stitch stripes

Garter stitch stripes have a different texture than the ones made in reverse stockinette stitch. The sample shown in Figure 2-3 is one way to arrange them. Try out some others.

Cast on any number of stitches.

Rows 1, 3, 5–11, 13, 15, and 16 (RS): Knit.

Rows 2, 4, 12, and 14: Purl.

Repeat Rows 1–16.

Figure 2-3:
Garter stitch
stripes

Making ribbing

Knit ribs are textured vertical stripes. Ribbing is made by alternating columns of knit stitches with columns of purl stitches. Instead of alternating knit rows with purl rows as you do when you make horizontal stripes, when you make a ribbed pattern, you change from knit stitches to purl stitches *within* a row.

Ribbing is the edging par excellence on most sweaters because of its elasticity — it stretches to let you in and out of cuffs and neckbands and then springs back into place to hug you. The most common combinations are k1, p1 ribbing (also known as 1 x 1 ribbing) and k2, p2 ribbing (2 x 2). Check out Figures 2-5 and 2-6 to see what they look like.

In general, ribbed borders are worked on needles one or two sizes smaller than the ones used for the body of the project. For less "hug," use a larger needle (the same size or one size less than what you plan to use for the rest of the project) and a larger rib pattern, 2 x 2 or 3 x 3, and so on.

The wider the ribs and larger the needle size, the less the elasticity.

Instructions for knit and purl patterns don't explicitly tell you to bring your yarn to the front or back of your work. They assume that you know where the yarn should be when you're about to knit or purl a stitch. When knitting a stitch, the yarn is in *back* of your work. To go from a knit stitch to a purl stitch, bring your yarn between the needles to the *front* of your work, as shown in Figure 2-4a. When purling a stitch, the yarn is in *front* of your work. To go from a purl stitch to a knit stitch, bring your yarn between the needles to the *back* of your work, as shown in Figure 2-4b.

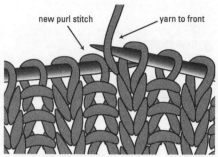
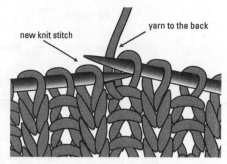

Figure 2-4: Knowing where to place the yarn.

A. Keeping your yarn in front of your work

B. Keeping your yarn behind your work

1 x 1 ribbing

The 1 x 1 rib pattern in Figure 2-5 is stretched out a bit. Stretch yours further to see the purls more clearly. In contracted form, most of the purl column is hidden by the knit column.

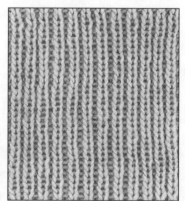

Figure 2-5: Looking at 1 x 1 ribbing.

Cast on an even number of stitches.

Work every row: *K1, p1; rep from *. (An asterisk (*) tells you to repeat what follows.)

Repeat this row for the length of your piece.

After the first row, you can tell by looking at your knitting whether you should be making a knit stitch or a purl stitch. If the next stitch on your LH needle is a purl (bump) stitch, purl it. If it's a knit stitch, knit it.

Get in the habit of looking at your work. The sooner you can "read" the pattern in your knitting — meaning that you recognize the sequence of knits and purls — the less dependent you'll be on the written instructions.

2 x 2 ribbing

Two-by-two ribbing alternates 2 knit stitches with 2 purl stitches. It pulls in slightly less than 1-by-1 ribbing. See Figure 2-6.

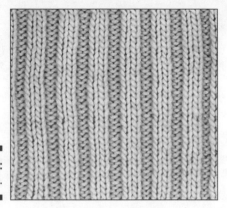

Figure 2-6:
2 x 2 ribbing.

Cast on a multiple of 4 stitches.

Work every row: *K2, p2; rep from *.

Note: If you want your piece to begin and end on two knit stitches, add 2 to the multiple given at the beginning. You then begin each even row as P2, k2.

4 x 2 and 2 x 4 ribbing

There's no reason to keep knit ribs and purl ribs the same number of stitches. You can work ribs in uneven combinations, such as knit 4, purl 2 or knit 2, purl 4, and so on, as shown in Figure 2-7.

Figure 2-7:
4 x 2 ribbing.

Cast on a multiple of 6 stitches, plus 4. (You can work this pattern over a multiple of 6 stitches but it won't be symmetrical.)

Row 1: *K4, p2; rep from *, end k4.

Row 2: *P4, k2; rep from *, end p4.

Repeat Rows 1 and 2 for pattern.

If you turn this swatch over, you'll have a very different looking pattern — thin vertical stripes instead of thick ones.

Knitting checkerboard patterns

You can create checkerboard patterns by alternating knits and purls horizontally and vertically. Seed stitch is one of the most common checkerboard patterns, but there are others, as well. Seed stitch consists of single knits and purls alternating horizontally and vertically. Other variations alternate pairs (or more) of knits and purls.

Seed stitch

Seed stitch, like garter stitch, lies flat, making it a good edging for a sweater border and cuffs. You can see in Figure 2-8 why it's called seed stitch — the little purl bumps look like seeds that have been scattered.

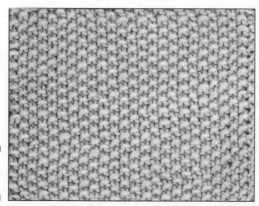

Figure 2-8:
Seed stitch.

Cast on an even number of stitches. (This pattern looks the same from both sides.)

Row 1: *K1, p1; rep from *.

Row 2: *P1, k1; rep from *.

Repeat Rows 1 and 2.

Moss stitch

Moss stitch, shown in Figure 2-9, is an elongated version of seed stitch. Instead of alternating the pattern every row, you work two rows of the same sequence of knits and purls before you alternate them.

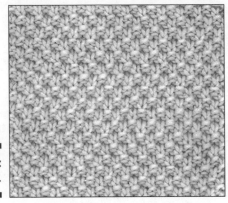

Figure 2-9: Moss stitch.

Cast on an uneven number of stitches. (An uneven number of stitches makes this pattern symmetrical. Either side can be the right side.)

Rows 1 and 4: *K1, p1; rep from * to end of row, end k1.

Rows 2 and 3: *P1, k1; rep from *, end p1.

Repeat Rows 1–4.

Double seed stitch

In this variation, you double seed stitch horizontally and vertically — 2 knits alternating with 2 purls for two rows and then reverse the sequence. Figure 2-10 illustrates double seed stitch.

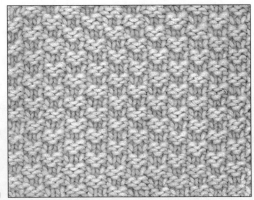

Figure 2-10: Double seed stitch.

Cast on a multiple of 4 stitches, plus 2. (Either side can be the right side.)

Rows 1 and 4: *K2, p2; rep from * end k2.

Rows 2 and 3: *P2, k2; rep from *, end p2.

Repeat Rows 1–4.

Knits and purls have a quirky but predictable relationship to each other. When lined up horizontally as in welt patterns, the purl-stitch rows stand out from the knit-stitch rows. Arranged in vertical patterns, like ribbing, the purl stitches recede, and the knit stitches come forward, creating an elastic fabric. When worked in a balanced manner (same number of knits and purls appearing on each side of the fabric), as in seed stitch and its variations, the fabric is stable — it lies flat and doesn't have the tendency to roll in on the edges. These qualities make seed and moss stitches, as well as garter stitch, good choices for borders that you want to lie flat and not pull in as ribbed borders do.

Knitting Notebook

The knit and purl stitch patterns in this section are a short introduction to the many designs you can make with these simple elements. As you work from one to the next, you'll see how a few simple adjustments can create a whole new pattern.

4 x 4 ribbing

The 4 x 4 rib shown in Figure 2-11 gives you a vertical stripe pattern that will pull in very little. It's symmetrical, a simple alternation of 4 knit stitches with 4 purl stitches.

Figure 2-11:
4 x 4 ribbing.

Cast on a multiple of 4 stitches, plus 4 more. (Either side can be the right side.)

Row 1: *K4, p4; rep from *, end k4.

Row 2: *P4, k4; rep from *, end p4.

Repeat Rows 1 and 2 for pattern.

Mistake stitch ribbing

Mistake stitch ribbing is a 2 x 2 rib worked over 1 less stitch than required to make it even. See Figure 2-12.

Figure 2-12:
Mistake
stitch
ribbing.

Cast on a multiple of 4 stitches, plus 3.

Work every row: *K2, p2; rep from *, end k2, p1.

Repeat this row for pattern.

Interrupted rib

The interrupted rib pattern looks different from each side, but both are handsome. Use whichever side you like best. Figure 2-13 gives you an idea of what it looks like.

Cast on an even number of stitches.

Rows 1, 2, and 3: *K1, p1; rep from *.

Row 4: Purl.

Repeat these 4 rows.

Rows 5,6,7: *P1, k1, rep from *

Row 8: Purl.

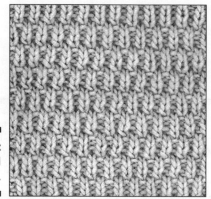

Figure 2-13:
Interrupted
rib.

Diagonal ribbing

The "ribs" in this fabric slant in one direction from one side and slant in the other direction from the reverse side. Figure 2-14 shows what diagonal rib looks like.

Figure 2-14:
Diagonal
ribbing.

Cast on a multiple of 8 stitches, plus 6.

Row 1: K1, *p4, k4: rep from *, end p4, k1.

Row 2: K4, *p4, k4; rep from *, end p2.

Row 3: K3, *p4, k4; rep from *, end p3.

Row 4: K2, *p4, k4; rep from *, end p4.

Row 5: P1, *k4, p4; rep from *, end k4, p1.

Row 6: P4, *k4, p4; rep from *, end k2.

Row 7: P3, *k4, p4; rep from *, end k3.

Row 8: P2, *k4, p4; rep from *, end k4.

Repeat Rows 1–8.

Basketweave

A glance at Figure 2-15 shows you how this pattern got its name. This is one of several variations on the woven theme. Look through a stitch dictionary for more alternatives.

Figure 2-15:
Basket-
weave
pattern.

Cast on a multiple of 8 stitches, plus 5.

Row 1 (RS): Knit.

Row 2: K5, *p3, k5; rep from *.

Row 3: P5, *k3, p5; rep from *.

Row 4: Repeat Row 2.

Row 5: Knit.

Row 6: K1, *p3, k5; rep from *, end last rep k1 instead of k5.

Row 7: P1, *k3, p5; rep from *, end last rep p1 instead of p5.

Row 8: Repeat Row 6.

Repeat Rows 1–8.

Double basket pattern

This pattern combines ribs and ridge patterns, as shown in Figure 2-16.

Figure 2-16:
Double basket pattern.

Cast on a multiple of 18 stitches, plus 10.

Row 1 (RS): *K11, p2, k2, p2, k1; rep from *, end k10.

Row 2: P1, k8, p1, *p1 (k2, p2) twice, k8, p1; rep from *.

Row 3: *K1, p8, (k2, p2) twice, k1; rep from *, end k1, p8, k1.

Row 4: P10, *p1, k2, p2, k2, p11; rep from *.

Rows 5, 6, 7, and 8: Repeat Rows 1, 2, 3, and 4.

Row 9: Knit.

Row 10: (P2, k2) twice, p2, * p10 (k2, p2) twice; rep from *.

Row 11: *(K2, p2) twice, k2, p8; rep from *, end (k2, p2) twice, k2.

Row 12: (P2, k2) twice, p2, *k8 (p2, k2) twice, p2; rep from *.

Row 13: *(K2, p2) twice, k10; rep from *, end (k2, p2) twice, k2.

Rows 14, 15, 16, and 17: Repeat Rows 10, 11, 12, and 13.

Row 18: Purl.

Repeat Rows 1–18.

Ripple stitch

Here the purl stitches make wavy lines, as you can see in Figure 2-17. For an experiment, you might try plotting this pattern on a piece of graph paper and then see whether you can change the contour of the waves and chart your variation.

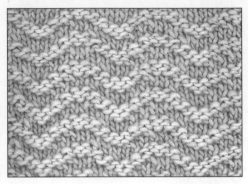

Figure 2-17:
Ripple
stitch.

Cast on a multiple of 8, plus 6 stitches.

Row 1 (RS): K6, *p2, k6; rep from *.

Row 2: K1, *p4, k4; rep from *, end p4, k1.

Row 3: P2, *k2, p2; rep from *.

Row 4: P1, *k4, p4; rep from *, end k4, p1.

Row 5: K2, *p2, k6; rep from *, end p2, k2.

Row 6: P6, *k2, p6; rep from *.

Row 7: P1, *k4, p4; rep from *, end k4, p1.

Row 8: K2, *p2, k2; rep from *.

Row 9: K1, *p4, k4; rep from *, end p4, k1.

Row 10: P2, *k2, p6; rep from *, end k2, p2.

Repeat Rows 1–10.

Diamond brocade

This pattern, as you can see in Figure 2-18, has a true brocade appearance.

Cast on a multiple of 12, plus 1.

Row 1 (RS): K1, *p1, k9, p1, k1; rep from *.

Row 2: K1, *p1, k1, p7, k1, p1, k1; rep from *.

Row 3: K1, *p1, k1, p1, k5, (p1, k1) twice; rep from *.

Row 4: P1, *(p1, k1) twice, p3, k1, p1, k1, p2; rep from *.

Row 5: K1, *k2, (p1, k1) 3 times, p1, k3; rep from *.

Row 6: P1, *p3, (k1, p1) twice, k1 p4; rep from *.

Row 7: K1, *k4, p1, k1, p1, k5; rep from *.

Row 8: Repeat Row 6.

Row 9: Repeat Row 5.

Row 10: Repeat Row 4.

Row 11: Repeat Row 3.

Row 12: Repeat Row 2.

Repeat Rows 1–12.

Figure 2-18:
Diamond
brocade.

Seed stitch diamonds

This pattern is a bit like diamond brocade (see the preceding section) in reverse. This time, the seed stitches are used to make solid diamonds instead of simply outlining them. See Figure 2-19.

Figure 2-19:
Seed stitch
diamonds.

Cast on a multiple of 10 stitches, plus 1.

Row 1 (RS): P1, *k3, p1, k1, p1, k3, p1; rep from *.

Row 2: P1, *k1, p3, k1, p3, k1, p1; rep from *.

Row 3: P1, *k1, p1, k5, p1, k1, p1; rep from *.

Row 4: P1, *k1, p1, k1, p3, (k1, p1) twice; rep from *.

Row 5: Repeat Row 3.

Row 6: Repeat Row 2.

Row 7: P1, *K3, p1, k1, p1, k3, p1; rep from *.

Row 8: P3, *(k1, p1) twice, k1, p5; rep from *, end last repeat p3.

Row 9: K2, *(p1, k1) 3 times, p1, k3; rep from *, end last repeat k2.

Row 10: P3, *(k1, p1) twice, k1, p5; rep from *, end last repeat p3.

Repeat Rows 1–10.

Combining Stitch Patterns

Knit-purl stitch patterns, such as the diamond brocade presented earlier in this chapter, can be worked as repeating motifs in all-over, predictable patterns. But you can also combine different motifs in the same fabric. (Think of the wonderful variety of patterns in traditional Aran and Guernsey sweaters.) Although it's possible to write these out as row-by-row instructions, it's easier to see the pattern if the instructions are in chart form. The stitch patterns in this section show you two ways to combine elements from the patterns above.

Knitted plaid

The pattern in Figure 2-20 combines reverse stockinette stripes, vertical ribs, and double seed stitch for a plaid effect. See Figure 2-21 for the chart.

Figure 2-20:
Knitted
plaid.

Cast on a multiple of 19 stitches.

Starting at the bottom right corner, work the first right-side row from right to left according to the chart in Figure 2-21. Work the next wrong-side row from left to right, remembering to work the stitches as they will appear on the right side. (See the section on working from a chart earlier in this chapter.) Continue to work all right-side rows (odd-numbered rows) from right to left, and wrong-side rows (even-numbered rows) from left to right.

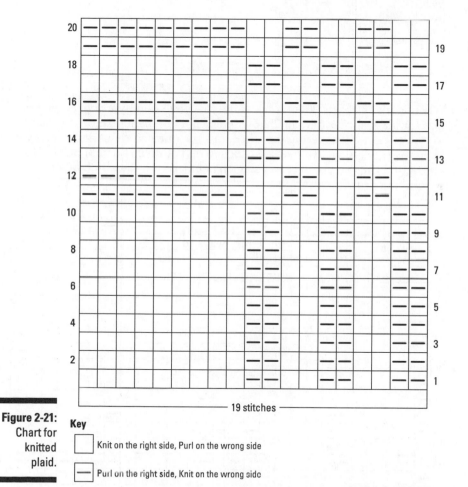

— 19 stitches —

Figure 2-21:
Chart for
knitted
plaid.

Key

☐ Knit on the right side, Purl on the wrong side

⊟ Purl on the right side, Knit on the wrong side

Guernsey knit-purl pattern

Figure 2-22 shows a traditional combination knit-and-purl pattern from a Guernsey-style sweater, and Figure 2-23 shows the chart. See the instructions for working a chart in the preceding "Knitted plaid" section.

Figure 2-22: Swatch showing a Guernsey knit-purl pattern.

When working charts, keep track of the row you're on by using a self-stick note or magnetic strip. (See Chapter 4 for more on handy knitting tools.) Mark your row by covering the row *above* the one you're working on. If you keep the row you've just worked exposed on your chart, you'll be able to check that the stitch you're working on lines up with the stitch below it.

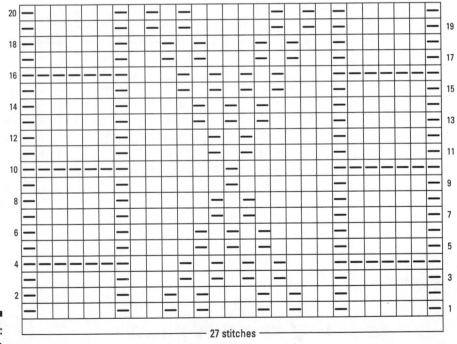

Figure 2-23: Chart for a Guernsey knit-purl pattern.

Key

☐ Knit on the right side, Purl on the wrong side

⊟ Purl on the right side, Knit on the wrong side

Chapter 3

Oops! Fixing Common Mistakes

· ·

In This Chapter

▶ Knowing what to do when you mess up

▶ Saving dropped stitches

▶ Removing extra stitches

▶ Ripping out without having to start over

· ·

As a beginning knitter, you may not notice the mistakes in your project, and that's understandable. After all, you're trying to figure out what to do with your hands, the needles, and the yarn. That's enough to worry about when you're just learning! But once you get the hang of it, you'll start paying attention to your work and notice those little bumps and twists that don't look right. Trust me, once you're up and running and making an otherwise perfect project, those little glitches will come to haunt you unless you fix them.

For your own sense of competence and satisfaction, discover how to see where you are in your work, how you made your mistake, and how to fix it and carry on. I know that advice sounds like hard work. But try to think of your mistakes as good teachers. More than anything else, they'll show you what you need to know to be an independent knitter.

 The sooner you spot a mistake, the easier it is to correct it and move on. Get in the habit of checking your work. As you practice, take the time to count your stitches after each row. One stitch more or less than you cast on frequently indicates that something has gone wrong in the last row you worked. Don't panic! You won't have to count your stitches forever. Soon your fingers will alert you to a missed move, and you'll be catching mistakes before they become a nuisance to correct.

Having Too Few Stitches on Your Needle

If you count the number of stitches on your needle and discover that you have one stitch less than you should have, you've probably dropped a stitch. It has imperceptibly worked its way off the needle, often before you've had a chance to work it.

Carefully spread out your stitches along the needle and slowly scan the row(s) just below the needle till you locate the dropped stitch. If it hasn't unraveled far, it will look like the one in Figure 3-1. A dropped stitch, contrary to knitting lore, will not immediately unravel itself into oblivion. (Thank goodness!)

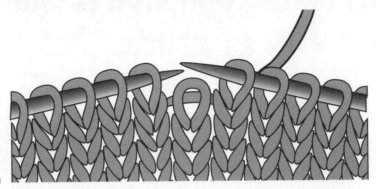

Figure 3-1:
Dropped
stitch from
the knit side.

When you find a dropped stitch, carefully work a small needle tip, the blunt point of a tapestry needle, a toothpick, a nail, a bobby pin (anything!) into it to secure it and stretch it out a bit. Find a safety pin (you should have some with your knitting supplies) and nab the stitch. Take a deep breath and follow the instructions in the following sections for getting that dropped stitch back on the needle.

Rescuing a dropped stitch in the row below

Continue working (knitting or purling) until you reach the pinned stitch. Take a good look at the situation. If the stitch slipped off while you weren't looking and you knit right past it, or it worked itself out of the old loop, you'll see a short horizontal strand of yarn that didn't get wrapped and pulled through as a new stitch. The strand will be either behind or in front of the dropped stitch. If you see no sign of an unknitted strand, simply put the stitch back on the LH needle in the ready-to-work position and carry on. (See Chapter 7 for more on the ready-to-work position.)

If you do see an unworked strand, you need to pull it through the dropped stitch. If you see more than one strand, the stitch has dropped more than one row, and you'll need a crochet hook to pick up stitches. Scan down to "Rescuing a dropped stitch from several rows below" to find out how to do this.

It's a simple matter to rescue a stitch that has one strand of yarn to pull through, but how you go about it depends on whether you want to make a knit stitch or a purl stitch.

To make a knit stitch

If the *knit* side of your work is facing, rescue the dropped stitch as follows:

1. **Insert your RH needle into the *front* of the dropped (pinned) stitch.**

   Look behind the stitch. You'll see the horizontal strand of yarn that didn't get pulled through.

2. **Using the RH needle, go under this strand from the front — strand and stitch are on the RH needle, as shown in Figure 3-2.**

3. **Insert the LH needle into the stitch from the back (Figure 3-3) and pull it over the strand (the strand has become a stitch).**

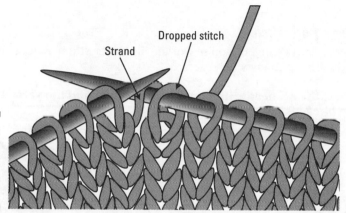

Dropped stitch

Strand

Figure 3-2: Dropped stitch ready to be worked.

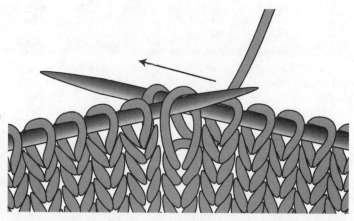

Figure 3-3: Insert LH needle into the dropped stitch.

4. **Put the new stitch on the LH needle in the ready-to-knit position, as shown in Figure 3-4.**

Check to see that you've made a smooth V stitch.

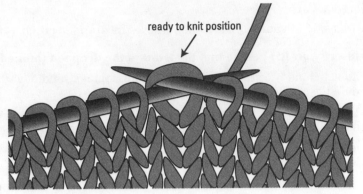

Figure 3-4: Transfer the stitch to the ready-to-knit position.

ready to knit position

To make a purl stitch

If the *purl* side is facing, or you're working in garter stitch, rescue the dropped stitch as follows:

1. **Insert the RH needle into the dropped stitch *and* the yarn strand from the *back*, as shown in Figure 3-5.**

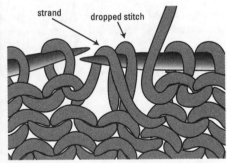

strand   dropped stitch

Figure 3-5: Picking up a dropped purl stitch.

A. Put RH needle through the dropped stitch and under the yarn strand as indicated by the arrow.

B. Picking up both the dropped stitch and the yarn strand.

2. **Using the LH needle, pull the stitch over the strand and off the needle, forming a new stitch on the RH needle, as shown in Figure 3-6.**

3. **Place the new stitch on the LH needle in the ready-to-work position. See this in action in Figure 3-7.**

Check to see that you have a bump below the stitch.

Figure 3-6:
Pulling the
dropped
stitch over.

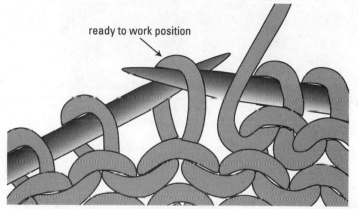

ready to work position

Figure 3-7:
Replacing
the rescued
stitch in the
ready-to-
work
position.

If you can't readily pick up a dropped stitch from the back or front, pick it up any way you can and put it on the RH needle. Check to see if it's in the ready-to-knit position. Pull the unworked strand through and then check to see that you've made the right kind of stitch — knit or purl depending on what you're making.

I hope you're practicing this as you read along!

Rescuing a dropped stitch from several rows below

If the dropped stitch has worked itself down several rows or if you didn't notice its absence immediately, you can still rescue it. Find the dropped stitch and secure it with a safety pin, a paper clip, or whatever you have on hand. Work to the spot the stitch dropped from. You'll see the wayward stitch at the bottom of a ladder of unworked strands that look like Figure 3-8. Each strand represents a row.

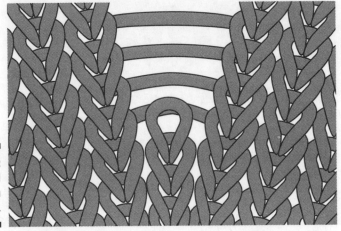

Figure 3-8:
Dropped
knit stitch
and ladder.

In stockinette stitch

Rescue a dropped stitch from the knit side (if the purl side is facing, turn it around) by following these steps:

1. **Use a crochet hook to reach through the errant stitch and pick up the bottom strand in the ladder, as shown in Figure 3-9.**

2. **Pull the strand through the stitch to form a new stitch.**

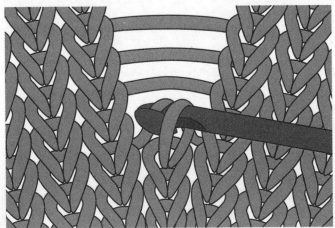

Figure 3-9:
Pulling
through the
first strand.

3. **Continue to pull each successive strand in the ladder through the loop on the crochet hook till the last strand has been worked.**

Take care to pull the stitches through in the right sequence (from the bottom of the ladder to the top), or you'll have a new mistake in your knitting.

Aim to make your "crocheted" stitches the same size as their neighbors. Give a little tug on your work in each direction when you've finished your rescue to blend the stitches.

In garter stitch

In order to pick up several rows of dropped stitches in garter stitch, you have to alternate the direction from which you pull the ladder strands through the dropped stitch — pulling through the front of the stitch if you want to create a knit stitch or pulling through the back of the stitch for a purl.

After you've secured the dropped stitch and before you insert your crochet hook, determine whether to pull the first strand at the bottom of the ladder through the secured stitch from the front or the back. To do this, follow the bottom strand to the side (either way) to see what the stitch connected to it looks like. (Pull gently on the strand to locate the neighboring stitches if you need to.) You can see the connected stitches in Figure 3-10.

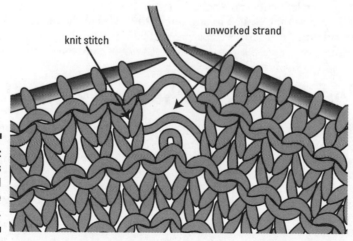

knit stitch

unworked strand

Figure 3-10: Stitches connected to the strand.

If the base of the next stitch is the bottom of a V, it's a knit stitch, and the dropped stitch should be picked up from the front (refer to Figure 3-9 to see what this looks like). If the base of the stitch is a bump, insert the crochet hook into the stitch *back to front* (toward you), pick up the strand, and pull it through, as shown in Figure 3-11. Check to make sure that the stitch you've made matches the ones next to it.

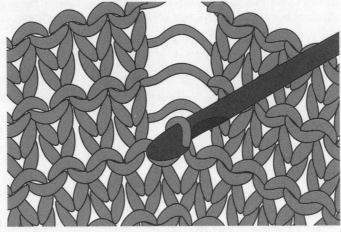

Figure 3-11:
Picking up a dropped stitch from the back.

Alternate pulling stitches from each direction until you've pulled through the last strand. Put the last loop onto the LH needle in the ready-to-work position.

Pick up the strands of yarn in the proper order. You'll have a major glitch in your work if you pull a loop through from a strand in the wrong row.

Some yarns, especially plied ones, are prone to splitting. When you're knitting and fixing mistakes, take care not to let your needle penetrate the yarn you're using. Make sure that you go in and out of the *holes* in the stitches, leaving the yarn strand intact.

Having Too Many Stitches on Your Needle

An extra stitch on your needle often means that the yarn has crossed the needle while you weren't looking, making an inadvertent *yarn over* — a knitting move that makes a "hole" in your knitting. Or it could mean that the wrap of yarn hasn't quite made it through the old stitch or that the old stitch wasn't completely dropped from the needle when you created a new stitch above it. Sometimes the extra stitch is just a mystery stitch. Who knows where it came from?

In any case, rip back. The following sections tell you how.

Ripping out: Stitch by stitch

If you're lucky enough to catch your mistake on the row you're working on before you've finished it, you can rip back to your mistake one stitch at a time. You'll be *unforming* the loops on the RH needle. Here's how:

1. **With the knit or purl side facing, insert the LH needle from *front to back* (away from you) into the stitch below the one on the RH needle, as shown in Figure 3-12.**

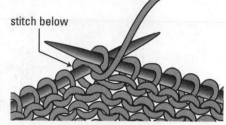

slide needle out

stitch below

stitch below

Figure 3-12: Unforming a stitch.

A. Into a knit stitch below   B. Into a purl stitch below

2. **Slide the RH needle out of the stitch and gently pull on the yarn to free it.**

   Your work won't unravel because your LH needle has secured the stitch below.

3. **Continue to rip back, stitch by stitch, to the point of your mistake.**

Ripping out: Row by row

What's the worst case scenario? You notice a mistake several rows down in your work — a bump or glitch that can't be rescued easily by backing up a few stitches. You may decide that to rip back one stitch at a time may take longer than to simply start over. Take a deep breath, do an unkinking exercise or two (see Chapter 20), and get ready to take your work off your needle. You *can* do this.

Because ripping out stitch by stitch is very time consuming, a better approach is to bite the bullet, take your work off the needles, rip out several rows of those carefully constructed stitches, and work them again. Or you can live with the glitch. What you decide depends on your personality. Some of you may find it easier than others to live with imperfections.

If you decide to rip out and fix your mistake, the following steps will gently guide you through this process:

1. **Locate the row your mistake is on and mark it with a safety pin.**

2. **Slide your needle out of the stitches.**

3. **Pull gently on the working yarn, undoing the stitches, until you're on the row above the mistake. Rip to the end of the row.**

4. **Hold your knitting with the working yarn on the right (flip it over if it's on the left). Following the direction of the arrow in Figure 3-13, insert the tip of the needle into the first stitch on the row below (from back to front toward you).**

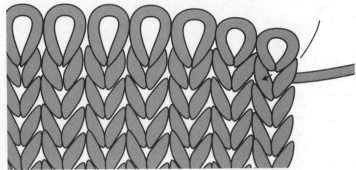

Figure 3-13:
Insert the needle into the stitch below.

5. **Pull gently to free the yarn from the stitch.**

   You'll have one stitch solidly planted on the RH needle.

6. **Repeat Step 5 until you reach your mistake.**

   Figure 3-14 shows what it looks like as you work across to your mistake.

7. **Rip out your mistake, turn your work, and start knitting again!**

Pull gently on the yarn
to unravel the stitching

Figure 3-14:
Stitches on your RH needle as you work across to your mistake.

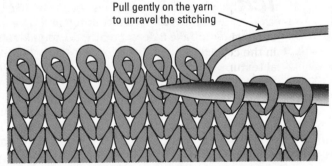

Use a needle several sizes smaller to pick up the last row of your ripped-out knitting. Work the next row with your regular needle.

Take the time to practice ripping out a little of your work. You should be familiar with this procedure before you tackle any project.

Chapter 4

Tools of the Trade

Some yarn and a pair of needles are all you really need in order to knit. However, these basic supplies can become a not-so-simple choice when you consider the array of beautiful yarns and designer needles available.

This chapter gives you the know-how to find the right yarn for your project, and the right needle for your yarn, and guides you in making your choice.

Yarn: The (Quick) Consumer's Guide

Yarn shops are bursting with colorful and imaginative novelty yarns. (You can see some pictured in the color insert.) Their jewel colors, undulating surfaces, and whimsical textures are hard to resist. (There's even a yarn called Eyelash, and guess what it looks like.)

Even the basics have gotten a facelift. Classic wool worsted (medium-weight) yarn shares the shelf with washable wool, felted wool, wool from designer breeds of sheep, wool blended with silk, mohair, cotton, alpaca, acrylics, boucléd wool, ribboned wool, plied wool, cabled wool, and (like everything else) wool in shades of kiwi, strawberry, and mango.

Whether you prefer your yarn plain or fancy, some knowledge of yarn basics will ensure that what looks great on the shelf will look great in your finished project.

Yarn 101

Yarn is made from short fibers (which come from animals, plants, or petroleum), which are combed (carded) to align them into a soft untwisted rope (called roving) and then spun (twisted) into a strand or ply of yarn that is usually combined with other plies to form the final yarn.

Variation in yarns come from four factors: the composition and combination of the fibers used, whether the final yarn is single or plied, tricks in the spinning process that create texture in the strand, and the dyeing process.

A weighty matter

Yarns come in different weights or thicknesses. The thickness of a yarn determines how many stitches it takes to knit 1 inch. A medium-weight yarn that knits up 5 stitches and 7 rows to the inch takes 35 stitches to make a square inch of knitted fabric. A bulky yarn at 3 stitches and 5 rows to the inch needs 15 stitches to make a square inch. You can see the difference in Figure 4-1.

Figure 4-1:
Knitting with yarn of different weights.

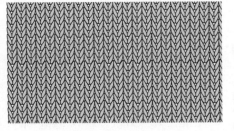 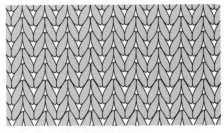

Medium-weight yarn   Bulky yarn

The weight of your yarn (among other things) determines the look of your project and certainly the amount of time it takes to knit up your project.

Although there aren't any standardized categories for yarn weights, there are some familiar terms for describing yarns by their thickness and the size of the needle they're usually worked on. Table 4-1 gives you a starting reference point.

Table 4-1	Common Yarn Weights	
Yarn Weight	*Needles*	*Stitches Per Inch*
Fingering or baby weight	1–3	7–8
Sport	3–6	5–6
DK (double-knitting)	5–7	5–5½
Worsted	7–9	4–5
Bulky	10–11	3–3½
Gigantic	13–15	2–2½

Yarn consists of one or more strands of yarn called *plies*. Plied yarns are made from several plies of yarn twisted together. The thickness of a given yarn is determined not by the *number* of plies, but by their individual thickness. If the plies are thin, a 4-ply yarn can be finer than a heavy single-ply yarn.

Multi plied and firmly twisted yarns are usually strong, smooth, and even. Lightly twisted plied and single-ply yarns are closer to their roving (unspun) state and, though sturdy enough when knitted up, can pull apart in strand form if they're overhandled. They can be slightly uneven and have more loft and softness and are warmer than their twisted sisters.

Fiber fundamentals

All yarn, whether curly or straight, solid or variegated, is made from fibers that come directly from nature (animals or plants) or are conjured from petroleum, coal, or wood (synthetics). More than anything else, the combination of fibers your yarn is made from determines its ultimate characteristics, feel, and wearable comfort.

Knitting style through the ages

In the 1600s, men's waistcoats were knit (by men) 11 stitches (and more) to the inch in fine silk thread on steel needles no thicker than wire. In the 18th and 19th centuries, the women of the Shetland Isles knit sweaters on fine needles while they walked and between chores, turning out several sweaters a year. Today, you can knit with yarn as thick as rope on needles that measure an inch or more around.

The matter at hand

A fabric's *hand* is how it feels to the touch. Just as pieces of woven fabric from silk or wool differ in drape and softness, so do knits from different fibers. But fiber isn't all that accounts for drape and softness. The size of the needle you use with a given yarn affects the feel of your knitted piece. The larger the needle and looser the stitch, the softer and drapier the fabric. The smaller the needle and tighter the stitch, the stiffer the fabric.

The real thing: Wool

Wool (made from the fleece of sheep) is the queen of yarns, so much so that it's almost impossible to hear the word *knitting* and not think of wool at the same time. There are excellent reasons why wool endures and remains a popular choice for knitters.

The crinkled nature of its microscopic fibers creates pockets of trapped air, making it a good insulator — warm in winter, cool in summer. Wool can absorb lots of moisture without feeling wet — think socks. It also absorbs dye beautifully. It's resilient, meaning that wool fibers can stretch and bend repeatedly but always return to their original shape without breaking — your garment will keep its shape, too. A little steam turns uneven stitches into smooth and even stitches. It's soft. It's relatively lightweight. It's beautiful to look at. And not least important, wool is a pleasure to knit with because it's soft to the touch and gives just enough to make it easy to get your needles in and out of the stitches.

Although all wool yarns are wonderful to work with, they vary tremendously depending on the breed of sheep or combination of breeds they come from, how they're spun, whether they're plied or single stranded, and whether they're treated for washability or not.

Yarns from the fleeces of other animals

Sheep aren't the only animals to give us fibers for yarns. Fuzzy mohair and luxurious cashmere come from Angora and Cashmere goats, respectively. Warm, soft alpaca comes from members of the llama family, the small, South American cousin of the camel. The belly of Musk oxen provides the lush and exceptionally warm and light qiviut. Lighter than air and fuzziest of all, angora comes from the Angora rabbit hair.

Silk, cotton, linen, and rayon

Silk, cotton, linen, and rayon yarns are the slippery yarns. Unlike rough yarns from the hairy fibers of animals, their smooth and often shiny surfaces will cause them to unravel quickly if you drop a stitch. They are inelastic and may stretch lengthwise over time. Often, they're blended with other fibers (natural and synthetic) to counteract their disadvantages. But silk and cotton, even in their pure state, are so lovely to look at and comfortable to wear that they're worth trying.

The other stuff

Originally, synthetics (nylon, acrylic, and polyester) were made to mimic the look and feel of natural materials. Just as wool yarn is spun from short lengths of aligned fibers from a sheep's fleece, synthetic yarns begin as a long extruded filament cut into short lengths and processed to look like wool yarn.

Knitters give mixed reviews to 100 percent acrylics. On the one hand, they are inexpensive and can go in and out of the washing machine. For those who are allergic to wool, they make (at least from a distance) a look-alike substitute.

On the downside, all-synthetic yarns don't have the wonderful insulating and moisture absorbing qualities of the real thing, and therefore, they can be uncomfortable to wear (imagine plastic wrap made into yarn). For the same reason, they can make your hands clammy when you're knitting. They pill more readily than wool or other fibers. And once exposed to heat (a hot iron is deadly), they lose all resilience and become flat. Nothing will bring them back to life.

Wooly words

Wool, far from being just one thing, comes to you in a variety of ways. Here are a few ways you'll come across wool yarn.

- **Lamb's wool:** This wool comes from a young lamb's first sheering. It's softer and finer than wool from an older sheep's fleece.

- **Merino wool:** Merino is the oldest breed of sheep and considered the finest of the fine breeds. Long, lustrous fibers make a soft and exceptionally lovely knitted fabric.

- **Pure new wool/ virgin wool:** "Pure new" and "virgin" refer to wool that is made directly from animal fleece and not recycled from wool garments.

- **Shetland wool:** This traditional 2-ply heathery yarn was originally from the small and hardy native sheep of the Shetland Islands and used in traditional Fair Isle sweaters. It's usually available in sport or fingering weight. This wool originally came in sheep's colors, including all shades of charcoal and deep brown to white. Shetland wool is now also available in an extraordinary range of beautiful dyed colors.

- **Icelandic wool:** This rustic, soft, single-ply, medium-weight to heavy-weight yarn was traditionally available only in natural sheep colors (black, charcoal, light gray, and white) and characteristically knitted up in patterned, round yoke sweaters. Frequently sold under the name Lopi, this yarn is now also available dyed in bright jewel and heathered colors and in a lighter indoor weight.

- **Washable wool:** This wool is treated chemically or electronically to destroy the outer fuzzy layer of fibers that would otherwise felt or bond with each other and shrink in the washing machine.

These complaints and their dubious reputation have encouraged manufacturers to come up with new and better applications for synthetics. Though synthetics will never be wool or cotton, the world of novelty yarns wouldn't be possible without them.

New millennium yarns

Perhaps the best use for synthetics is in combination with other fibers. Manufacturers now engineer blended yarns for certain qualities. For example, nylon is extremely strong and light. Blended in small amounts with more fragile fibers such as mohair, nylon adds durability. A little nylon blended with wool makes a superb sock yarn. In elastic form and spun with wool, nylon can add to wool's natural resilience by preventing elbow or rear-end (in a skirt) pouch. A little acrylic in cotton makes the yarn lighter and promotes "memory" so that it won't stretch out of shape.

If you like to make socks and want to reinforce heels and toes without resorting to using nylon throughout, you can make a do-it-yourself blend by working a separate strand of nylon (designed especially for sock heels) along with your regular yarn for spot blending.

Yarnspeak made easy

When you're looking around at different yarns, here are some terms you'll come across as you check out their labels. A little time browsing in a good yarn shop, and it won't be long before you're an old hand at identifying the different varieties of yarns to knit with.

Blends: A yarn made from fibers of different origins — for example, wool/cotton, wool/silk, alpaca/cotton.

Boucle: A highly bumpy textured yarn.

Chenille: Velvety in appearance, tricky to knit with, but very attractive. Usually in rayon (for sheen) or cotton.

Felted: Yarn that has been treated to look in the strand like a felted piece of knitting. Soft and a little fuzzy.

Heather: A yarn that has been spun with a mix of dyed and/or natural gray fleece. Heather yarns are muted in color. Think of them as the yarn equivalent of watercolors.

Marled (ragg yarn): A plied yarn in which the plies are different colors.

Mohair: *Mohair* refers to a fiber and also to a fuzzy, lightweight yarn.

Ribbon: Just what it says, although it usually refers to a knitted ribbon in rayon with wonderful drape.

Tweeds: Usually wool, a yarn with a background color flecked with bits of fiber in different colors.

Variegated yarn: Yarn dyed in several different colors or shades of a single color.

Looking at yarn packaging

Yarn is packaged (sometimes called "put up") in different ways — balls, skeins (rhymes with canes), and hanks. Each ball, skein, or hank comes wrapped with a label. Read the label carefully. It gives you useful information and lets you know whether the yarn is a good candidate for the project you have in mind. If the yarn begs to be purchased before you know what you want to make with it, the information on the label will let you know what kind of project would best suit it.

Label talk

Though you'll find lots of vital information on the label (Figure 4-2 shows what you can expect to find there), probably the first thing you'll want to look for is the gauge (how many stitches and rows per inch) and the size needle suggested. This will give you an idea of what the final knitted fabric will look like. A size 11 needle and a gauge of low numbers (3 stitches and 5 rows to the inch) will yield a heavy chunky fabric. A size 5 needle and a gauge of 5 stitches and 7 rows to the inch will yield a finer more traditional fabric. Fiber content will let you know whether the yarn is wool, cotton, acrylic, a blend, or something else. If you intend to make a washable garment, check to see whether the yarn is machine or hand washable or strictly a dry-clean fiber.

1. Name and identifying number of color
2. Dye lot number
3. Company's name or symbol
4. Yarn's brand name
5. Care instructions
6. Company's name and address
7. Length of yarn in meters and in yards
8. Weight in grams and ounces
9. Ply (number of thin strands twisted together to make the yarn)
10. Yarn content (type of fiber or fibers)
11. Suggested knitting needle size to achieve expected gauge (number of stitches to the inch) for this yarn

Figure 4-2: Sample yarn label.

The dye lot number given on the label along with the color number identifies a batch of yarn dyed together. Even if you can't detect any difference in color between two balls of different dye lots, when you knit them up one after the other, there's a good chance that you'll see a line where one ball ends and the other begins. Avoid this problem by checking for dye lot numbers and buying enough yarn for your project at one time. If you have to buy more later, you may not be able to find yarn from the right dye lot.

If you absolutely can't make the whole project with yarn from the same dye lot, you can fudge the join between balls by alternating rows of different dye lots for several inches before switching entirely to the new dye lot. This blurs the line between the yarns of different dye lots. This method is better than an out-and-out switch.

Ball, skein, or hank?

Yarn is packaged in different forms: balls, skeins, and hanks, as shown in Figure 4-3. Balls and skeins come ready to knit. Once you find the end you can cast on and go. Hanks need to be wound into a ball before you can use them. If you try to knit with the yarn in hank form, you'll quickly end up with a tangled mess.

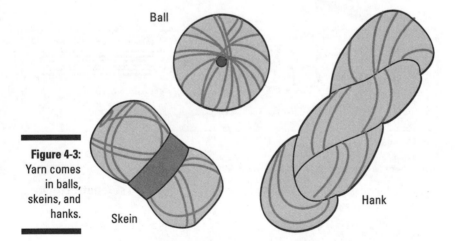

Ball

Figure 4-3:
Yarn comes
in balls,
skeins, and
hanks.

Skein

Hank

Balls and skeins are knittable as is. They don't need to be rewound. If possible, start knitting with the yarn end that comes from the *inside* of the skein or ball. This way the skein or ball will remain in place as you knit and not roll around the floor attracting the attention of the attack cat.

If you're lucky, the inside end will already be pulled to the outside — ready to go. If not, you'll have to reach in and pull out a small hunk of yarn in order to find this end, but rewrapping a little yarn around your skein is less work than trying to retrieve it after it's rolled (for the third time) under the couch.

Making a yarn ball

Hanks of yarn have to be wound into a ball before you can use them. To do this, follow these simple steps:

1. **Carefully unfold the hank (it's formed into a large circle) and drape it over a chair back, a friend's outstretched arms, or, if you're sitting, your bent knees.**

2. **Locate the ends of the yarn and, if they're tied, cut or unknot them.**

3. **With either end, begin by making a butterfly. Leaving an end of 8 inches or so, wrap the yarn in a figure eight around the thumb and little finger of your left hand (or your right hand if you're left-handed), as shown in Figure 4-4.**

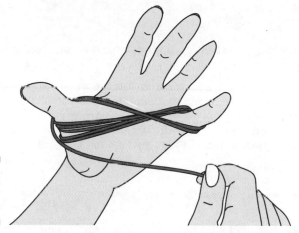

Figure 4-4:
Making a
butterfly.

Make about 20 passes if you're winding a medium-weight yarn, more for a finer yarn, or less for a thick yarn.

4. **Take the "wings" off your finger and thumb and fold the butterfly in half, holding it between thumb and fingers.**

5. **Continue wrapping yarn *loosely* around the folded butterfly (and your fingers), as shown in Figure 4-5.**

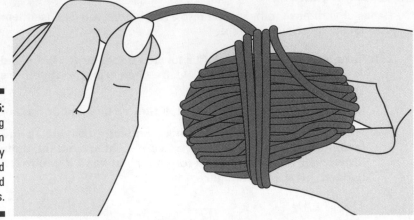

Figure 4-5:
Wrapping
the yarn
loosely
around
thumb and
fingers.

6. **When the package gets bulky, slip it off, turn it, and continue to wrap the yarn into a ball.**

   Neatness isn't important. *Looseness* is. Always wrap the yarn around as many fingers as you can, slipping them out when you change position. The space they take up will ensure that the yarn isn't stretched as it waits to be knitted. If you knit with stretched yarn, guess what happens to your knitted piece when the yarn springs back to size?

Choosing yarn for a specific project

Yarns, garment shapes, and stitch patterns must work together for your project to be successful. If you plan to knit a scarf or a blanket, go ahead and let the yarn you fall in love with dictate the outcome of your project. However, if you plan to make a sweater, using a sweater pattern as your starting point is the simplest way to get going on a project. You can purchase the yarn specified in the pattern or something similar enough (check with a knowledgeable salesperson) to ensure that the completed garment will look like the one in the picture.

Remembering gauge

If an irresistible yarn is your starting point and you want to make a sweater, find a pattern written especially for the kind of yarn you've chosen and hope that you like the style. Another option is to select a pattern calling for another yarn that works up to the same gauge as the yarn you've chosen. If the pattern you've chosen expects you to get 4 stitches and 6 rows to the inch and your yarn gives you something different, your sweater will turn out a different size than the one given in the pattern. See Chapter 5 for more on gauge.

Just because two yarns have the same gauge doesn't mean that they can sub-stitute for each other successfully in a given pattern. If they have different characteristics — texture, drape, fiber, and color — the final garment will look and feel different from the one pictured on your pattern.

It isn't easy to predict what yarn in a ball will look like when it's knitted up. This is especially true of novelty yarns. Jewel-colored hanks may look beauti-ful when displayed in a basket, but like mush when knitted up. Even plainer traditional yarns can surprise you. Their drape and feel will vary greatly depending on how tightly spun they are, the fiber they're made of, and the dye used to color them.

Check to see whether the yarns you're interested in have been knitted into a sample. Many yarn shops knit up sample swatches or entire sweaters in the yarns they carry so that you can see what they look like worked up.

Thinking about texture and color

If you want to work cables and stitch patterns, a smooth plied yarn in a solid color gives your stitches a crisp look, showcasing your effort. Cables and pat-tern stitches worked in soft single plies have a slightly softer appearance than when worked in highly twisted yarns. In general, plied and twisted yarns are sophisticated and classic. Single plies are rustic and relaxed.

If color is what you're after, a simple stockinette sweater knitted up in a color-ful hand-painted or sparkling novelty yarn will make a knock-out sweater with relatively little knitting effort. Simple stitch patterns are best. Don't knock yourself out with tricky stitch work if you're using a variegated yarn. The tex-ture won't show up, and all your stitch-making effort will be for naught.

If you love Fair Isle patterns, smooth plied yarns in contrasting colors give you clear and readable patterns. But don't overlook the possibilities of using a hand-painted yarn as one of your colored yarns. A variegated yarn in a single color that shades from light to dark has the subtlety of a watercolor.

Some novelty yarns can be tricky to work with. If you're dying to work with a novelty yarn, start with a variegated dyed or painted simple plied yarn. These give lots of color variation and interest, but the strand of yarn is itself easy to see. Identifying individual stitches in highly textured yarns is difficult if not impossible, making it hard to fix mistakes or rip out stitches.

The wilder the yarn, the simpler the sweater shape and pattern stitch should be. The plainer the yarn, the more texture and shaping details will show up.

Considering fiber content

For cotton, silk, and other yarns that are inelastic, look for patterns that don't depend on rib for fit. Find patterns that hang straight to highlight the drape of these yarns.

If you have your heart set on a cotton sweater with a ribbed border and you want the ribbing to pull in and not hang straight, ask the people at your yarn shop whether they have an elastic thread that you can work along with your regular yarn in the rib or edging pattern.

If you shop in a specialty yarn store, chances are that the people who work there have experience with their yarns and with knitting in general. They're there to help you and encourage you. Feel free to ask questions about the yarn you're considering for your project. Here are some good questions to keep in mind:

✔ Does it pill?

✔ Is it colorfast?

✔ Will it stretch?

✔ Is it easy to knit with?

✔ Does it work with the pattern I've chosen?

✔ What size needle will it work best with?

Whatever yarn you choose, remember that you're going to be seeing a lot of it. Hundreds of yards of it will be passing through your fingers as you build — stitch by stitch — your knitted project. Make sure that what you choose is worth your effort. You don't always have to spend more money for good quality, but if you do, you'll save yourself a headache or two, and you'll have a beautiful garment or project to show for your effort.

Knitting Needles

For knitters, variety doesn't end with yarns. Knitting needles come in a stunning assortment of materials, styles, and sizes to mesh with your knitting style, the particular project you're working on, your aesthetics, and your budget.

Exploring needle types

You can choose from three kinds of knitting needles: straight, circular, and double-pointed (see Figure 4-6).

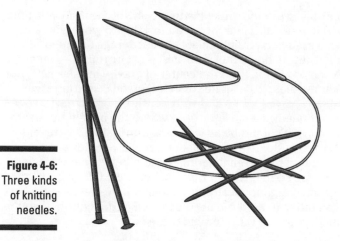

Figure 4-6:
Three kinds
of knitting
needles.

Telling it straight

Straight needles are generally used for *flat knitting* — knitting on the right side, turning and knitting on the wrong side. Straight needles come in standard lengths of 10, 13, and 14 inches. The larger your project, the longer the needle you'll need. Figure 4-7 shows the various parts of straight needles.

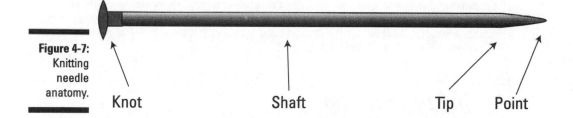

Figure 4-7:
Knitting
needle
anatomy.

Knot   Shaft   Tip   Point

Going in circles

Circular needles are really a pair of straight knitting needle tips joined by a flexible cable. They make it possible to knit spiral-like, creating a seamless tube large enough for a sweater body or small enough for a neckband. They can also be used like straight needles to work back and forth. Circular needles are available in standard lengths of 16, 24, 29, and 36 inches. Although you can sometimes find circular needles in shorter lengths, double-pointed needles are more comfortable to work with on smaller circumferences.

If you're knitting a particularly wide project with lots of stitches, say an afghan or shawl, a roomy circular needle is far more comfortable to work with and much less likely than a cramped straight needle to encourage dropped stitches. In fact, some knitters do all their knitting — flat or round — on circular needles. They like to be able to keep the center of gravity in their laps, not spread out along their needles. It's a matter of your personal knitting style.

When choosing circular needles, check the spot where the needle tip meets the cable (called the *join*). It should be as seamless as possible to prevent stitches from snagging on it. Some of the smaller circular needles are made from a continuous strand of nylon, eliminating the join between needle and cable. These, however, are so lightweight that they can feel flimsy. Some circular needles are designed ergonomically with a bend in the needle tip, making it easier for a knitter to hold the needle in a curved position. If you're ergonomically inclined, you may want to seek these out.

Needle size is not always marked on circular needles. Invest in a small needle gauge with graduated holes to help you determine the size of your needle if you forget to put it back in its labeled package.

Double-pointed needles

Double-pointed needles have a point at each end and are sold in sets of four or five needles. They work the same way as circular needles — in rounds. They're generally used to make smallish tubes where the number of stitches is too small to stretch around the circumference of a circular needle, such as sleeve cuffs, tops of hats, socks, mittens, and so on. They come in 7- and 10-inch lengths and recently have shown up in 5-inch lengths — a great boon to those who enjoy making socks and mittens.

Sizing them up

A needle's size is determined by its diameter. The smaller the size, the narrower the needle and the smaller the stitch it makes.

Before knitting needles were imported from Europe and Japan, they were available only in American sizes, 0 to 15. These days a full range of metric sizes, which include more gradations than the American system, is available. Although American and metric sizes are somewhat equivalent (see Figure 4-8), you can't always count on a size 8 (American) being the same as a size 5 (metric) any more than you can count on one manufacturer's size 8 being the same as another manufacturer's size 8. This may sound like a drawback, but the variety of needles on the market actually affords greater possibilities for gauge (stitches per inch) tweaking.

Popular Knitting Needle Sizes

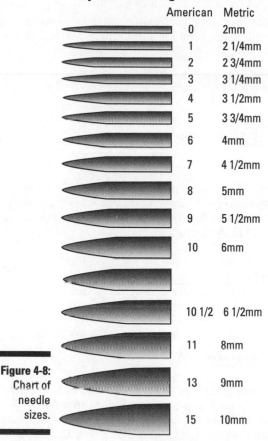

	American	Metric
	0	2mm
	1	2 1/4mm
	2	2 3/4mm
	3	3 1/4mm
	4	3 1/2mm
	5	3 3/4mm
	6	4mm
	7	4 1/2mm
	8	5mm
	9	5 1/2mm
	10	6mm
	10 1/2	6 1/2mm
	11	8mm
	13	9mm
	15	10mm

Figure 4-8:
Chart of needle sizes.

The perfect match

Yarn labels *suggest* appropriate needle sizes, but the best needle size for your project will be dictated by your yarn, your gauge, and/or the *hand* (the way the knitted fabric feels in your hand) you want your final project to have. In general, medium- or worsted-weight yarn is knit on needles anywhere from size 6 to size 9 depending on how tightly you knit and how you want the final fabric to look and feel.

After knitting a sample with the suggested needle size, you may feel that the fabric is more open than you'd like (needle too large) or too stiff (needle too small). In that case, try another needle size. Keep in mind that if you're making a garment or project and you want to achieve the finished measurements given in the pattern, you'll need to meet the gauge and live with the "hand" of the sample. If you're making a scarf or project where getting the exact number of stitches per inch isn't important, you can experiment to your heart's content with different needle sizes until you find you have a fabric you like.

Getting to the point

Whether you use straight, circular, or double-pointed needles, you're going to make your stitches on the tips of your needles. Needle tips vary — some are pointy and a bit concave, and others are rounder and blunter. See Figure 4-9.

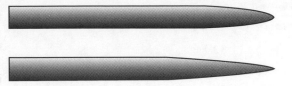

Figure 4-9:
Two kinds of
needle tips.

If you're working a project with a lot of stitch manipulation (lace or cables) or if you're a snug knitter, you'll have an easier time if you use a needle with a long tapered tip. If you're knitting with a loosely spun yarn and/or you are a relaxed knitter, you may prefer a blunter point.

If you're a new knitter and not sure what you prefer, ask your local yarn shop if you can sample a few different needles with your chosen yarn. You may find that you have a preference, or you may decide that different needle tips don't make a whit of difference.

The stuff they're made of

First mass-produced in steel, knitting needles have been made in ivory, tortoiseshell, silver, whale bone, and more. Today you can find them made in ebony and rosewood, sherbet-colored pearly plastic, Teflon-coated aluminum, and 14-carat gold plated (I kid you not). And that's only the beginning. Whatever your needles are made of, the material will contribute more or less to your knitting comfort, speed, and the quality of your stitches.

If you're knitting in stockinette or a straightforward stitch pattern, a slippery needle makes sense. The fastest ones are nickle-plated brass and call themselves Turbo. Use these and watch your stitches fly by before your eyes. (Also watch for more easily dropped stitches.)

If you're new to knitting, working on double-pointed needles, or executing color patterns, wood (bamboo, walnut, and so on) and plastic are good choices. Wood and some plastics have a very slight grip, giving you more control over your work and discouraging dropped stitches.

A recent innovation from Europe is straight needles that feature a standard tip (where the stitches are made) that tapers to a thin shaft, enabling the needle to carry more stitches comfortably and facilitating their glide along the needle.

The material of your needles determines other characteristics as well. When choosing needles, ask yourself the following questions:

- ✔ Is the shaft of the needle smooth or very slippery?
- ✔ Is it rigid or flexible and springy?
- ✔ Are the needles quiet or clicky (or screechy)?
- ✔ Are they warm or cool to the touch?

Although all needles look pretty much alike, there is a difference in the feel of various kinds of needles and in their interaction with your knitting style and the yarn you're using. If you find that some feature of their construction or material is annoying you or interfering with the flow of your project, try a different kind of needle. Switching may make the difference between a knitting experience on cruise control or one that stops and starts and sputters along.

Gizmos and Gadgets

Lots of knitting gadgets are on the market. Some make life a little easier, others are out-and-out lifesavers. Some you have to buy, but you can improvise others from what you already have on hand.

The essentials

Knitting gadgets are, for the most part, small and portable. Keep the essentials in a little zippered bag, and you can carry them anywhere your knitting goes.

Scissors

Small portable scissors are a must. In a pinch, you can break certain yarns with your hands, but others have to be cut with scissors. Collapsible scissors that fold up and don't leave any sharp points exposed are great. You'll find them in most knitting stores. Other small scissors come with a little case that covers the tips. You can carry them in your knitting bag without finding them poking through.

Tape measure

A small retractable tape measure marked for inches and centimeters can go anywhere. Use it to measure your gauge swatch and to check your knitted pieces as you go along. A short plastic ruler is also good to have for such things as checking how many inches of ribbing you've worked.

Tapestry needles

A tapestry needle is simply a large-eye needle with a blunt point. You use this to sew knitted pieces together. When joining pieces of knitted fabric, you're working in the spaces around the stitches, not through the yarn strand. A blunt point ensures that you won't split the yarn. Knitting stores frequently sell gigantic plastic needles. These needles are good for sewing together a *very* bulky sweater, but don't make the mistake of using them for the average knitted project. Instead, try to use the smallest needle you can comfortably thread your yarn through.

Safety pins

Safety pins are handy for a variety of tasks. Pinned to your piece at strategic points, they can help you keep track of when to increase or decrease or signal the right side of reversible fabric. They work well as mini stitch holders for small groups of stitches and for securing dropped stitches. In knitting shops and specialty catalogs, you can find coil-less pins in several sizes. These stand a better chance of not catching on your yarn.

Needle gauge and tension gauge

Needle gauges and tension gauges are indispensable. A needle gauge is a small rulerlike gadget with graduated holes in it for measuring the size of your knitting needles. If you knit a lot on circular needles, which frequently aren't labeled for size, or if you're prone to finding a lost double-pointed needle under the sofa cushions, a needle gauge is essential for size identification.

Because needle sizes vary from manufacturer to manufacturer and metric and American sizes are not always equivalent, a needle gauge will help you determine whether one size 8 is bigger or smaller than another size 8. This tool is helpful if you're close to but not on gauge. Buy one that shows both metric and American sizes.

A tension gauge often comes as part of a needle gauge. It's a flat piece of metal or plastic with a 2-inch L-shaped window for measuring stitches and rows. You lay the tension gauge (often called a stitch gauge) over your knitting, lining up the window along a row of stitches horizontally and vertically, and count the rows and stitches exposed. The drawback to using this tool is that 2 inches isn't always a large enough measure for an accurate gauge count. See a typical combination needle-tension gauge in Figure 4-10.

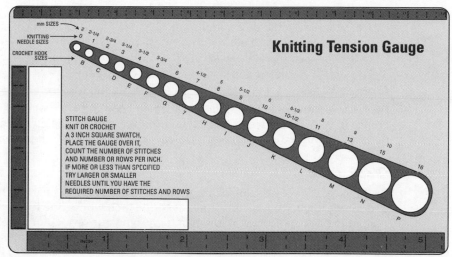

Figure 4-10:
A common tension gauge.

KNITTING TIP

You can make a great tension gauge by cutting a very accurate 4-inch window in a piece of sturdy but thin cardboard. Lay this over your knitting, and you'll be able to clearly count 4 inches worth of stitches and rows.

Cable needles

A cable needle is a short needle that's pointed at both ends and used to hold stitches temporarily while you work on their neighbors. There are several different versions of the two main types: U-shaped or straight. Try out a couple different styles and notice which one you find yourself reaching for when you work your next cabled project. Buy more of the same when you're in the market for another cable needle. Figure 4-11 shows some basic cable needles.

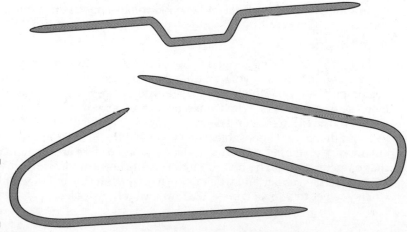

Figure 4-11:
Cable needles.

In a pinch, you can use a double-pointed needle or even a long nail or tooth-pick as a cable needle, but a tool especially designed for this task is the best one and a small price to pay for its convenience. Obviously, if you don't plan to ever knit any cables, leave this item off your list.

Crochet hooks

Even if you don't plan to crochet edgings on your knits, a crochet hook comes in very handy when picking up dropped stitches. They're sized by number and/or letter. A medium-size one is good for your supply basket.

Graph paper

Graph paper is very useful for diagramming patterns and charting designs and motifs. Figuring on 5 or 8 squares to the inch works fine for sweater plot-ting and texture patterns. If you plan to design your own color patterns or motifs, look in your local yarn shop for knitter's graph paper, which has flat-tened-out squares (5 squares across and 7 squares up to the inch) to reflect the grid of knitted fabric — more rows per inch than stitches. If you want graph paper the exact proportions of your gauge, you can make it yourself. (See the "Software for Knitters" section later in this chapter).

Small calculator

A calculator comes in handy for figuring gauge and plotting patterns.

Not necessarily essential but nice to have

You can get by without buying the gadgets in this section, but you may find some of them worth the small investment. For example, after years of using strands of yarn tied in a circle for my yarn markers, I marvel at how much I prefer the little rubber rings I now use. I find myself using markers in ways I never thought of before. Figure 4-12 shows some of my favorite knitting gadgets.

Stitch markers

A marker is a small ring slipped onto your needle between stitches and used to alert you to places in your knitting that you need to pay attention to: the beginning of a round, the beginning and end of a repeat, the spot to work an increase or a decrease. When you reach a marker, you slip it from the LH needle to the RH needle and carry on. You may not use markers in every pro-ject, but they're indispensable when you need them. Several styles of mark-ers are on the market. Some are wafer thin, and others are small plastic coils that open up and can be placed on the needle in the middle of a row. Some are made from rubber and won't come whizzing off the end of your needle when you get to them. Figure 4-12 shows what they look like.

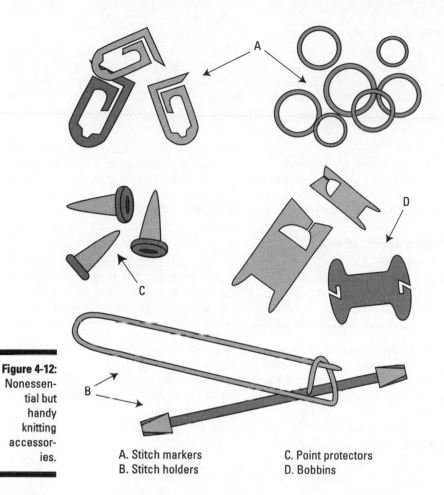

Figure 4-12:
Nonessen-
tial but
handy
knitting
accessor-
ies.

A. Stitch markers   C. Point protectors
B. Stitch holders   D. Bobbins

If you don't have any bona fide knitting markers, you can always tie a loop of yarn in a contrasting color and use it around the needle instead. If you're going for the homemade version, use cotton or some other nonfuzzy yarn in a bright color.

Stitch holders

Stitch holders resemble large safety pins and are used to secure stitches that will be worked up or finished off later. They come in a variety of lengths, from 1¾ inches to 8 inches. If you don't have any, you can always transfer the stitches to a spare circular needle (put point protectors at each end) or to a contrasting yarn threaded on a tapestry needle. These are the best ways to hold a lot of stitches. Check them out in Figure 4-12.

Point protectors

Point protectors are small rubber pointed caps to fit over the tip of your needles to protect them and more generally to prevent your stitches from sliding off when you put down your work. If you use a circular needle as a stitch holder, point protectors will secure the stitches on it. They come in different sizes to fit your needles. See Figure 4-12.

Bobbins

Bobbins are small, flat, plastic items for winding small amounts of yarn onto. They're used for intarsia color work, not Fair Isle (see Chapter 9 for information about intarsia and Fair Isle knitting). Some people find bobbins more trouble than they're worth. Figure 4-12 shows some common bobbins.

Magnetic board and strips

If you plan to knit anything from a chart, a magnetic board with strips is a wonderful item to have. You put your chart on top of the magnetic board and align the magnetized strip on the row of squares *on top* of the row you're working on. After you've worked the row shown on the chart, you move the strip up, exposing the next row to knit.

You can, of course, use self-stick notes for marking your row. The problem with them, however, is that they're often shorter than the width of your chart and more vulnerable to cats skittering across the table or someone grabbing the note to use for something more important than your place on the knitting chart.

Magnetic line magnifier

A magnetic line magnifier is a see-through ruler that works like the magnetic board and strips but also magnifies the line you're working on.

Pompom maker

After years of wimpy, lopsided pompoms, I bought a pompom maker. What a difference. I can now make rainbow pompoms in three sizes. This small and inexpensive gadget is one of those simple but brilliant ideas (like a bucket) that turn a tedious job with questionable results into something quick with spectacular results. You may find yourself adding pompoms to everything.

Tassel and fringe maker

Everything I say about the pompom maker also applies to the tassel and fringe maker. A tassel maker is a small adjustable plastic frame that allows you to wrap any number of threads around it, before cutting the wraps for fringe or tassels. No more hunting around for the book or piece of cardboard just the right size for wrapping.

Notebook or folder

You'll probably find many good reasons to keep a notebook or folder among your knitting supplies. It's a good place to keep a knitting diary — someplace where you can record your projects and save labels from the yarn you're using. (Never throw away the label that comes with your yarn. You may need it to match the color and /or dye lot numbers if you run out of yarn.) You can also write down the needle size you ended up using and the gauge you got. In addition, you can jot down ideas, technical questions to ask your knitting mentor, patterns you'd like to swatch, and so on.

Blocking Equipment

Blocking is the process of using steam or water to smooth out and gently uncurl and flatten your knitted pieces so that you can easily join them together. Blocking equipment makes the difference between a tiresome awkward task and an easy streamlined one. Don't shirk this step. If you find yourself dreading the blocking part of sweater construction, invest in good blocking equipment. It'll make all the difference.

Steam iron

You probably already have a steam iron. The more steam the better.

Blocking board

A blocking board is not your ironing board. It's a flat surface made from a material that you can stick a pin into. It should be large enough to hold at least one pinned-out sweater piece. Ideally, it should be marked with a 1-inch grid so that you can pin out your knitted piece to its proper dimensions without using your tape measure. If you have enough space, you can leave the blocking board up all the time for checking your project's measurements as you go along.

Ready-made blocking boards or kits for making one are available from sources listed in the appendix. Or you can make one from scratch with a few easy-to-find and inexpensive materials. The simplest blocking board is made from a piece of Styrofoam-type board insulation, readily available at your local hardware store. Just follow these steps:

1. **Cut Styrofoam board to a convenient size with a utility knife. A great size is 36 x 54 inches.**

2. **Using a sharp blade and a yardstick or other rigid straight edge, score a 1-inch grid into the surface.**

When you block your sweater, you can line up your project pieces with the grid lines. Styrofoam allows you to pin into it.

Another option is to find a piece of plywood (5 x 3 feet), cover it with old blankets to make a padded surface about 1 inch thick (check out your local Goodwill for old blankets), and top it off with a purchased canvas grid (available through sources listed in the appendix. To make this kind of blocking board, follow these steps:

1. **Cover the board and blankets with a purchased canvas grid.**

2. **Staple or tack the edges of the grid cloth to the underside of the board.**

   Figure 4-13 shows how this goes together.

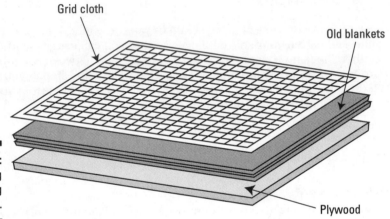

Grid cloth

Old blankets

Figure 4-13:
Assembling
a blocking
board.

Plywood

Blocking wires

Blocking wires are long, slightly flexible stainless steel wires in various lengths. Threaded through the edges of your knitted piece, blocking wires allow it to be pinned into shape so that the edges don't become scalloped at the pin sites. They're a wonderful invention and well worth the investment.

T-pins

Large T-shaped straight pins help you pin out the edges of your project pieces. T-pins are easy to get a grip on, and because they don't have any plastic parts (like the straight pins with colorful plastic heads), they won't melt under your iron while you're steaming your knitted piece.

Organizing Your Equipment

You'll probably end up filing your straight needles in an artful arrangement in a jar or vase. Most knitters want to put their hands on their needles at a moment's notice. However, if you splurge on some especially lovely needles — such as rosewood or ebony — you may want to invest in a case just for them. (Wouldn't you store your pearls in a jewelry box?)

A needle case is also a good idea when you're traveling. Spare needles rattling around your knitting bag are prone to getting lost, bent, or even broken. Fabric needle cases have narrow pockets for filing your needles, and you can roll them up and tie them for storage and travel. If you come across a hard needle case in wood or plastic, buy it. Think of your needles as your violin.

For circular needles, you can keep track of their sizes by storing them in the size-identifying plastic containers they come in. However, this also keeps them curled up. Before you can comfortably knit with them, you need to unkink them in hot water. You can also purchase a canvas wall holder with slots for each size. Stored this way, the needles rest in their slot with their point ends hanging down, unkinked and ready to knit.

If you find yourself collecting more yarn than you can knit up in a given year (or more), store your precious skeins with a few moth balls in a bin of some kind that allows air to circulate. If you want to put your yarn in a plastic bin, leave the lid off it a bit or drill a hole or two in the sides so moisture and air can flow in and out. Some yarns are already mothproofed. Those that aren't are susceptible to moths, and it's a frustrating thing indeed to be knitting along and suddenly find your yarn strand has ended while a full ball remains in the basket. A good many yarns fade in direct sunlight, so never store them where they'll be exposed to daily sunshine

When you're on the move, you want a bag that's roomy enough to stow your project and essential equipment. But don't buy anything so roomy that your equipment gets lost in it. If your bag has pockets of various sizes, all the better. And it should look good, too. My favorite is a backpack designed for school kids. It's got plenty of pockets of various sizes with little compartments in them and a roomy big pocket for my project. And it's comfortable to carry. Canvas beach bags and the fashion fabric totes carried in yarn shops are also good choices. If you have a nice shoulder bag for your laptop computer, take out the laptop and put in your knitting.

As for your essential small gadgets, a small zippered bag works great. Look for a clear plastic one you can see through. You might find one in the cosmetics section of your local department store.

Software for Knitters

If you're familiar with letting a computer help you do your job or hobby, you may want to look into the different kinds of software available for knitters. Some software programs do relatively basic (and necessary) tasks, such as indexing your soon to be growing collection of knitting magazines. Others enable you to design garment types and/or color and texture stitch patterns and put them together.

To keep you organized, some programs let you track your projects (such as what yarn and how much of it you used, gauge, comments on fit, pitfalls to look out for, and tricks to remember). In addition, they can index patterns and magazine articles and list yarns that you can substitute for each other.

One of the simplest software programs, called "Print a Grid," provides an invaluable service: It creates and lets you print out graph paper that matches your knitting gauge. If you start to design color patterns or want to do intricate or unusual shaping, graph paper in the exact gauge of your fabric will help immensely.

Stockinette fabric has more rows than stitches per inch. Anything you draw on a square grid will be wider and shorter when knitted. Accurate graph paper can also help you design garment details and figure out where cables will stop and start relative to your garment piece.

Several programs, such as Sweater Wizard 2001, enable you to plug in your own dimensions and/or yarn gauges and will spit out a pattern for you. This is definitely less work than using your calculator.

For more advanced designing, programs are available that take you from A to Z. Some are more sophisticated than others and enable you to use a graphics program in conjunction with them. You can scan an image into a paint program and convert it to a knitted image, change the scale, play with colors, repeat it vertically, repeat it horizontally, and so on.

The more the program can do, the more it costs. But if you put in the time to learn your program, you may find that what it can do is well worth the investment. But you have to like sitting at a computer. Three sources to investigate include

- ✔ **Designaknit:** Distributed by Knitcraft, 215 North Main, Independence, MO 64050; phone 816-461-1248; e-mail knitcraft@knitcraft.com, Web site www.knitcraft.com

- ✔ **Stitch Painter and Garment Styler:** Distributed by Cochenille Design Studio, P.O. Box 234276, Encinitas, CA 92023-4276; phone 858-259-1698; fax 858-259-3746; e-mail info@cochenille.com

- ✔ **Stitch and Motif Maker:** Available at www.knittingsoftware.com

Chapter 5

Friendly Math (Gauge) for Knitters

- -

- -

Gauge is the number of stitches and rows it takes to make 1 square inch of knitted fabric. Understanding how to measure and work with gauge is what allows you to go from a knitted swatch or sample to a finished project — a project that measures what you want it to. Without knowing your gauge, you wouldn't know before you picked up needles and yarn whether your envisioned sweater would go around you once or would comfortably house two of you.

Understanding how gauge works makes it possible to ensure that what you make will hit the mark (or at least come near it). It enables you to follow a pattern, confident that what you make will look like what's pictured. It also enables you to plan and make your own projects and garments.

If you've spent some time around knitters, you may already know that mention of the word *gauge* often elicits a groan. (If you're unaware of this reaction to the word, skip the next paragraph. There's no point in encouraging a prejudice this soon.)

Gauge has a bad reputation among many knitters for three reasons. First, it represents an unpleasant "should." Second, it's a tedious task that has to be accomplished before the fun part of the project — the *knitting* — can begin. Finally, it involves math. However, getting comfortable with gauge gives you a leg up in knitting. If you know how to think in terms of gauge, you can do the following:

✔ Knit away on your project in the comfortable knowledge that when you've completed the thousands of stitches required to complete it, it will fit.

✔ Substitute another yarn for the one given in the pattern.

✔ Use the size needle that makes the best fabric for your chosen yarn, even if it means you don't match the pattern's gauge.

✔ Design your own projects and sweaters.

Getting to Know Gauge

Every knitted fabric is made up of stitches and rows. The stitches and rows that make up 1 square inch of a stockinette swatch can be seen in Figure 5-1. Note that in stockinette and most other knitted fabrics, there are more vertical rows per inch than stitches. Though the stitch:row ratio changes from swatch to swatch, for medium (frequently called *worsted*) weight yarn, it's usually around 5 stitches to 7 rows an inch.

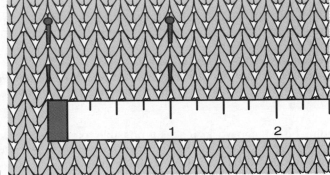

Figure 5-1:
One square inch of stockinette measured.

Gauge varies depending on the yarn, the needle size, and the stitch pattern you use. It can also vary with the time of day you're knitting, how long you've been knitting at a stretch, and what you're thinking about. The tension you put on the yarn traveling around the needle contributes to stitch size. Being tired or tense can affect the flow of your yarn and stitch size.

Needles and stitch size

The same yarn knitted on different size needles will have different gauges. Since a knit stitch is made by wrapping yarn around a needle, the size (circumference) of the needle determines the size of the stitch. The bigger around the needle, the bigger the stitch.

Figure 5-2 shows three different possible fabrics using the same yarn and stitch pattern, but using different size needles. The smaller the needle, the tighter the stitches and the denser the knitted fabric. The larger the needle, the looser the stitches and the drapier (and stretchier) the fabric.

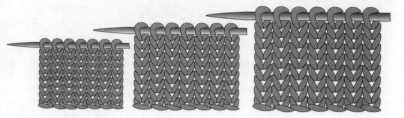

Figure 5-2:
Gauge on three different needle sizes.

Stitch patterns and stitch size

The same yarn knitted on the same needles but in different stitch patterns will have different gauges. Cables and ribs pull in, requiring more stitches to make a square inch, while lace and slip stitch or garter stitch patterns spread the fabric out, so they require fewer stitches to make an inch. Figure 5-3 compares the gauges of various stitch patterns.

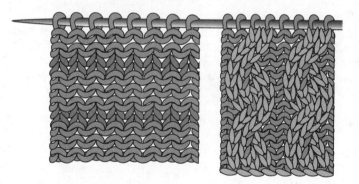

Figure 5-3:
Gauge on different stitch patterns.

Working with Gauge

The first step in any knitting project is to determine the gauge of the knitted fabric you're making. Gauge (sometimes called 'tension') is listed at the beginning of a pattern before the instructions proper begin. It's given as a number of stitches and rows over 4 square inches or 10 square centimeters. It tells what needle and what stitch pattern were used to determine the gauge. Check your pattern to see how many stitches and rows should make up 4 inches of knitted fabric. (See more on the setup of knitting patterns in Chapter 13.)

You need to measure *your* gauge against that given in the directions. To find out whether your gauge matches the pattern, you begin by making a gauge swatch.

Making a gauge swatch

A gauge swatch is a small sample worked in the pattern stitch specified with the gauge numbers and using the same yarn, needles, and stitch pattern you intend to use for your project. It's important that you use the *same* yarn, not the same brand in a different color. Different dyes can affect how a specific yarn knits up, and believe it or not, a yarn in one color can give you a different gauge from the same yarn in a different color. Needles can vary, too. A size 8 needle from one manufacturer can vary from the size 8 of another.

Cast on the number of stitches given in the pattern for 4 inches, plus 6 more stitches, and work in the stitch pattern specified for the number of rows required to make 4 inches, plus 6 more rows. For example, if the gauge is given as 18 stitches and 22 rows over 4 inches, cast on 24 stitches and work in the pattern given for 28 rows. Then bind off loosely or cut the strand of yarn, leaving an 8-inch tail and draw it through the loops of the last row. The extra 6 stitches and rows will give you a border around the area you're measuring. Edge stitches are frequently distorted and shouldn't be included in what you measure unless your swatch is a good 6 inches square. If the stitch pattern needs to be worked in a specific multiple, cast on any multiple that will yield a swatch larger than 4 inches in order to enable you to get an accurate gauge measurement. (For more on stitch patterns and multiples, see Chapter 2.) For example, if the pattern is worked on a multiple of 6 stitches, plus 1 more, and the gauge given is 4 stitches to an inch, cast on *at least* 25 stitches (a multiple of 6 + 1). At 4 stitches to the inch, your swatch will be more than 4 inches wide, giving you a good area for measuring.

Patterns written in countries other than the United States often give dimensions in centimeters rather than inches. You can calculate inches from centimeters by dividing the centimeter number by 2.5. For example, 10 centimeters divided by 2.5 equals 4 inches.

Measuring your gauge

Before measuring your swatch, steam or block it in the same manner you plan to use for your finished project. (Your stitches may shrink in a bit when they're steamed.) *Then* you're ready to measure it.

Smooth out your swatch on a flat surface (your lap is not flat). A blocking or ironing board is good for this task. Pin the edges down if they're curling in, or thread short blocking wires along the edges to line everything up. Just *don't* stretch your swatch.

To be as accurate as possible, you need to know gauge over a 4-inch square. The following sections present two methods for taking an accurate gauge

measurement. Method 1 works for most situations. However, if you're working with a textured or fuzzy yarn where it's hard to distinguish actual stitches, use Method 2.

Method 1

Once you've steamed or blocked your swatch and it's lying nice and flat, you're ready to measure.

1. **Lay a ruler along a row of stitches and mark the beginning and end of 4 inches with pins.**

   If your second pin lands at half a stitch, don't be tempted to stretch or slightly squish your knitting to make the 4 inches end on a whole stitch.

2. **Note the number of stitches in 4 inches, fractions and all.**

3. **Lay your ruler along a vertical line of stitches, aligning the bottom of the ruler with the bottom of a stitch (the bottom of a V), and put a pin in to show where the first stitch begins. Place another pin 4 inches up.**

4. **Count the stitches between the pins and note the number of rows.**

These steps give you gauge over a 4-inch (10-centimeter) square. Check to see whether your 4-inch gauge matches the one in the pattern.

Method 2

With fuzzy or highly textured yarns, it can be difficult to see your stitches clearly enough to take an accurate measurement by counting stitches. In this case, the following steps enable you to measure your gauge:

Swatch watch

If you (like many of your fellow knitters) think of gauge swatches as a waste of time and yarn, it wouldn't hurt to work on an attitude adjustment. Here are some things you can do with a gauge swatch to help you see gauge making as time well spent:

- Use it as a base for experimenting with edgings and embroidery.

- Sew two together for a potholder.

- Collect swatches and sew them together for a great afghan.

- If your pattern calls for a pocket, knit the pocket and use it as a gauge swatch.

- Make a *big* swatch and turn it into a pillow or purse.

- Throw your swatch into the washing machine and see how it felts for your next project.

- Put it in your knitting notebook for future inspiration.

1. **Make a swatch larger than 4 inches and write down the total number of stitches and rows in your swatch.**

2. **Measure the entire swatch side to side and top to bottom.**

3. **With your handy calculator, plug your numbers into the formulas that follow:**

   To find *stitch gauge* (number of horizontal stitches per inch): Divide the number of stitches in the swatch by the width of the swatch in inches. This gives you the number of stitches per inch.

   To find *row gauge* (number of vertical stitches per inch): Divide the number of rows by the overall length of the swatch in inches. This gives you the number of rows per inch.

To find your gauge over 4 inches, multiply stitches per inch or rows per inch by 4.

For information on measuring gauge over cable or lace patterns, see Chapters 9 and 10.

Comparing your gauge to the pattern's gauge

If your gauge swatch doesn't match the one specified in the pattern you want to use and you want your project to come out the same size as the pattern measures, you must change the needle size you're working on. If your swatch is smaller than specified, use larger needles. If your swatch is larger than specified, use smaller needles.

Keep adjusting your needle size until you get the same number of stitches and rows in a 4-inch square that your pattern requires. If you can't get both stitch and row gauge to match the pattern's gauge, work with the needle that gives you the right *stitch* gauge.

The cumulative effect of knitting at a gauge as small as half a stitch less than the pattern calls for can be disastrous. If your project piece is supposed to measure 20 inches and calls for a gauge of 5 stitches per inch, your finished piece will measure 22 inches if you're knitting at 4 stitches per inch. If you're off by 2 inches on both the front and back of a sweater, the total difference between the pattern and your sweater will be 4 inches overall. That's why gauge gets so much attention in knitting books and why taking the time to measure is so important — but it's not hard.

Numbers refer to two different things in knitting: inches and stitches. The *inches* identify the dimensions of your project pieces or your gauge swatch. *Stitches* refer to the number of stitches in your project or gauge swatch. Knitting math is simply a matter of converting inches to stitches or stitches to inches.

Designing with Gauge

As you begin to knit projects, you may find yourself imagining sweaters and hats you'd like to make but can't find a pattern for. Making your own pattern for a project isn't all that difficult. No matter how fancy the pattern stitch or shaping, how large or small the project, it all comes down to stitches and inches — figuring out your gauge on the yarn and needles you want to use and then determining the dimensions of the finished project.

To determine the number of stitches to cast on for a project you're imagining, you can work the formula for determining gauge in reverse. First, decide how wide you want your piece to be and then multiply that number by your gauge. For example, if you're imagining a scarf in one of the patterns in Chapter 2, make a gauge swatch. If your gauge is 5 stitches to the inch and you want your scarf to be 7 inches wide, cast on 35 stitches and start knitting.

Chapter 6

Getting Started with Simple Projects

Knitting swatches is fun for a while, but the point of knitting is to make things that you can use — or that you can give as gifts to the people you care about. The projects in this chapter give you practice on working the basic knit stitches, reading and understanding patterns for knitted garments, and, if you decide to give them your own dimensions, working with gauge. *And* you end up with a scarf, a bag, or a hat (and multiple variations thereof) that you can wear yourself or give to friends and family.

You can use the yarn I specify or another yarn with a similar stitch gauge. Check the label on the yarn you'd like to use to see if the stitch gauge matches or ask a yarn shop employee to suggest something. You needn't be overly concerned about matching gauge. (See Chapter 5 for detailed information about gauge.) If these projects turn out an inch bigger or smaller either way, it won't be a catastrophe. Just knit until the piece you're working on measures the length given in the pattern. You can see many of these projects pictured in the color insert.

Garter Ridge Scarf

This scarf is quick and cozy, and you don't have to worry about sewing any seams. Make it in a soft yarn and a favorite color, or try the suggested yarn.

Dimensions: 8½ inches x 42 inches

Materials: 3 1.75-ounce (50 gram) skeins of Maya (Classic Elite Yarns), 50% wool, 50% llama, color #3081; one pair of size 8 needles; tapestry needle for weaving in the ends (Because this scarf takes 3 skeins of yarn, you'll have to know how to join a new skein when you run out of the first one. For instructions, see the sidebar "Joining yarns," in Chapter 1.)

Gauge: 18 stitches to 4 inches in the stitch pattern (4½ stitches to the inch)

Garter ridge pattern: This pattern doesn't require a specific multiple or an odd or even number of stitches. The pattern is similar to the garter stripes shown in Chapter 2. Simply cast on and knit up this scarf in any number of stitches. Just follow these instructions:

Rows 1, 3, 5–11, 13, 15, and 16: Knit.

Rows 2, 4, 12, and 14: Purl.

Repeat these 16 rows until your scarf reaches the desired length.

To discourage the edges from rolling in, work a selvedge stitch on the edges by knitting the first and last stitch of every row.

Making your scarf

To make this simple scarf, follow these steps:

1. **Cast on 38 stitches.**

2. **Beginning with Row 3, work in garter ridge pattern for 17 repetitions.**

   The scarf begins on Row 3 of the pattern because the cast-on row works as the first garter ridge — a ridge consisting of 2 rows.

3. **End the scarf by working Rows 1–5 of the garter ridge pattern.**

4. **With the wrong side facing, bind off by *knitting* every stitch for the final garter stitch ridge.**

To finish your scarf, weave in the loose ends and gently steam or wet it down to block it. (See Chapter 15 for ways to weave in the ends, block, and otherwise learn how to finish your scarf like a pro.)

If you want your scarf to be wider, cast on more stitches. If you want it to be narrower, cast on fewer stitches. If you have a specific width in mind, multiply the number of inches you want your scarf to be by your gauge. (You'll have to make a sample swatch and measure your gauge — the number of stitches per inch.) That's the number of stitches you'll cast on. For detailed information about gauge, see Chapter 5.

Varying your scarf

You can express your creativity — and practice newly learned skills at the same time — by altering the basic garter ridge scarf in any of the following ways:

✔ Work the scarf in a yarn of a different weight and with the appropriate needles. If you stick with the cast-on number of 38 stitches and you work it in a finer yarn (say 5 stitches to the inch), it will measure 7½ inches wide; if you work it in a heavier yarn (say 4 stitches to the inch), it will measure 9½ inches wide.

✔ Substitute a different pattern stitch for the garter ridge pattern following the guidelines in the "Substituting one stitch pattern for another" sidebar later in this chapter.

✔ Work the scarf for 16 inches in the pattern you've chosen, then work 10 inches or so in 2 x 2 or 3 x 3 rib, and then work the last 16 inches in your pattern again. The ribbed part will fit nicely into the contour of your neck.

✔ Buy another skein of yarn and make your scarf longer.

✔ Make a sampler scarf by working 3 or so inches of as many different patterns as you like.

✔ Make a striped scarf. For stripe ideas and information on how to work with more than one color, see Chapter 11.

Everywhere Bag in Garter Stitch

This basic bag is handy for carrying your wallet, keys, and some lip balm. Make it larger and throw in your glasses case and a notebook. Make it even bigger, add a pocket, and use it for a knitting bag. You'll find several ways to vary this project at the end of this section. So cast on and get started!

Finished measurements: This pattern makes a bag 8 inches wide by 9 inches long, with a 4-inch flap.

Materials: One 3.5-ounce (100 gram) skein Tahki Donegal Tweed (100% wool) in any color, one pair of size 7 needles, one button any size

Gauge: 18 stitches to 4 inches in garter stitch (4½ stitches to the inch)

Making the bag

All you need to do to make this versatile bag is knit a rectangle, sew up the sides, make and attach a cord for the strap, make a button loop, attach a button, and voilà!

Knitting the rectangle

Follow these simple steps to get started:

1. **Cast on 38 stitches.**

2. **Knit until the piece measures 22 inches in length.**

    In garter stitch, you never have to purl; just knit every row.

3. **Bind off and steam lightly. (See Chapter 15 for tips on steaming.)**

Sewing up the sides

Next you need to close the sides of your bag so that your stuff doesn't fall out.

1. **Measure down 9 inches and fold your piece with wrong sides together.**

    Even though garter stitch is reversible, your cast-on edge will look different from each side. Choose which side you like better and make that side the right side.

2. **Sew the sides closed. You'll have 4 inches left over for the flap.**

    It doesn't really matter how you sew the sides closed. But to make a neat seam, use a tapestry needle and a strand of the same yarn and try the basic mattress stitch for this task. Flip to Chapter 15 for specifics on sewing up seams.

Making and attaching the cord strap

Cords can be made in a variety of ways. Here's a good one to get you started. You'll find other ways to make a cord later in the chapter.

1. **Cast on 42 inches' worth of stitches.**

    To determine how many stitches it's going to take to make 42 inches, you need to test your gauge — for example, 42 inches × 4½ stitches (your gauge) = 189 stitches (the number of stitches you need to cast on). Go back to Chapter 5 if you need help with this.

2. **Work in garter stitch for 3 rows.**

3. **Bind off.**

4. **Sew the ends of the strap to either side of the top of the purse.**

Elizabeth Zimmerman and her idiot cord (I-cord)

Elizabeth Zimmerman, author of *Knitting Without Tears,* was the first person to bring her simple method for working a cord to knitters' attention and give it the name idiot cord (I-cord). Her books are an indispensable part of any knitter's library. Zimmerman's "unvented" techniques and her novel way of thinking about knitting and designing have converted many half-hearted knitters into knitting enthusiasts. These are the steps to follow:

Using a double-pointed needle the same size as, or one size smaller than, the one you used for your project, cast on 4 stitches.

With a second double-pointed needle, knit the 4 stitches.

3. Instead of turning your work, slide the stitches you just worked to the opposite end of the needle, right side still facing.

4. With the yarn end at the *left* end of your work, knit another row, pulling slightly on the yarn after you make the first stitch.

5. Continue knitting a row and then sliding the stitches to the opposite end of the needle in order to knit them again until your cord is as long as you want it.

Forming the button loop and attaching the button

You can make a small button loop just as you would make the cord strap — just make it shorter. For an easy garter stitch loop, do the following:

1. **Cast on 8 stitches.**

2. **Knit 1 row.**

3. **Bind off.**

4. **Center the loop on the bag flap with the ends 1 inch or so apart and attach it with yarn.**

5. **Position your button to fit the button loop and sew it on with embroidery floss or sewing thread.**

   If you've worked the bag in a plied yarn, you can separate a single ply and use that to sew on your button.

Varying your bag

You can alter this basic bag in a number of ways. By changing the details, adding a pocket, or using more than one color, you can create entirely different bags. You can even alter this pattern a bit to make a pillow — just leave off the strap and stuff it!

Use a different stitch pattern

You don't have to knit this bag in garter stitch. Instead, try stockinette stitch, a combination of garter stitch and stockinette stitch, or any of the stitch patterns presented in Chapter 2. See the sidebar "Substituting one stitch pattern for another" for tips. Remember that textured pattern stitches show up better in a smooth plied yarn. Consider knitting your project in one stitch pattern and then knitting a pocket for it in a different stitch pattern.

Try a different cord

If you'd like to make a tube-like cord, cast on 4 stitches, knit Row 1 (RS), and purl Row 2. Repeat these rows until the cord measures 44 inches (or as long as you'd like it to be). Because stockinette fabric rolls to the wrong side, the strip will form a tube. You don't need to seam it.

If you want to save yourself a little sewing, rather than knitting a separate strap that you'll have to sew onto the bag later, pick up 4 stitches at the edge of your purse and start knitting on those to create a tube strap. At the end of your cord, you can graft the stitches to the other side of the purse opening. (See Chapter 13 for how to pick up and graft stitches.)

If you'd like a closed tube for a cord, you can work a cord in the round on two double-pointed needles. Cast on 4 stitches and follow the instructions for making I-cord in the sidebar "Elizabeth Zimmerman and her idiot cord (I-cord)." Use a needle the same size or one size smaller than you used in your bag.

Make a different closure

For the tube-like button loop, cast on 2 or 3 stitches, work for 2 inches, and then bind off. Center the loop on the bag flap with the ends 1 inch or so apart and attach with yarn.

Embellish your bag

Work embroidery on your bag before stitching it up. Add beads, fringe, or tassels.

Make a pillow instead of a bag

To convert your bag into a pillow, cast on 63 stitches. Work in garter or stockinette stitch until the piece measures 16 inches from the beginning. Join a second color and continue working in garter stitch until the piece measures 15 inches from color change. Bind off. Fold the piece in thirds, overlapping the ends by 2 inches.

Using mattress stitch, sew the side seams together (see Chapter 15).

To make button loops, cast on 2 stitches and work in St st until the piece measures 2¼ inches. Cast off. Fold the loops in half and sew the ends of the

Substituting one stitch pattern for another

If you decide to substitute a different knit/purl pattern for garter or stockinette stitch in any of the projects in this chapter, don't start knitting until you've mapped out how the pattern will be centered on your project piece. You want to be sure that your pattern will come out symmetrically. Use graph paper and plot your pattern by using knit and purl symbols to see that it begins and ends symmetrically. Remember, to be symmetrical, a pattern with a single center stitch needs to go on an uneven number of stitches. A pattern with 2 center stitches needs to go on an even number of stitches.

button loops evenly spaced along the overlapping edge of the pillow. Or try working five eyelet buttonholes (see Chapter 16) evenly spaced across the row about 1 inch before you bind off.

Sew the buttons under button loops or buttonholes and button up!

Make or buy a 14-x-14-inch fabric pillow form for the inside of the pillow.

Three-Way Hat

With this pattern, you can make three different hats. The Tassel Hat is the basic beginning hat — a knitted rectangle with a fold-up cuff. The Envelope Hat and Tie Hat diverge from the basic hat by ending in different ways. Try these in the different versions shown and experiment with the other variations given at the end of the pattern.

Sizes: Small (baby), medium, and large. The numbers given in the pattern before the parentheses are for the small size. The numbers given within the parentheses are for the medium and large sizes, respectively. You may want to highlight or circle the numbers you're using.

Measurements: 18 (20 and 22) inches in diameter.

Materials: Three 1.75-ounce/50-gram skeins (approximately 138 yards) of Classic Elite Waterspun (or any yarn that yields the necessary gauge), one pair of size 7 needles, tassel maker for Tassel Hat (optional)

Gauge: 20 stitches and 28 rows to 4 inches in stockinette stitch (5 stitches to the inch)

Knitting the base

No matter which style you choose, all three hat versions start out the same.

1. **Cast on 90 (100, 110) stitches.**

2. **For the cuff: Work in stockinette stitch until the piece measures 3" (3½", 4"), ending on a wrong side row. (The last row worked is a *purl* row). Begin the body of the hat: Purl the next row. Now knit the next row and continue in stockinette stitch until the piece measures 9" (10½", 11") from the beginning, ending with a wrong-side (WS) row. (The last row worked is a *purl* row).**

3. **Work the next row (RS): Bind off 1 stitch, knit to the end of the row — 89 (99, 109) stitches.**

4. **Work the next row: Bind off 1 stitch, purl to the end of the row — 88 (98, 108) stitches.**

5. **Continue making the hat according to the instructions for the specific hat you want in the following sections.**

To work these hats in the round, cast on 2 fewer stitches to eliminate the 2 seam stitches. See Chapter 17 for more about knitting in the round (or circular knitting).

Making a Tassel Hat

Work the base of the hat as described in Steps 1 through 4 of the "Knitting the base" section and then finish as follows to make a Tassel Hat like the one in Figure 6-1.

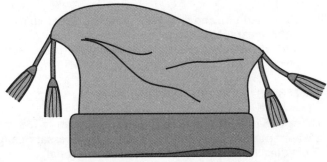

Figure 6-1:
Tassel Hat.

1. **Bind off all stitches.**

2. **Seam the hat at the center back by using the mattress stitch.**

3. **Seam the top of the hat by using the backstitch.**

See Chapter 15 for instructions on how to sew knitted pieces together.

4. **Steam the seams.**

5. **Make tassels for each hat corner — as many as you like — as follows (see Figure 6-2):**

   1. With a single color or several different colors, wrap the yarn 25 times or more around a piece of firm cardboard 3½ inches wide as shown in Figure 6-2a.

   2. Thread three 12-inch strands of yarn through the yarn wraps at one end of the cardboard and tie firmly with a knot.

   3. Cut the wraps of yarn at the opposite end of the tie as shown in Figure 6-2b.

   4. Wind another strand of yarn tightly several times around the tassel about an inch down from top to secure the tassel as shown in Figure 6-2c.

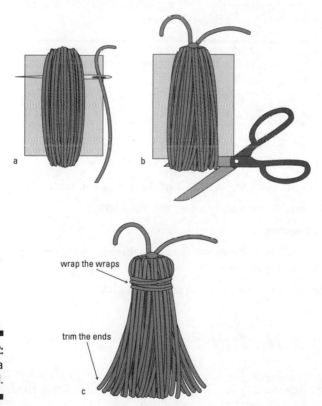

a

b

wrap the wraps

trim the ends

c

Figure 6-2:
Making a
tassel.

5. Knot and hide the ends in the tassel.

6. Braid the yarn tails to make a cord and bring it through the corners of the hat with a tapestry needle.

7. Secure the ends inside the hat.

Making an Envelope Hat

Work the base of the hat as explained in Steps 1 through 4 of the "Knitting the base" section earlier in this chapter. Then follow these simple steps to finish your Envelope Hat so that you end up with the top of the hat matching the one in Figure 6-3. (For detailed information about how to sew up seams, see Chapter 15.)

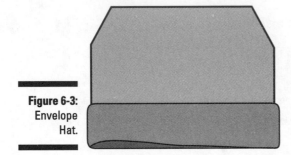

Figure 6-3:
Envelope
Hat.

1. **Bind off all stitches.**

2. **Seam the hat along the center back by using the mattress stitch.**

3. **Seam the top of the hat by using the backstitch.**

4. **Steam the seams.**

5. **Tuck the outside corners at the top of the hat to the inside so that the top of the hat tapers in.**

6. **Tack the corners to the wrong side of the hat.**

Making a Tie Hat

Before you try to make a Tie Hat, check out Figure 6-4 to see what the finished product looks like. Then, beginning at Step 5 of knitting the base, continue to work in stockinette stitch as follows:

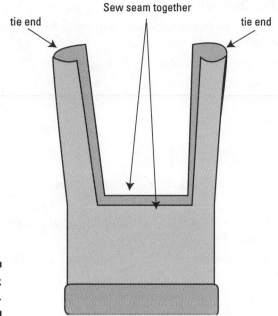

Figure 6-4:
Tie Hat.

1. **Work the next row (RS):**

    1. Bind off 15 (16, 18) stitches.

    2. Knit 14 (17, 18) stitches.

    3. Bind off the next 30 (32, 36) stitches.

    4. Knit 14 (17, 18) stitches.

    5. Bind off the remaining 15 (16, 18) stitches.

    This gives you two sets of "live" stitches that ultimately will become the two strands that you tie together at the top of the hat.

2. **Place one of the "live" sets of stitches on a holder.**

3. **Work the other group of 14 (17, 18) live stitches until it measures 8 (9, 9½) inches in length.**

4. **Bind off.**

5. **Work the other tie the same way (repeat Steps 3 and 4).**

6. **Seam the hat at the center back by using the mattress stitch.**

    Find out how to do this in Chapter 15.

7. **Seam the top of the hat.**

   Use the backstitch to sew the seam. (See Chapter 15 for how to sew knitted pieces together.)

8. **Steam the seams.**

   Chapter 15 offers tips on how to do so. When you finish making the hat, tie the ends together.

Varying your hat

- Work the basic hat using a garter or seed stitch variation from Chapter 2 for the cuff.

- Make a striped hat by using various colors and different stripe arrangements. (See Chapter 11 for stripe ideas.)

- Make the cuff in a contrasting color. See Chapter 11 for how to join two colors together.

- Turn the Envelope Hat into a Slouch Hat by knitting the hat a total of 13 (15, 16) inches before binding off.

- Put pompoms on the ends of the ties on the Tie Hat.

Part II
Manipulating Stitches

The 5th Wave   By Rich Tennant

In his later years, Capt. Hook gave up on chasing Peter Pan and took up knitting.

In this part . . .

Now that you have the basics down and you've practiced making knit and purl stitches, it's time to move onto other things that you can do with needles and yarn. In this part, you discover how to manipulate stitches in new ways to make different kinds of stitch patterns. You find out how to make a basic cable and how to vary twists and turns to make new and different cable patterns. I explain the basics of knitted lace — what makes up the simple building block and how it's used to create myriad open work fabrics. Put your new cabling and lace-making skills to work by making the practice samplers and simple projects you find here.

Chapter 7

Vital Stitchtistics: Manipulating Stitches

In This Chapter

▶ Manipulating stitches: slipping, twisting, and increasing

▶ Adding techniques to your Knitting Notebook

Playing around with knit and purl patterns can keep you busy for a long time, but you can do a lot more with knitted stitches. Cables, lace, and color work all lie ahead. As you begin to explore different stitch patterns and follow patterns for projects and garments, you'll want to familiarize yourself with the different stitch maneuvers that crop up in instructions for more demanding knitted fabrics.

When you come across "slip," "twist," "knit into the stitch below," and "yarn over" in pattern instructions, flip back to this chapter for a reminder of how to work them.

Slipping Stitches (sl)

If your directions tell you to *slip a stitch* (abbreviated sl), they mean for you to move a stitch from the left-hand (LH) needle to the right-hand (RH) needle without knitting or purling it *and* without changing its orientation. It remains in the ready-to-work position. To do so, insert the RH needle *purlwise* (as if you were going to purl) into the first stitch on the LH needle and slip it off the LH needle onto the RH needle. Unless your instructions specifically tell you to slip a stitch *knitwise*, always slip a stitch as if you were going to purl it. Figure 7-1 shows stitches being slipped purlwise and knitwise.

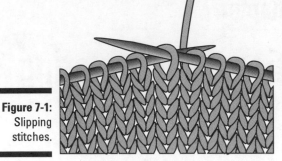
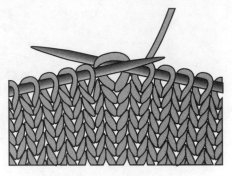

Figure 7-1:
Slipping
stitches.

A. Slipping a stitch purlwise.   B. Slipping a stitch knitwise.

Slipped stitches are used in different ways. You frequently run across them in methods for decreasing stitches — when you want to reduce the number of stitches you have on your needle. They also form the basis of a family of stitch patterns. Like garter stitch, slip-stitch patterns are stable and lie flat — and they're a breeze to knit.

Knitting into the Stitch Below (k1b or k-b)

Knitting into the stitch below is a technique that's often used for increasing stitches — when you need to add another stitch to your needle. Also, the family of soft and densely textured Brioche stitch patterns is built around the method of knitting into the stitch in the row below.

If your instructions tell you to "knit (or purl) into the stitch below," insert your needle into the stitch you've already made, which is directly below the next stitch on the LH needle and then wrap and knit as you normally would. You'll be knitting the stitch below and the one on the needle at the same time. When you've completed the stitch, look at the purl side of your work. You'll see 2 purl bumps for the stitch you've made. You can see how to do this in Figure 7-2.

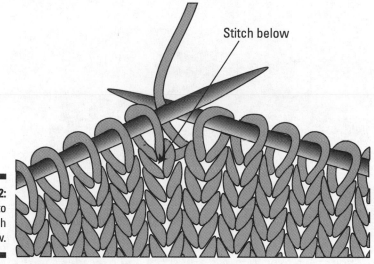

Stitch below

Figure 7-2:
Knitting into
the stitch
below.

Making a Yarn Over (yo)

A *yarn over* is a way of making an extra stitch on your needle and creating a deliberate little hole in your fabric. To make a yarn over, you bring the knitting yarn (the "over" strand) over the needle between two existing stitches on one row, and then work the "over" strand as a stitch when you work your way back to it in the next row.

A yarn over is formed differently depending on the kinds of stitches it goes between — 2 knit stitches, a knit stitch and a purl stitch, 2 purl stitches, or a purl and a knit stitch. Here are the methods to use in each situation:

✔ **If your yarn over goes between 2 knit stitches (k1, yo, k1):**

1. Knit the first stitch.

2. Bring the yarn forward between the needles into purl position.

   When you knit the next stitch, the yarn automatically crosses the RH needle, forming a yarn over. (See Figure 7-3.)

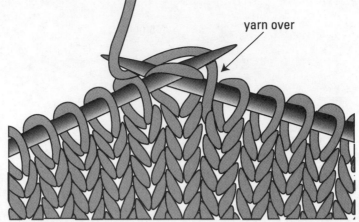

Figure 7-3:
Making a
yarn over
between 2
knit stitches.

yarn over

✔ **If your yarn over follows a knit stitch and precedes a purl stitch (k1, yo, p1):**

1. Knit the first stitch.

2. Bring the yarn to the front between the needles to purl position, and then bring it back over the top of the RH needle to the back and return to the front into purl position again.

3. Purl the next stitch. (See Figure 7-4.)

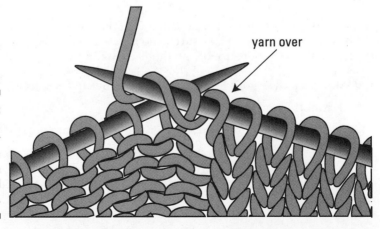

Figure 7-4:
Making a
yarn over
between a
knit stitch
and a purl
stitch.

yarn over

✔ **If your yarn over goes between 2 purl stitches (p1, yo, p1):**

1. Purl the first stitch.

2. Bring the yarn over the top of the RH needle front to back and into purl position again.

3. Purl the next stitch. (See Figure 7-5.)

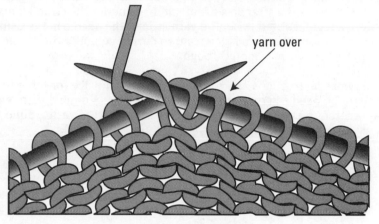

yarn over

Figure 7-5:
Making a yarn over between 2 purl stitches.

✔ **If your yarn over follows a purl stitch and precedes a knit stitch (p1, yo, k1):**

1. Purl the first stitch and leave the yarn in the front on your work.

2. With the yarn remaining in the *front* of your work, knit the next stitch. The yarn automatically crosses the RH needle when you knit this next stitch. (See Figure 7-6.)

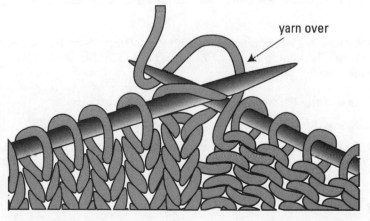

yarn over

Figure 7-6:
Making a yarn over between a purl stitch and a knit stitch.

As you work the row following the row in which you performed your yarn over, you'll recognize the yarn over by the big hole that suddenly appears on your needle where a stitch should be. Above the hole is the strand of yarn that you've crossed over the needle (well, you actually yarned it over). Think of the strand as a stitch. You can go under it as if to knit it, or under it as if to purl it. To work the strand as a knit stitch, go under the strand knitwise, as if it were a regular stitch, wrap the yarn around the needle in the usual way, and draw a loop through. If you want to purl it, go under the strand purlwise, wrap, and draw a new loop through.

Sometimes instructions ask you to wrap the yarn twice (or more times) around the needle in order to make a bigger hole. A double yarn over is usually written "yo twice." Figure 7-7 shows wrapping the yarn around the needle twice for a yarn over.

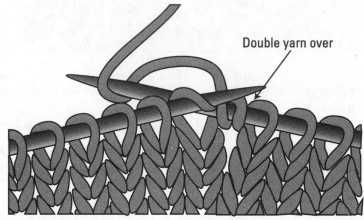

Double yarn over

Figure 7-7:
A yarn over
with the
yarn
wrapped
twice
around the
needle.

Every once in a while, particularly in lace patterns, a pattern calls for a yarn over at the beginning of a row. If the first stitch in the row is a knit stitch, do the following:

1. **Insert the RH needle into the first stitch knitwise.**

2. **Bring the yarn strand to the front *under* the RH needle.**

3. **Knit the stitch. The yarn will automatically cross the needle, making a yarn over. You'll see 2 stitches on the RH needle after knitting the first stitch.**

The yarn will cross the needle, creating a yarn-over stitch.

For a yarn over at the beginning of a purl row, insert the RH needle purlwise into the first stitch, bring the yarn from the front to the back *under* the needle, and purl the first stitch. The yarn crosses the needle automatically, making a yarn-over stitch.

Yarn overs are an indispensable part of lace knitting (see Chapter 10 for more about using yarn overs in lace). They have a multitude of other applications as well, such as decorative increases, buttonholes, and novelty stitch patterns.

Twisting Stitches

A *twisted stitch* is a single stitch rotated so that the strands that form the little V cross at the bottom. When stitches are lined up in the ready-to-work position, they have a front and a back. The front of the stitch is the part of the loop on *your* side of the needle. The back of the stitch is, well, on the side of the needle facing away from you. (See Figure 7-8.)

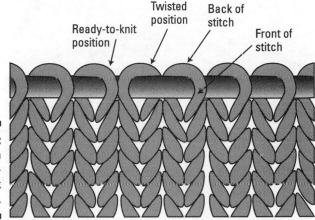

Ready-to-knit position

Twisted position

Back of stitch

Front of stitch

Figure 7-8: Stitches in the ready-to work position.

When you knit in the usual fashion, you work into the front of the loop. This means that you insert your RH needle into the stitch from left to right, lifting and spreading the front of the loop — the side of the loop on your side of the needle — when you insert your needle. Try this to see it in action. To work into the *back of the loop*, insert your needle from right to left, with the RH needle *behind* the LH needle, lifting and spreading the back of the loop — the side of the loop on the opposite side of the needle. Then you wrap the yarn around the needle and pull a new loop through.

In general, you work into the front of a stitch to make a normal knitted stitch (to avoid twisting the stitch). If your instructions tell you to knit through the back of the loop, they're asking you to change the direction from which your needle enters the stitch. When you work into the back of a stitch, you're deliberately twisting it. Figure 7-9a shows knitting into the front of a loop, and Figure 7-9b shows knitting into the back of a loop.

Figure 7-9:
Knitting into the front and the back of stitches.

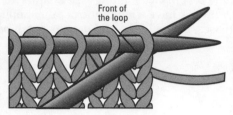

Front of the loop

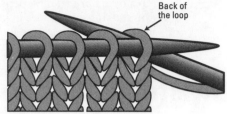

Back of the loop

A. Knit into the front of the loop.

B. Knit into the back of the loop.

You can purl into the front and back of a stitch as well. Figure 7-10 shows purling into the front and back of a loop.

Figure 7-10:
Purling into the front and the back of stitches.

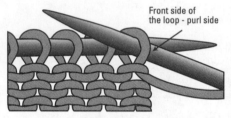

Front side of the loop - purl side

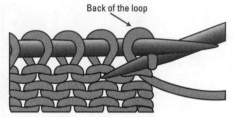

Back of the loop

A. Purl into the front of the loop.

B. Purl into the back of the loop.

Stitch patterns that use twisted stitches have an etched linear quality. You can see this in the Twisted Rib and Garter stitch pattern in the Knitting Notebook that follows. On a background of reverse stockinette stitch, a vertical or wavy line of twisted stitches stands out in sharp definition. Frequently, you find twisted stitches combined with cables in traditional Aran patterns.

Abbreviations can vary from pattern to pattern. Don't confuse knitting in the stitch below with knitting through the back loop. Check your pattern for which abbreviation they are using for what.

Doing the Twist: Making Mini Cables

Twists are diminutive cousins of the cable. (See Chapter 9 for the twist on cables.) A twist consists of 2 stitches, 1 stitch crossing over its neighbor. You can twist in either direction: left over right or right over left. To make a 2-stitch twist, you can use a cable needle to take 1 stitch to the front or back while you knit the other stitch. But there's another way to accomplish the crossing that doesn't require a cable needle, saves time, and is easier to do.

Twisting to the right

To work a twist to the right, do the following:

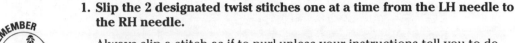

REMEMBER

1. **Slip the 2 designated twist stitches one at a time from the LH needle to the RH needle.**

   Always slip a stitch as if to purl unless your instructions tell you to do otherwise.

2. **With the tip of the LH needle in back, go past the slipped stitch on the left, enter the second stitch left to right, as in Figure 7-11, and leave it there.**

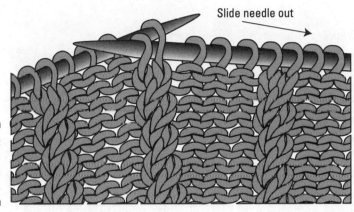

Slide needle out →

Figure 7-11:
Inserting the
needle from
left to right.

3. **Gently slide the RH needle out of both stitches, leaving the one on the left hanging.**

4. **Bring the tip of the RH needle around to the *front* and insert it into the stitch that you left hanging. (See Figure 7-12.)**

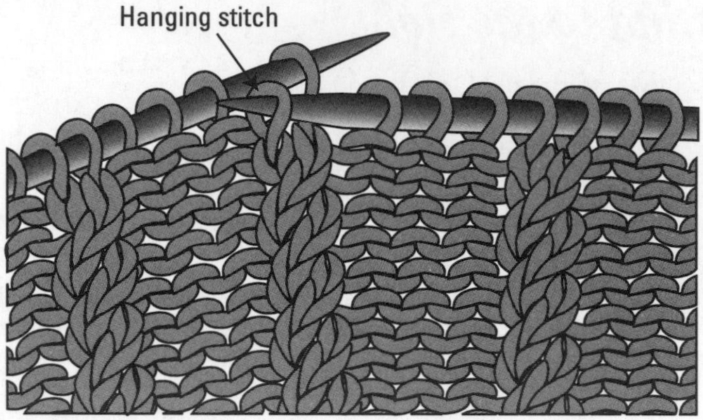

Hanging stitch

Figure 7-12:
Insert the
needle tip
into the
hanging
stitch.

5. **Transfer this stitch to the LH needle.**

   Both stitches are back on the LH needle, with the second one overlapping the first to the right.

6. **Knit both stitches in the usual way.**

Twisting to the left

To work a twist to the left, work your stitches this way:

1. **Slip the 2 designated twist stitches one at a time from the LH needle to the RH needle.**

2. **With the tip of the LH needle in front of your work, go past the slipped stitch on the left, insert it into the second stitch from left to right (see Figure 7-13), and leave it there.**

Figure 7-13:
Inserting the
needle from
left to right.

3. **Gently slide the RH needle out of both stitches, leaving 1 stitch hanging.**

4. **Keeping the RH needle in** *back* **of the LH needle, insert the tip of your RH needle into the stitch you left hanging. (See Figure 7-14.)**

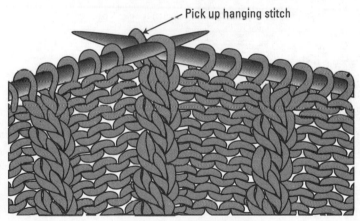

← Pick up hanging stitch

Figure 7-14:
Pick up the
hanging
stitch.

5. **Transfer this stitch to the LH needle.**

   Both stitches are back on the LH needle, with the first one overlapping the second to the left.

6. **Knit both stitches in the usual way.**

Knitting Notebook

The examples of stitch patterns in this section make use of the stitch maneuvers explained in this chapter. You'll find many, many more in the stitch dictionaries listed in the Chapter 19. Try to knit as many patterns as you can (and as much as you can) to become familiar with these moves and how they're used.

Garter slip-stitch pattern

Working this garter stitch pattern with slipped stitches (see Figure 7-15) is as simple as working regular garter stitch — maybe even more so. They look a bit the same, but the slipped stitches break up the strong horizontal lines of basic garter stitch. To make it, cast on a multiple of 2 stitches, plus 1 extra, and then work as follows:

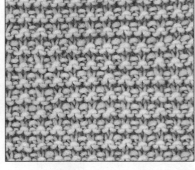

Figure 7-15: Garter slip-stitch pattern.

Row 1 (RS): Knit.

Row 2: Knit.

Row 3: K1, * slip 1 pwise, k1; repeat from * to end.

Row 4: K1, * yf (bring the yarn to the front of your work), slip 1 pwise, yb (bring the yarn to the back), k1; repeat from * to end.

Repeat these 4 rows.

Fisherman's rib

Fisherman's rib (see Figure 7-16) makes a fabric with a ribbed appearance but with more depth and softness than a standard rib. To make it, cast on an even number of stitches and work as follows:

Figure 7-16:
Fisherman's
rib.

Row 1: Purl.

Row 2: *P1, knit next st in the row below, allowing old stitch to drop from needle; rep from *, end p2.

Repeat Row 2 only.

Twists

To make a sample of twist stitches, cast on 28 stitches.

CR = cross right. Slip 2 stitches to the RH needle one at a time. With the LH needle behind the RH needle, go past the first stitch on the needle and insert the tip into the second stitch. Slide the RH needle out of both stitches, bring the tip around and insert it in the hanging stitch, and then transfer it to the LH needle. The stitch crossing to the right is on top. Knit the 2 stitches as you normally would.

CL = cross left. Slip 2 stitches to the RH needle one at a time. With the LH needle in front of the RH needle, go past the first stitch on the RH needle and insert the tip of the LH needle into the second stitch. Slide the RH needle out of both stitches, insert it into the hanging stitch, and transfer it to the LH needle. The stitch crossing to the left is on top. Knit the 2 stitches as you normally would.

Row 1 (RS): P3, (CR, p2) 3 times, (CL, p2) 3 times, end p1.

Row 2: K3, *p2, k2; rep from *, end k1.

Repeat Rows 1 and 2.

Twisted rib and garter stitch

This pattern (see Figure 7-17) consists of two stitch patterns that you're already familiar with if you read Chapter 2: 1 x 1 rib and garter stitch. The difference is that in the ribbed section presented here, you work the knit columns on the right and wrong sides with twisted stitches for a sharp, crisp look.

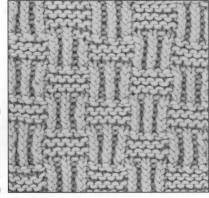

Figure 7-17:
Twisted rib and garter stitch.

Cast on a multiple of 10 stitches, plus 5.

Rows 1, 3, and 5 (RS): *K5, (k1tbl, p1) twice, k1tbl; rep from *, end k5.

Rows 2, 4, and 6: *K5, (p1tbl, k1) twice, p1tbl; rep from *, end k5.

Rows 7, 9, and 11: *(K1tbl, p1) twice, k1tbl, k5; rep from *, end (k1tbl, p1) twice, k1tbl.

Rows 8, 10, and 12: *(P1tbl, k1) twice, p1tbl, k5; rep from * end (p1tbl, k1) twice, p1tbl.

Repeat Rows 1–12.

Chapter 8

Shaping: The Ins and Outs of Knitting

• •

• •

Not all knitted pieces are square. Being able to increase or decrease one or more stitches along the edge or within the body of a knitted piece enables you to create knitted pieces with edges that taper and expand. When you increase stitches, you add them to your needle. When you decrease stitches, you get rid of stitches on your needle.

The techniques in this chapter enable you to tailor your knitting in many ways, including

✔ Decreasing at each edge of a neckline to make an opening that follows the contour of the neck.

✔ Increasing along a sleeve seam to expand the sleeve toward the shoulder, just as your arm does.

✔ Decreasing and then increasing in the body of a sweater to contour it to your body, making it fit better.

Increases and decreases also enable you to make more variations in stitch patterns. With increases and decreases, you can slant a group of stitches to the right or left. You can make pointed or scalloped edges. And, most notably, you can make lace (see Chapter 10).

As with everything else in knitting, there are several ways to increase and decrease stitches. Some methods are almost invisible, and others are decorative and meant to be seen. And because increases and decreases are often worked as pairs (picture adding stitches at either end of your needle when you're shaping a sleeve), if one slants to the right on the right side of your work, the other slants to the left on the left side.

Working Increases (inc)

You can work increases (add stitches) into your knitting in various ways. Each method has a different appearance. If the increase is part of a fabric stitch pattern, the pattern will almost always tell you how to make the increase. Sometimes garment patterns specify which increase to use when shaping, but others leave it up to you to decide what will look best. Having a few techniques up your sleeve (pun intended) gives you the flexibility to decide which increase will look best in your current project. Various knitting patterns require that you knit a single increase, work a double increase, or distribute several increases along a given row. Try some of the fundamental techniques in this section to learn what your choices are.

Although most shaping is done on the right (or knit) side of your work, there are times when the purl side is the right side. The following methods are given for knitting and purling.

Adding a single stitch

You can add a stitch by making two stitches in one, as in the bar increase described later, or you can create an independent new stitch *between* two stitches on your needle, as in the make 1 increase. These two increases are basic and easy to do, and either one will more than adequately suit your increasing needs. You can get familiar with how to make them and how they look by working the sampler in the "Practice Projects" section at the end of this chapter.

Using a bar increase (K1f&b)

If you're increasing 1 stitch on the very edge of your knitting, you use this increase, which is called a *bar increase* because it leaves a telltale horizontal bar under the increased stitch. It's good to use on edge stitches that will be enclosed in a seam. You can use it elsewhere too if you like the way it looks.

Knitting directions for the bar increase read, "Knit into the front and back of the stitch." (See Chapter 7 for information about the front and back of a stitch.)

Here's how to make a bar increase when you're working on the *knit* side:

1. **Knit 1 stitch as you normally would, but don't slide the old stitch off the LH needle.**

2. **Bring the tip of the RH needle to the right, behind the LH needle, and enter the same stitch through the back.**

3. **Knit the stitch again, but through the back this time (flip back to Figure 7-9b to see how to knit through the back of the loop).**

You've worked two stitches in one.

Here's how to make a bar increase when you're working on the *purl* side:

1. **Purl 1 stitch as you normally would, but don't slide the old stitch off the LH needle.**

   Your RH needle is behind the LH needle.

2. **Keeping the RH needle behind the LH one, bring the tip of the RH needle to the left and enter the stitch again through the back from left to right.**

3. **Purl that stitch again.**

   You've worked 2 stitches from a single stitch.

If you're using this bar increase several stitches in from the edge as part of a paired increase, adjust the position of the stitch in which you make the increase so that the bar shows up in the same place on each side. (Make the sampler given in the "Practice Projects" section at the end of this chapter to see how this works.)

Working a make 1 (m1)

To work the m1 increase, you create a new, separate stitch between 2 stitches that are already on the needle. When you get to the point where you want to make an increase, pull the LH and RH needle slightly apart. You'll notice a horizontal strand of yarn, called the *running thread*, connecting the first stitch on each needle. You use the running thread to make the new stitch. The increased stitch will be a twisted stitch (see Chapter 7) and will cross to the right or to the left depending on how you work it.

Twisting to the right

When you want your m1 increase to twist to the right, follow these steps if you're working on the *knit* side:

1. **Work to the point between 2 stitches where you want to increase.**

2. **Bring the tip of the LH needle under the running thread from back to front.**

   The running thread will be draped over the LH needle as if it were a stitch. See Figure 8-1a.

3. **Go to the left of that draped strand and knit it as if it were a stitch, as shown in Figure 8-1b.**

Figure 8-1:
Working an
m1 increase
that twists
to the right.

A. Insert the tip of the LH needle under the
running thread from back to front.

B. Knit the strand as if it were a stitch.

When you're working a right-twisting m1 increase on the *purl* side, do the
following:

1. **Bring the tip of the LH needle under the running thread from back to front.**

2. **Purl the strand by going into the front of the loop (the part of the loop that's closest to you) instead of the back of the loop — see Figure 8-2.**

Figure 8-2:
Purling the
strand
through the
front of
the loop.

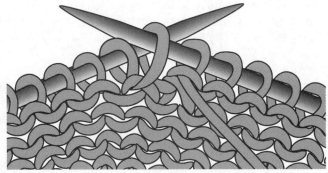

Twisting to the left

When you want your m1 increase to twist to the left, follow these steps if
you're working on the *knit* side:

1. **Work to the point between 2 stitches where you want to increase.**

2. **Insert the tip of the LH needle under the running thread from front to back (see Figure 8-3a).**

3. **With the RH needle, knit the strand through the back of the loop crossing it, as shown in Figure 8-3b.**

Figure 8-3:
Working an
m1 increase
that twists
to the left.

A. Insert the tip of the LH needle under the
running thread from front to back.

B. Knit the strand through the back of the loop.

When you want your m1 increase to twist to the left and you're working on
the *purl* side, do the following:

1. **Work to the point between 2 stitches where you want to make your
   increase.**

2. **Bring the tip of the LH needle under the running thread from front
   to back.**

3. **With the RH needle behind the LH needle, reach around the back of
   the strand, inserting the RH needle tip from left to right between the
   strand and the LH needle.**

4. **Purl the stitch, as shown in Figure 8-4.**

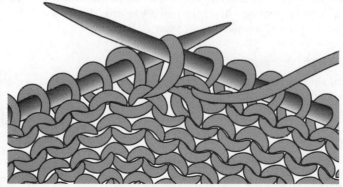

Figure 8-4:
Purling the
strand
through the
back of
the loop.

After you make an increase or decrease, always check to make sure that it's
twisted in the direction you intended. If it isn't, undo your new stitch — it will
only unravel as far as the running thread — and try it again.

You can make this a decorative "eyelet" (makes a little hole) increase by knitting or purling into the running thread without twisting it.

Making a double increase

There are occasions in knitting — in certain stitch patterns or when working a raglan sweater from the neck down — when you want to increase *2* stitches in the same place. This is called *working a double increase*, and it often utilizes an existing stitch as the increase point.

Doubling your increase with a yarn over (yo)

This technique results in 3 stitches being made from 1 stitch. To make a double increase with a yarn over, follow these steps:

1. **Work to the stitch in which you plan to make the increase.**

2. **Insert your RH needle as if to knit.**

3. **Wrap the yarn around the needle and bring the new loop through to the front, but don't slide the old stitch off the LH needle.**

4. **Bring the yarn between the needles to the front.**

5. **With the yarn in front and down, insert the RH needle as if to knit into the same stitch again.**

6. **Bring the yarn over the RH needle to the back.**

7. **Wrap the yarn around the tip of the RH needle as you normally would, pull the loop through, and slide the old loop off. You'll see 3 stitches clustered together on your RH needle.**

Doubling your increase with a make 1 (m1)

This technique makes a new stitch on either side of an existing center stitch. Make the increase symmetrical by having the m1 increase before the center stitch twist to the right and the m1 increase after the center stitch twist to the left. See the section just preceding for instructions on how to work these twisted increases. To create a double increase with a make 1, follow these steps:

1. **Work to the stitch marked for the increase.**

2. **As in the make 1 (m1) increase presented earlier in this chapter, insert your RH needle below the running thread between the stitch just made and the stitch designated as the center stitch. Work an m1 that twists to the right.**

3. **Knit the next (center) stitch.**

4. **Knit into the running thread between the center stitch and the stitch just after it, making the new stitch twist to the left.**

If you want to see more ways to work a double increase, check out *Knitting from the Top* by Barbara Walker. She gives a whopping ten ways to make a double increase.

Increasing multiple stitches in one place

In certain knitting situations, such as buttonholes and dolman sleeves, you need to add a series of stitches all together. Essentially, you cast on in the middle of a row or at the edge of your project or garment. The cast-on techniques that I talk about in this section come in handy in these situations.

Cable cast-on (cable co)

The cable cast-on, or "knitting on," is less elastic than the two-strand cast-on introduced in Chapter 1. Use it to cast on over buttonholes (see Chapter 16) or when you need a sturdy, not-too-stretchy edge. If you're making a brand-new cast-on row, start with Step 1. If you're adding on at the beginning of an existing row or making new stitches over a buttonhole, start from Step 2.

Follow these steps:

1. **Make a slip-knot stitch.**

   For this cable cast-on, you can leave a short tail.

2. **Knit into the first stitch in the usual way, but instead of slipping the old loop off the LH needle, bring the new loop to the right and slip it onto the LH needle, as shown in Figure 8-5a.**

3. **Insert the RH needle *between* the 2 stitches on the LH needle (see Figure 8-5b).**

4. **Wrap the yarn around the RH needle as you do when you knit, and then bring a new loop through to the front (see Figure 8-5c).**

5. **Bring this loop around to the right and place it on the LH needle, as shown in Figure 8-5d.**

6. **Repeat Steps 3 through 5 until you have the number of cast-on stitches called for.**

A. Knit the first stitch through the slip-knot stitch.

B. Insert the RH needle between the two stitches.

C. Bring the new loop through to the front.

Figure 8-5:
Working
a cable
cast-on.

D. Add the next stitch to the LH needle.

Thumb cast-on

The thumb cast-on is quick and easy, but it doesn't look as nice as the cable cast-on, and it isn't easy to knit into. Still, it has its uses (for example, for replacing cast-off stitches in a buttonhole or for a quick and easy increase stitch in the middle of a row), and learning how to do it is worthwhile. Follow these steps (If you're using the cast on at the beginning or in the middle of an existing row, skip Step 1.):

1. Make a slip-knot stitch (no need to leave a long tail).

2. Wrap the yarn around your left thumb, as in Figure 8-6a, and hold the needle in the right hand.

3. Insert the needle through the loop around your thumb (see Figure 8-6b), slide your thumb out, and pull gently on the yarn strand to tighten the stitch.

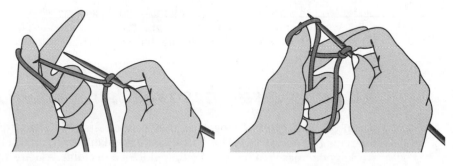

Figure 8-6: Working a thumb cast-on.

A. Wrap the yarn around your left thumb.   B. Insert the RH needle into the thumb loop.

Increasing at several points in a single row

Patterns sometimes ask you to increase several stitches evenly across a row. It's up to you to figure out the best spacing. To do so, follow these steps:

1. **Take the number of stitches to be added and add 1.**

   This gives you the number of spaces between increases.

2. **Divide the total number of stitches on your needle by the number of spaces between the increases.**

   For example, if you have 40 stitches and you need to increase 4 stitches, there will be five 8-stitch sections between the increases. If your pattern calls for you to work bar increases into existing stitches,

make your increases in every eighth stitch across the row (stitches 8, 16, 24, and 32). When you're counting the stitches between increases, don't include the increased stitches.

If your numbers don't come out even and you have a remainder of several stitches, you can

- Divvy up the extra stitches and knit them before the first increase and after the last increase.

- Alternate working an extra stitch into every other section of stitches between increases until you've used up the extras.

Graph paper is great to have on hand for charting out increases — and all other manner of knitting math.

Doing Decreases

A decrease is a method for getting rid of a stitch on your needle. You use decreases for shaping at the edges and/or in the middle of a knitted piece. They're also used in conjunction with increases in various stitch patterns, most notably in lace.

A decreased stitch looks like 1 stitch overlapping another. Depending on the design you're working with, you can make your decreases slant to the left or right. When a stitch overlaps to the right, the decrease slants to the right. When a stitch overlaps to the left, the decrease slants to the left.

Knitting 2 stitches together (k2tog)

When you knit 2 stitches together, they become 1 stitch. The stitch on the left overlaps the one on the right — the decrease slants to the right. If you're working decreases in pairs (on either side of a neckline you are shaping, for example), use the k2tog on one side and the ssk decrease that follows on the other side.

To knit 2 stitches together (k2tog) on the right (knit) side of your knitted fabric, follow these steps:

1. **Bring the tip of the RH needle 2 stitches to the left on the LH needle.**

2. **Insert the RH needle knitwise into the first 2 stitches on the LH needle at the same time.**

3. **Knit them together as if they were 1 stitch (see Figure 8-7).**

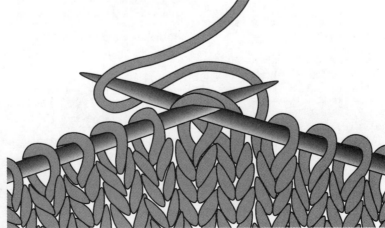

Figure 8-7:
Knitting 2
stitches
together
(k2tog).

Full-fashioning

Increases and decreases can be worked on the edge or several stitches in from the edge. If a series of increases or decreases are worked 2 or more stitches from the edge, they create a visible line, and the shaping is described as "full-fashion." This shaping technique is peculiar to knits and sometimes distinguishes a sweater that's cut and sewn from knitted fabric from one that has been knitted to shape. Not only attractive, working increases or decreases several stitches from the edge also makes it easier to sew knitted pieces together. You have two untampered stitches at the edges to seam between.

Purling 2 stitches together (p2tog)

Although most knitting patterns have you decrease on right-side rows only, sometimes you may be asked to work a decrease from the purl side. When you do, you can purl 2 stitches instead of knitting them together. When you look at a p2tog decrease from the knit side, the stitches will slant to the right, just as they do with a k2tog decrease.

When you need to work a single p2tog decrease on the wrong side of your knitting (the purl side), follow these steps:

1. **Insert the RH needle purlwise into the next 2 stitches on the LH needle.**

2. **Purl the 2 stitches together as if they were 1 stitch (see Figure 8-8).**

Figure 8-8:
Purling 2
stitches
together
(p2tog).

Slip, slip, knit (ssk)

Ssk stands for "slip, slip, knit" and results in a left-slanting decrease. The ssk decrease is the mirror image of k2tog: It slants to the left. Use it when you want to work symmetrical decreases.

To work an ssk on the knit side, follow these steps:

1. **Slip the first stitch on the LH needle (as if to knit) to the RH needle without actually knitting it.**

2. **Do the same with the next stitch.**

    At this point, the 2 slipped stitches should look like the stitches in Figure 8-9a.

3. **Insert the LH needle into the front loops of these stitches (left to right), as in Figure 8-9b.**

4. **Wrap the yarn in the usual way around the RH needle and knit the 2 slipped stitches together.**

Figure 8-9: Working a slip, slip, knit (ssk) decrease.

A. Two stitches slipped knitwise.

B. Insert the LH needle into the front of the loops.

To work an ssk on the purl side, follow these steps:

1. **Slip the first stitch on the LH needle as if to knit to the RH needle.**

2. **Do the same to the next stitch.**

3. **Keeping the 2 slipped stitches facing in this direction, transfer them back to the LH needle.**

4. **Purl these stitches together through the *back* loops.**

    Figure 8-10 shows this step in action.

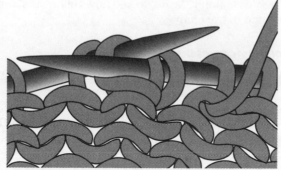

Figure 8-10:
Purling the slipped stitches through the back of the loops.

Pass slipped stitch over (psso)

Psso refers to a less attractive version of the left-slanting ssk decrease, but one that's still used in certain stitch patterns and in double decreases (decreasing 2 stitches at once). Essentially, psso makes a bound-off stitch in the middle of a row. You can work it from the knit or purl side of your work.

Here's how to work a psso on the knit side:

1. **Slip 1 stitch** *knitwise* **from the LH needle to the RH needle.**

2. **Knit the next stitch from the LH needle.**

3. **Insert the tip of the LH needle into the slipped stitch and bring it over the knitted stitch and off the needle as if you were binding off.**

To work a psso on the purl side, do the following:

1. **Purl 1 stitch.**

2. **Slip the next stitch knitwise and return it in this changed direction to the LH needle.**

3. **Return the purled stitch from the RH needle to the LH needle.**

4. **Insert the RH needle into the slipped stitch and bring it over the purled stitch and off the needle.**

"Pass a stitch over" means to bind it off.

Making double decreases

Sometimes you need to decrease 2 stitches at the same time. Certain stitch patterns depend on decreasing 2 stitches at the same time for their effect, and sometimes you'll need to use a double decrease in garment shaping. Like single decreases, they can slant to the left or right. Or they can create a single vertical line at the decrease point. Again, to see how this works, make the sampler given at the end of the chapter.

Right-slanting double decrease

To work a right-slanting double decrease on the knit side, follow these steps:

1. **Work an ssk.**

   This means that you need to slip 2 stitches knitwise one at a time to the RH needle, insert the LH needle into the front of the loops, and knit them together. (Flip back to the previous section, "Slip, slip, knit (ssk)," for instructions on making an ssk decrease.)

2. **Slip the stitch you just worked back to the LH needle.**

3. **Bring the second stitch on the LH needle over the decreased stitch and off the needle.**

4. **Return the decreased stitch to the RH needle.**

To work a right-slanting double decrease on the purl side, do the following:

1. **Slip the next stitch from the LH needle to the RH needle.**

2. **Purl the next 2 stitches together.**

   Refer to the earlier section, "Purling 2 stitches together," to find out how to do so.

3. **Pass the slipped stitch over the decreased stitch.**

Left-slanting double decrease

To work a left-slanting double decrease on the knit side, follow these steps:

1. **Slip the next stitch on the LH needle as if to knit.**

2. **Knit the next 2 stitches together.**

   Refer to the earlier section, "Knitting 2 stitches together," to find the instructions for doing so.

3. **Bring the slipped stitch over the decrease stitch as if you were binding off.**

To work a left-slanting double decrease on the purl side, do the following:

1. **Purl 2 stitches together.**

   Flip back to the section, "Purling 2 stitches together," to find out how to do so.

2. **Slip this decreased stitch back to the LH needle.**

3. **With the RH needle, bring the second stitch on the LH needle over the first (decreased) stitch and off the needle.**

4. **Return the decreased stitch to the RH needle.**

Vertical double decrease

This double decrease creates a vertical line instead of a line that slants to the left or right. To make a vertical double decrease, follow these steps:

1. **Insert the RH needle into the first 2 stitches on the LH needle as if you were knitting them together.**

2. **Transfer these 2 stitches (without knitting them) to the RH needle.**

3. **Knit the next stitch.**

4. **With the LH needle, bring both slipped stitches together over the knitted stitch and off the needle, as in Figure 8-11.**

Figure 8-11:
Bringing the slipped stitches over in a vertical double decrease.

Reading Shaping Charts

Increases and decreases in stitch patterns can be charted just as textured stitches can. Although symbols for increases and decreases may vary from one publication to another, most symbols for decreases show which way they slant.

To show an increase, the pattern inserts a symbol in the square that represents the new stitch being made. Symbols for decreases are shown in a single square as well, even though they involve 2 or 3 stitches. When you come to a symbol indicating a decrease, work the next 2 stitches together in the manner indicated by the symbol and then work the next stitch on your needle according to the symbol in the square just after the one that shows the decrease.

When you're working with increases and decreases, the number of stitches in a row doesn't always remain constant. When the shape of a sweater piece, or part of one like the armhole or neckline, is charted, the chart indicates the shaping along the edge of the piece — that is, stitches increased or decreased — by adding or subtracting squares along the edge (see Figure 8-12).

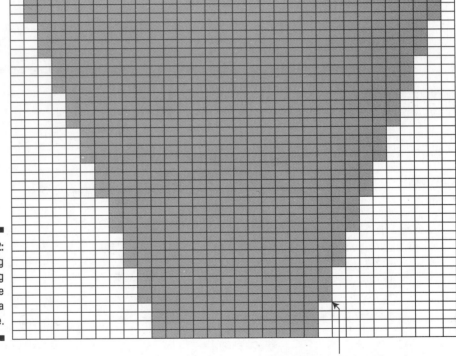

Figure 8-12:
Charting shaping along the edge of a piece.

Increased stitch along the edge

In texture and lace patterns that involve changes in the number of stitches in a row, a "no-stitch" symbol may be used. Often, it's simply a filled gray square indicating that it's holding a place for a stitch that's temporarily not there. Using a "no-stitch" symbol in the pattern repeat to indicate a decrease allows you to maintain a consistent number of stitches (squares) in the chart. Your chart key will alert you to a no-stitch symbol. If you follow the no-stitch square up along a vertical row, you see that it becomes active again after an increase. When you come to a "no-stitch" symbol, just skip over it and work the next squares as indicated in the chart. (See Chapter 10 for an example.)

Shaping with Short Rows

Short rows are just that: They allow you to taper the outside edge of your knitted piece without having to work specific decreasing techniques. Instead of knitting to the end of the row, you knit part of a row, stop, turn your work, and work back in the direction you came from, making a short row (or, more accurately, two short rows).

Why would you want to work only part of a row? Because short rows, though not used as frequently as increases and decreases, are an ingenious shaping tool. When you increase and decrease stitches, you shape your piece in and out widthwise. Short rows enable you to tinker with length. They also enable you to

✔ Shape a sloped shoulder and leave the stitches "live" so that you can use the 3-needle bind-off later.

✔ Add subtle darts to a sweater.

✔ Shape certain kinds of collars.

✔ Knit a sweater border along with the front, even when the gauge of the border is different from the gauge of the sweater body.

✔ Turn the heel of a sock.

Short rows are sometimes called "partial knitting" or, more quaintly, "stitches in waiting."

Working a short row with the knit side facing

Making a short row that doesn't leave a telltale little hole in the spot where you turn around is a two-step process: wrapping a stitch at the turning point and knitting the wrapped stitch on the return row as shown in the following steps:

1. **Knit to the point where you want to turn your work.**

2. **Leave the yarn in back and slip the next stitch to the RH needle.**

3. **Bring the yarn forward between the needles.**

4. **Return the slipped stitch to the LH needle.**

5. **Bring the yarn between the needles to the back of your work.**

   Before you turn your work, take a good look at the base of the slipped stitch. You'll see that you have wrapped the strand of yarn around it. The way you work this wrap together with the slipped stitch on a later row creates a smooth transition between the different levels of your knitting.

6. Turn your work.

Your yarn is in back of your work, ready to purl back.

If you're working in garter stitch, or if the next stitch after you turn your work is a knit stitch, simply leave the yarn on the front side of your work, turn, and start knitting back — the stitch will be wrapped automatically.

When you're ready to knit back over the turning point where you've wrapped the stitch, you need to knit the wrapped stitch in a special way. Otherwise, you'll have an unsightly hiccup in your work. To knit the return row:

1. Work to the wrapped stitch.

2. Insert the RH needle into the wrap and the stitch and knit the wrap and the stitch together.

Make sure that the wrap goes over the end of the needle with the old stitch. The wrap will fall to the purl side of your work. See Figure 8-13.

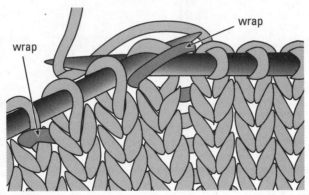

Figure 8-13:
Inserting the RH needle into the wrap *and* the stitch and knitting them together.

wrap

wrap

Working a short row with the purl side facing

Again, there are two steps in the process of working a short row: wrapping a stitch at the turning point and purling the wrapped stitch on the next full row. To work the first row:

1. Purl to the point where you want to turn your work.

2. Slip the next stitch from the LH needle to the RH needle.

3. Bring the yarn between the needles to the back of your work.

4. **Return the slipped stitch to the LH needle.**

5. **Bring the yarn back between the needles, encircling the stitch.**

6. **Turn your work.**

   The yarn is in the back of your work, ready to knit back to the beginning of the row.

To work the next full row:

1. **Purl to the wrapped stitch.**

2. **Insert the tip of the RH needle from the back into the wrap and put it on the LH needle (see Figure 8-14).**

3. **Purl the wrap and the next stitch together.**

   The wrap will fall to the purl side of your work.

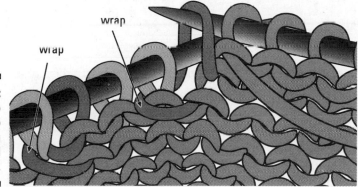

wrap

wrap

Figure 8-14:
Picking up
the wrap
and putting
it on the LH
needle.

Knitting Notebook

The stitch patterns in this section show you how you can use increases and decreases to create texture and interest in knitted fabric. Notice as you work these patterns that they always contain the same number of increases and decreases, which keeps the number of stitches in the piece consistent.

When you're working patterns with a lot of stitch manipulation, you'll have an easier time if you use a needle with a sharp tip and make an effort to keep a relaxed tension on your stitches. If you find yourself tensed up, take a moment to do some of the unkinking exercises described in Chapter 20.

Bobbles

You make bobbles (see Figure 8-15) by increasing several stitches in 1 stitch and then knitting back and forth on them before binding off, creating a knob on the surface of the fabric. The more stitches you increase in a single stitch and the more rows you work on them, the larger the bobble.

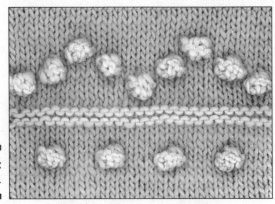

Figure 8-15:
Bobbles.

To practice making bobbles, cast on a multiple of 6 stitches, plus 5 more, and then do the following:

Rows 1 and 3 (RS): Knit.

Rows 2, 4, and 6: Purl.

Row 5: K5, * (knit into the front of the stitch, then the back, then the front, then the back, then the front one last time, and slide the old stitch off — 5 stitches in 1). Turn your work so that the wrong side is facing — the stitches will be on the LH needle. Knit the 5 stitches. Turn the work around again and knit the 5 stitches again. With the tip of the LH needle, pull the 2nd stitch over the first and off the RH needle. Repeat with the 3rd, 4th, and 5th stitches. (One bobble made!) K5; rep from *.

These instructions make a textured bobble — by knitting on the right side and wrong side of the bobble, you make a garter stitch bobble. For a smooth bobble, purl the 5 stitches when the wrong side of the bobble is facing.

If things start to feel tight as you work into the front and back of the stitch, insert just the *tip* of the LH needle into the stitch. After you wrap, however, be sure to bring your needle far enough out through the wrap that the new stitch forms on the thickest part of the needle.

Chevron

When you stack increases on top of increases and decreases on top of decreases, the stitches slant away from the column of increases and toward the column of decreases, creating chevron and wavy patterns (see Figure 8-16). The bottom edges of these patterns form points or scalloped borders, depending on whether the decreases and increases are worked in a single stitch or spread over several stitches. Although they look like they're tricky to make, they're relatively simple.

Figure 8-16: Chevron pattern.

Cast on a multiple of 12 sts, plus 6 (includes 1 extra st on each side for a selvage stitch).

Row 1 (rs): K1, k2tog, * k4, (k1, yo, k1) in next st (double decrease using yo), k4, sl next 2 sts together as if to knit, k1, psso (double decrease); rep from *, end ssk, k1.

Row 2: Purl.

Repeat Rows 1 and 2 for pattern.

See the Scalloped Scarf pattern in the "Practice Projects" section, later in this chapter, for a variation of the chevron pattern.

Wildflower knot

Some patterns make subtler use of increases and decreases, like the little wildflower knot pattern shown in Figure 8-17.

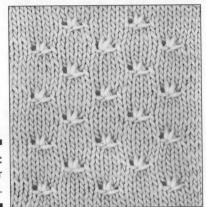

Figure 8-17:
Wildflower
knot pattern.

Cast on a multiple of 8 stitches, plus 5, and then do the following.

> Rows 1 and 3 (WS): Purl.
>
> Row 2: Knit.
>
> Row 4: K5, *p3tog, leave sts on LH needle; yo, purl same 3 sts together again, k5; rep from *.
>
> Rows 5 and 7: Purl.
>
> Row 6: Knit.
>
> Row 8: K1, *p3tog, leave on needle, yo, purl same 3 sts tog again, k5; rep from *, end last rep k1.
>
> Repeat Rows 1–8.

Practice Projects

You can use increases and decreases to create texture in stitch patterns, as in the fabrics in the "Knitting Notebook" section earlier in this chapter, and also to shape and sculpt knitted pieces. The Increase/Decrease Sampler shows how the decreases and increases given earlier can shape the edges of your knitted piece. To see how increases are used in sculpting 3-D fashion, check out the Easy Knit-from-the-Top-Down Hat in Chapter 17.

Increase/Decrease Sampler

The best way to see how these increases and decreases work in garment shaping is to try them out yourself. The sampler given here lets you practice the moves to see how they work and what they look like. Figure 8-18 shows this sampler, but if you want to see it in color, check out the color insert.

Figure 8-18:
Increase/
Decrease
Sampler.

When working a sampler, use medium-weight yarn in an easy-to-read color — white or something bright — and size 7 or 8 needles. Refer to the "Knitting Notebook" if you have any questions on how to work the specific increases and decreases.

To make the edges on your swatch (called selvages) attractive, slip the first stitch of every row knitwise (go into the first stitch as if to knit it and move it over the RH needle without working it) and knit the last stitch of every row.

Cast on 21 sts.

Work 4 rows of St st (knit one row, purl one row).

Next row (RS) *beg decs*: K4, k2tog, knit to last 6 sts, ssk, k4 — 19 sts.

Next row: Purl. Repeat these 2 rows 4 more times — 11 sts.

Work 6 rows in St st.

Next row (RS) *beg incs*: K3, knit into the front and back of next stitch (bar increase), knit to last 5 sts, work bar increase in next stitch.

Next row: Purl — 13 sts. Repeat these 2 rows 4 more times — 21 sts.

Note: In order to position the bar symmetrically, you work the increase asymmetrically in the 4th stitch on the right and the 5th stitch on the left.

Work 6 rows in St st.

Next row (RS) *beg decs*: K4, ssk, knit to last 6 sts, k2tog, k3 — 19 sts.

Next row: Purl. Repeat these 2 rows 4 times more — 11 sts.

Work 6 rows in St st.

Next row (RS) *beg incs*: K4, m1(right or left twist, you decide), knit to last 4 sts, m1(twist it in the opposite direction as your first m1), knit to end.

Next row: Purl — 13 sts.

Repeat these two rows 4 times — 21 sts.

Work 6 rows in St st.

Next row (RS) *beg decs*: K 9 sts (2 sts before center st), sl 2 tog as if to knit, k1, pass slipped stitches over stitch just knit, k to end.

Next row: Purl. Repeat last 2 rows, knitting 1 less stitch before dec on each RS row, until 11 sts remain.

Work 6 rows in St st.

In this next set of increases, when you see "m1," pick up the running thread with the LH needle by going under it from front to back. Then knit the strand without twisting it for a small decorative eyelet.

Next row (RS) increase row: K3, m1, k to last 3 sts, m1, k3 — 13 sts.

Next row: Purl. Repeat last 2 rows 4 times more — 21 sts.

Knit 4 rows in St st. Bind off.

Scalloped Scarf

This pattern uses stacked increases and decreases to create graceful scalloped edges. You create the wavy texture of this scarf by working increases and decreases in vertical columns. The stitches dip down at the decrease column and curve back up at the increases. To make the ends match, you work the scarf in two pieces from bottom up. You work the center portion of the scarf in a 2 x 2 rib that hugs your neck. See this scarf pictured in the color insert.

Dimensions: 54 inches by 8 inches

Materials: Three 50-gram (1 ¾ oz.) skeins (each approximately 123 yards) of Classic Elite Lush (50% angora/50% wool), or any yarn with a comparable gauge; one pair each of size 8 and 9 needles.

Gauge: Rather than try to match gauge, work up a swatch in stockinette stitch on size 9 needles. If you like the way it looks, start the pattern. If it feels tight and doesn't have enough drape, go up a needle size. If your swatch appears too loose, go down a needle size.

With the larger needles, cast on 41 stitches.

Rows 1 (RS): Knit.

Rows 2, 3, 4, 5, and 6: Knit.

Rows 7, 9, 11, and 13 (rest): K2, * knit in front and back of next st (bar inc), k3, ssk, k1, k2tog, k2, knit in front and back of next st (bar increase); rep from *, end k3.

Note: It may seem from the instructions that the pattern isn't symmetrical because there are 3 stitches on one side of the decrease and 2 on the other side. But because the increase creates a bar to the *left* of the increase stitch, the knitted fabric is the same on both sides of its center. You'll be able to see this after you've worked a few rows.

Rows 8, 10, and 12: Purl.

Repeat Rows 2–13 nine times. Then work Rows 2–6 once more. The piece should measure approximately 20 inches in length.

Change to the smaller needles and begin k2, p2 rib as follows. You'll be decreasing 1 stitch in the first row in order for the rib pattern to come out evenly.

Next row (RS): K3, p2tog, p1, *k2, p2; rep from *, end k3 — 40 sts.

Next row: P3, *k2, p2; rep from *, end k2, p3.

Continue in rib for 7 inches. Bind off or transfer the stitches to a holder, depending on whether you want to seam the pieces or graft the ends together. (See Chapter 15 for finishing tips.)

Work the second scarf piece as above. Block the pieces gently and seam or graft the center back ends of the scarf together.

Variations:

- Turn the scarf into a shawl by making it wider (cast on another 12 stitches, or a multiple of 12 plus 5).

- Use decorative yarn-over increases instead of bar increases. To do this, work Rows 7, 9, 11, and 13 as follows: K3, *yo, k3, ssk, k1, k2tog, yo, k1; rep from *, end yo, k3.

✔ Work the pattern in colored stripes (see Chapter 11) or in a light-weight mohair yarn on large needles.

✔ Use the chevron pattern and make the scarf pointy instead of scalloped. Cast on a multiple of the chevron pattern plus 4 extra stitches to work a 2-stitch garter edge.

Chapter 9

Cable Musings: Knitting Over and Under

Cables, like knit and purl patterns, offer an endless source of design possibilities. If you're familiar with the cream-color cabled sweaters of the Aran Isles, with their intertwining cable motifs in vertical panels arranged symmetrically across a sweater front, then you're already aware of the wealth of traditional cable designs.

The simple technique of cabling — crossing one group of stitches over another — lends itself to many interpretations. Once you've mastered the basic technique, and it's very easy to do, you can make all kinds of interesting and imaginative cable patterns. All it takes is a little patience and practice.

The simplest cables form a vertical rope of stockinette stitches on a contrasting background, usually reverse stockinette (the back, or purl, side of stockinette fabric). The following are a few other possibilities:

- ✔ Put a right-crossing cable next to a left-crossing cable and you have a double cable that looks like a horseshoe.

- ✔ Cross stockinette cable strands over the background fabric and you can open and close a cable.

- ✔ Use three cable strands and you have a braided cable.

- ✔ Arrange the crossings to repeat horizontally as well as vertically and you have an allover cabled fabric.

And that's just the beginning. This chapter presents cable basics that beginners can follow, as well as some more intricate cables for when you want to stretch your cabling skills.

Understanding Cables

You can make any kind of cable by suspending (holding) a number of stitches on a cable needle (cn) while you knit that same number of stitches from the LH needle. Then you knit the suspended stitches either by returning them to the LH needle and knitting them or by knitting them straight from the cable needle. (See Chapter 4 for more on cable needles.) This process of knitting stitches out of order enables you to cross stitches, creating cables. Whether you're making simple or intricate cables, all you're doing is crossing stitches. Easy, right? Right!

Standard or rope cables are the most basic cables. They generally cross stitches predictably up a single column of stitches. You can make a rope cable over almost any even number of stitches from two to twelve — or more.

- ✔ If you want to make a cable that looks like it's twisting to the *left*, you hold your suspended stitches in *front* of your work while you knit from the LH needle.

- ✔ If you want to make a cable that twists to the *right*, hold the suspended stitches in *back*.

Instructions for a 6-stitch left-twisting cable usually read something like this: Sl 3 sts to cn, hold in *front*, k3, k3 from cn. Instructions for that same cable, but twisting to the right, read like this: Sl 3 sts to cn, hold in *back*, k3, k3 from cn.

You may also see abbreviations like C3F and C3B. The *C* before the number tells you that these stitches are cable stitches. The number tells you how many stitches are involved with this particular maneuver. The *F* or *B* indicates whether you should suspend the stitches to the front or the back of your work.

Knitting a standard cable

When you knit cables, you don't have to cross stitches on every row. (Thank goodness!) The row on which the stitches are crossed over each other is called the *turning row*. After the turning row, you work several plain rows, and then you work another turning row. Standard cables have the same number of plain rows between turning rows as there are stitches in the cable. If the cable is 6 stitches wide, for example, you work the turning row every 6 rows.

Finding the right kind of needle

Various styles of cable needles (abbreviated as cn) are available. I prefer to work with a needle shaped like a U with a short leg, which seems to stay out of my way better than the other kinds, and the stitches on hold don't slide off. The other versions have different advantages. The straight needle type makes it easier to knit cable stitches being held directly from the cable needle, but I sometimes lose stitches with this version and never have been able to figure out what to do with my LH needle while I knit stitches from the cable needle. Try the different types as you practice cables to see which type best suits your knitting style.

To try a 6-stitch left-twisting cable, cast on 14 stitches and then follow these steps:

1. **Work Row 1 (RS): P4, k6, p4.**

   The first and last k4 (knit four) stitches make up the background fabric for your cable. The six stitches in the middle are where you'll form your cable stitches.

2. **Work Row 2: K4, p6, k4.**

3. **Work Row 3: P4, k6, p4. (same as row 1).**

4. **Work Row 4: k4, p6, k4 (same as row 2).**

5. **Work Row 5, the turning row: P4, sl 3 sts to cn and hold in front (see Figure 9-1a), k3 from LH needle (see Figure 9-1b), k3 from cn (see Figure 9-1c), p4.**

6. **Work Row 6: K4, p6, k4 (same as Row 2).**

   Instead of knitting stitches directly from the cable needle, you may prefer to return the suspended stitches to the LH needle before you knit them. Try both ways and use whichever technique is more comfortable to you.

   When you suspend stitches on the cable needle, let the cable needle dangle down in front of your work, giving the yarn a slight tug to keep it taut (you don't need to close the gap).

7. **Repeat Steps 1 through 6 and watch your stockinette stitches become a cabled rope.**

When you work cables, you go back and forth from purl stitches to knit stitches. From a knit to a purl stitch, bring your yarn between the needles to the front before you make the next stitch. From a purl to a knit stitch, bring your yarn between the needles to the back before you make the next stitch.

  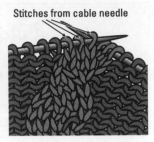

Stitches from cable needle

Figure 9-1:
Working the
turning row.

a. Slip the cable stitches to
the cable needle and hold
in front.

b. Knit 3 from the LH needle.

c. Knit the stitches from the
cable needle.

Checking gauge in a cable pattern

The combination of knit panels with purl panels (think ribs) and crossing
stitches over stitches causes cable patterns to pull in widththwise. A sweater
worked in a cable pattern will be significantly narrower than one worked in
the same number of stitches in stockinette stitch. You'll need more yarn and
more stitches for a cable sweater than for one of the same dimensions in a
knit/purl pattern.

If you decide to add a cable (or several) to a plain sweater, be sure to
increase enough stitches after you knit your border to maintain the overall
width. Although there are no hard and fast rules, you'll be safe if you add 1 to
2 for every 4 stitches in your cable. If you have a ribbed border, you can add
the stitches evenly on the last ribbed row. See Chapter 8 for more on making
increases.

If you're making a project in a repeating cable pattern, be sure to work a large
enough swatch to be able to measure gauge accurately. The swatch should
include at least two repeats of the cable pattern horizontally and vertically. If
you're working several different cables, you have to check your gauge over
each one.

Feel like you're wasting time making swatches to check gauge? Make two
gauge swatches and sew them together for a cabled pillow or bag.

Starting and stopping

Cables should begin and end on a row between turnings where the cable
stitches are relaxed and the fabric is smooth. Because the cable stitches
spread out a bit between turning rows, for the smoothest transition between
the beginnings and endings of cables, plan to increase a stitch or two over
the cable stitches when beginning a cable and decrease a stitch or two when
binding off over a cable.

Counting cable rows

Learn how to count the rows between cable crossings and you won't have to rely on your memory. (It's always good to have an alternative to memory.) Look carefully at the turning row. If the cable crosses to the right, you will see a small hole created by the pull of the stitches just to the left of the cable crossing. You may have to stretch the knitting vertically a bit to see it. If the cable crosses to the left, the hole will be on the right. Just below the hole is a horizontal running thread stretching between the last crossed stitch and the background. Check out the following figure to see what to look for.

Starting with the running thread *above* the hole, count up running threads to determine the number of rows worked since the last turning row. Alternatively, you can follow the thread to the stitch it connects to — the knit stitch in the cable or the purled stitch in the background. Starting with the stitch *above* the connected stitch, count up to and include the stitch on the needle for the number of rows worked. If you're working a 6-stitch cable and you count 6 running threads or stitches, you're ready for a turning row.

Small hole

To start a cable pattern

If you're adding a cable(s) to an uncabled sweater pattern, for every 4 stitches in the planned cable(s), add 1 or 2 stitches to the number of stitches to cast on. Then work a few rows in the knit/purl pattern you've established for your cables before working a turning row.

To end a cable pattern

When you're binding off cables, decrease across the top of the cable 1 or 2 stitches for every 4 stitches in the cable to prevent the bound-off edge from flaring out. Follow these steps for a neat finish:

1. **Bind off the background stitches as they present themselves (knit the knits and purl the purls as you bind off) until you reach the cabled stitches.**

   If you need a refresher on how to bind off stitches, flip back to Chapter 1.

2. **When you get to the cable stitches, bind off as follows: *k1, bind off, k2tog, bind off, k1, bind off; rep from * to the end of the cable (stockinette) stitches.**

3. **After binding off the cable stitches, go back to binding off the stitches of the background as they present themselves.**

Reading Cable Charts

Most knitting patterns give cable instructions in chart form that show the cable stitches, turning rows, and often some background stitches. Depending on how complicated the cable pattern is, the chart may show you one repeat of the cable or an entire piece.

Although chart symbols aren't standardized, every pattern has a key to the symbols used. Figure 9-2 shows a chart for a 6-stitch left-twisting cable.

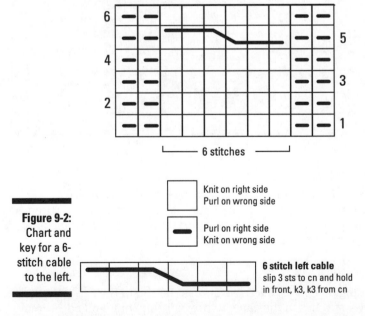

Figure 9-2: Chart and key for a 6-stitch cable to the left.

The chart represents the front side of your knitting. Each square in the chart represents a stitch. A horizontal line in the square indicates a purl stitch. The cable stitches (knit stitches) are pictured as plain (empty) squares. The cable symbols on the turning row indicate (via the key) which way to cross the cable — whether to hold the stitches on the cable needle in the front or the back.

When following cable charts, you may find it helpful to color in the turning rows. Use a magnetic board and strip to mark your place on the chart to help you stay on track. Sticky notepaper works well, too. If you're knitting a pattern that has several panels of different cables, use stitch markers on the needle to help delineate the separate panels.

Remember to pay attention to your knitted piece as well as your chart or instructions. Check to see whether you are cabling in the right direction and have worked the correct number of rows. If you learn to read what's happening in your work, you'll hardly need the chart or the markers after you've knitted a couple of repeats of the entire pattern. Trust me.

Trying an Open Cable

Not all cables are worked on the same stitches over and over. Using basic cabling techniques, you can cross stitches over the background as well to make open cables (sometimes called *traveling cables*). Picture the strands of a basic rope cable separating and moving away from each other and then returning and twisting around each other again, as in Figure 9-3.

Figure 9-3: Cable strands moving over the background.

To work a traveling cable pattern, you simply cross stitches as in a basic cable, but instead of crossing stockinette stitches over stockinette stitches, you cross stockinette stitches over one or more background (usually purl) stitches. You can open a cable and have the strands move away from each other by using the same crossing technique that you used for the 6-stitch rope cable earlier in this chapter.

Moving cable strands to the right

To turn a basic 6-stitch cable into an open cable, do the following:

1. **Work to 1 stitch before the cable stitches (this brings you to the last background stitch before the cable stitches begin); slip the background stitch to the cn (as in Figure 9-4) and take it to the back.**

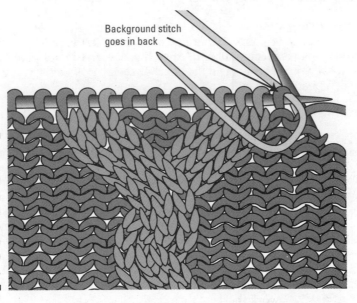

Background stitch goes in back

Figure 9-4: Slipping a background stitch to the cable needle to move the cable to the right.

2. **Knit 3 cable stitches from the LH needle.**

3. **Slip the background stitch back to the LH needle.**

4. **Purl the background stitch.**

Moving cable strands to the left

When you get to the next 3 cable stitches, follow these steps to move the second strand to the left:

1. **Slip 3 cable stitches to the cn and bring them to the front, as in Figure 9-5.**

2. **Purl the next (background) stitch.**

3. **Slip the 3 cable stitches to the LH needle.**

4. **Knit the 3 cable stitches.**

5. **Purl to the end of the row.**

You've moved the cable strands apart 1 stitch on either side; you have 2 background stitches between them. To continue opening the cable strands, work the preceding steps, moving the cable stitches 1 stitch to the right or left on every right-side row. When you're ready to bring the cable strands back in, reverse the procedure by working first to the left and then to the right.

Strand stitches on cable needle stay in front

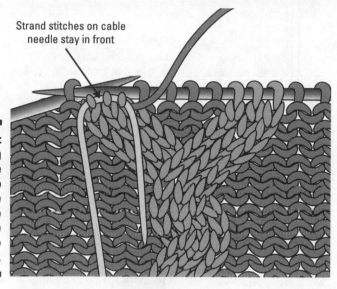

Figure 9-5: Slipping cable stitches to the cable needle to move the cable to the left.

Generally, when you're moving a cable strand across the background to open up your cable, you work the crossing on every right-side row. If you move the cable strands over 2 background stitches at a time, the strand will travel outward at a wider angle. You can practice open cables by knitting the cable sampler presented in the project section later in this chapter.

Varying a Cable

Even the simplest cable lends itself to variation. Here are some ideas to try when you're in an experimental mood (keep some graph paper nearby):

- ✔ Change the width of the cable strands.
- ✔ Play around with the number of rows between turning rows. (See the Eccentric Cable Scarf in the projects section later in this chapter.)
- ✔ Change the background stitch. Instead of stockinette stitch, work the cable on garter stitch, seed stitch, moss stitch, or whatever.
- ✔ Work one cable strand in a different color (see Chapter 9 on intarsia knitting).

KNITTING TIP

The stubborn stitch

Often, the left end knit stitch on a rib or in a cable is noticeably larger than the other knit stitches. When you move from a knit to a purl stitch, the yarn travels a tiny bit farther than it does between two knit or two purl stitches, resulting in this looser stitch. You can remedy this problem by working the first *2* purl stitches after the cable tighter than you normally would. After you knit the last stitch, insert your needle into the neighboring purl stitch, and then give a good tug on the yarn before wrapping and making the stitch. Do so again for the next stitch. This technique helps tighten up the last cable stitch. *Don't* let it tighten up the rest of your stitches.

If you find that you still have a sloppy knit stitch on the left edge of your cable, try this trick: On the right side, work the last knit stitch of the cable. Bring the yarn to the front, slip the next (purl) stitch, and continue on. When you come to the slipped stitch on the next wrong-side row, go into it as if to knit and, at the same time, go under the unworked strand on the right side. With the tip of the LH needle, bring the slipped stitch over the strand, transfer the newly formed stitch to the LH needle in the ready-to-work position, and knit it.

- ✏ Work one cable strand in a different pattern stitch.
- ✏ Work a mini cable in one of the strands.
- ✏ If you work an open cable with strands that travel out and in, consider the opening as a little frame and put something in it — a different pattern stitch, a bobble (see Chapter 8), or some embroidery, for example.

Knitting Notebook

The following patterns are designed to give you an idea of the many ways this simple technique can be used to create a rich variety of cable patterns. Practice them to improve your cabling technique. Each cable panel includes 3 set-up stitches on both sides of the cable. These set-up stitches make a crisp transition between the background fabric and the cable itself.

Double cable

Also known as a horseshoe cable, a double cable (see Figure 9-6) consists of a panel of 16 stitches (the cable is 12 stitches wide, with 3 set-up stitches on either side of it). The double cable pattern is as follows:

Cast on 18 sts.

Rows 1 and 3 (RS): P3, k12, p3.

Rows 2, 4, and 6: K3, p12, k3.

Row 5: P3, sl next 3 sts to cn, hold in back, k3, k3 from cn, sl next 3 sts to cn, hold in front, k3, k3 from cn, p3.

Repeat Rows 1–6.

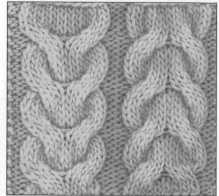

Figure 9-6:
Double
cable.

Did you notice that this is nothing more than a right cable next to a left cable? You can turn the cable upside down by working a left cable first and then a right one.

Wave cable

A wave cable (see Figure 9-7) consists of a panel of 10 stitches (the cable itself is 6 stitches wide). This cable gets its appearance from crossing inconsistently, to the right on one turning row and to the left on the next turning row. Work the wave cable as follows:

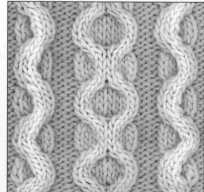

Figure 9-7:
Wave cable
(outside
patterns)
and chain
cable
(center
panel).

Cast on 12 stitches.

Rows 1, 3, 7, and 9 (RS): P3, k6, p3.

Rows 2, 4, 6, 8, 10, and 12: K3, p6, k3.

Row 5: P3, sl next 3 sts to cn, hold in back, k3, k3 from cn, p3.

Row 11: P3, sl next 3 to cn, hold in front, k3, k3 from cn, p3.

Repeat Rows 1–12.

Chain cable

A chain panel (shown in Figure 9-8) consists of 14 stitches; the cable itself is 8 stitches wide. Work this cable as follows:

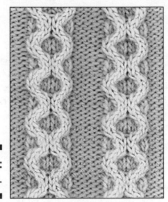

Figure 9-8:
Chain cable.

Cast on 14 stitches.

Rows 1 and 5 (RS): P3, k8, p3.

Rows 2, 4, 6, and 8: K3, p8, k3.

Row 3: P3, sl 2 sts to cn and hold in back, k2, k2 from cn, sl next 2 sts to cn and hold in front, k2, k2 from cn, p3.

Row 7: P3, sl next 2 sts to cn and hold in front, k2, k2 from cn, sl next 2 sts to cn and hold in back, k2, k2 from cn, p3.

Repeat these 8 rows.

Did you notice that a chain cable is two wave cables waving in opposite directions and lined up side by side?

Honeycomb cable

A honeycomb cable (see Figure 9-9) is made of a multiple of 8 stitches. Because this cable pattern is an allover pattern (it makes up the whole knitted fabric), it's set up as a multiple of stitches rather than as a panel. Knit this pattern as follows:

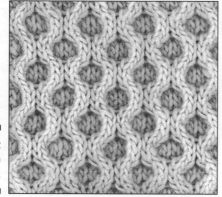

Figure 9-9: Honeycomb cable.

Cast on a multiple of 8 stitches.

Rows 1 and 5 (RS): Knit.

Row 2 and all wrong-side rows: Purl.

Row 3: * Sl 2 sts to cn and hold in back, k2, k2 from cn, sl 2 to cn and hold in front, k2, k2 from cn; rep from * to end.

Row 7: * Sl 2 sts to cn and hold in front, k2, k2 from cn, sl 2 sts to cn and hold in back, k2, k2 from cn; rep from * to end.

Repeat Rows 1–8.

Braid cable

A braid cable (shown in Figure 9-10) consists of a panel of 15 stitches; the cable itself is 9 stitches wide. Knit this pattern as follows:

Cast on 15 stitches.

Rows 1 and 5 (RS): P3, k9, p3.

Rows 2, 4, 6, and 8: K3, p9, k3.

Row 3: P3, sl next 3 sts to cn and hold in front, k3, k3 from cn, k3, p3.

Row 7: P3, k3, sl next 3 sts to cn and hold in back, k3, k3 from cn, p3.

Repeat Rows 1–8.

Figure 9-10:
Braid cable.

You can make a more petite version of this braid cable simply by reducing the number of cable stitches (the stitches between the set-up stitches on the edge) to 6. Cross 2 stitches over 2 for this version.

Open cable

The open cable pattern consists of a panel of 11 stitches. An open cable (see Figure 9-11) has the cable strands separate and move apart and then come back together to cross each other again. Where they cross is simply a 4-stitch cable turning row.

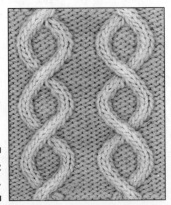

Figure 9-11:
Open cable.

To knit an open cable and make the strands travel across the background, you need two new techniques:

- ✔ **Back cross:** Sl next p stitch to cn and hold in back, k2, p the stitch from the cn.
- ✔ **Front cross:** Sl the next 2 sts to cn and hold in front, p1, k2 from cn.

Knit the open cable pattern as follows:

Rows 1 and 3 (WS): K3, p2, k1, p2, k3.

Row 2: P3, sl next 3 sts to cn (1 p st and 2 k sts) and hold in back, k2, sl the next p st back to LH needle and p it, k2 from cn, p3.

Row 4: P2, back cross, p1, front cross, p2.

Row 5: K2, p2, k3, p2, k2.

Row 6: P1, back cross, p3, front cross, p1.

Rows 7 and 9: K1, p2, k5, p2, k1.

Row 8: P1, k2, p5, k2, p1.

Row 10: P1, front cross, p3, back cross, p1.

Row 11: K2, p2, k3, p2, k2.

Row 12: P2, front cross, p1, back cross, p2.

Repeat Rows 1–12.

Practice Cable Projects

Cables lend themselves to almost anything you can knit: hats, pillows, scarves, sweaters. Even the most basic cables look intriguing, whether alone or in combination. Follow the patterns for the projects in this section as they are, or use them as guidelines and plug in different cables or substitute a column of bobbles (see Chapter 8) for one of the cables. The basic instructions for making the scarf and the pieces for the hat are written out, but instructions for making the cables are given in chart form.

Making a cable sampler

Making a cable sampler (see Figure 9-12) offers a great opportunity to practice working with cables and to see how easy it is to vary this basic technique for different effects. The more you practice, the more comfortable you'll become with the basic cable moves.

Use a medium-weight wool yarn and size 8 or 9 needles. You can work cables on a larger needle than you would normally use, but don't try working them on a smaller size unless you're making a suit of armor — the fabric will be so dense it will stand up on its own. This cable sampler includes the following cable patterns:

- ✔ A simple rope cable
- ✔ A wave cable
- ✔ An open cable
- ✔ A varied cable

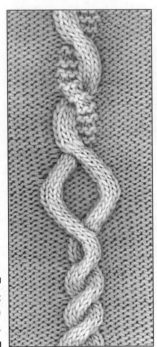

Figure 9-12:
Cable
sampler.

Figure 9-13 includes all the charts you need to make your sampler. You can see a completed sampler in the color insert.

Remember that charts for stitch patterns show the *right* side of the fabric. When you're working a right-side row, you work the symbol given in the square that represents the stitch you're making. When you're working a wrong-side row, you must work each stitch shown on the chart as it will appear on the right side of the fabric. If the chart shows a knit stitch, you must purl the stitch so it shows on the right side as a knit stitch. Use the key to interpret the symbols.

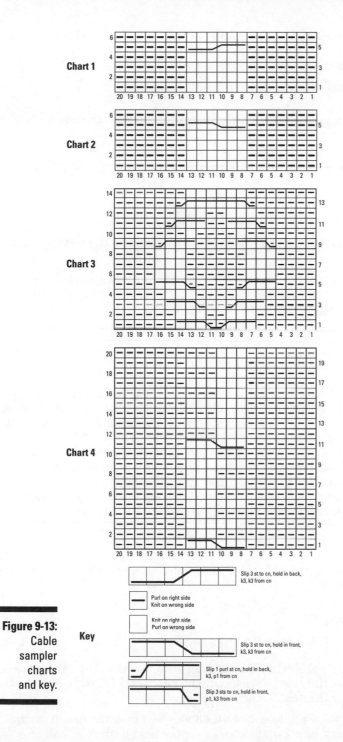

Figure 9-13:
Cable sampler charts and key.

Key

Slip 3 st to cn, hold in back, k3, k3 from cn

Purl on right side
Knit on wrong side

Knit on right side
Purl on wrong side

Slip 3 st to cn, hold in front, k3, k3 from cn

Slip 1 purl st cn, hold in back, k3, p1 from cn

Slip 3 sts to cn, hold in front, p1, k3 from cn

To make a cable sampler, follow these steps:

1. **Cast on 20 stitches.**

2. **Work 3 repeats of a rope cable (Chart 1) as follows:**

   1. Beginning at the bottom-right corner, work Row 1 of the chart from right to left.

   2. Work the next (wrong-side) row reading the chart from left to right.

   3. Continue to work the chart through Row 6 for three repetitions.

3. **Make a wave cable by working Chart 2 once.**

4. **Make an open cable by working 14 rows of Chart 3.**

5. **Finish your sampler with a varied cable by working 20 rows of Chart 4 twice.**

   In this final cable variation, you work one of the cable strands in garter stitch instead of the usual stockinette. The crossings are separated by 10 rows to show off the different pattern stitch.

Eccentric Cable Scarf

This scarf shows off three eccentric cables — eccentric because the turning row alternates between 6 and 10 rows. The middle cable is turned on different rows than the ones on either side of it. Staggering the turning rows allows the cables to fit into each other — when the outside cables are expanding, the center cable is contracting and vice versa. If you want to make the project easier, work the turning rows on all three cables at the same time. The background for the cables is garter stitch — a good stitch to use for a scarf because it's reversible and lies flat. Figure 9-14 shows the chart you need to make this scarf. You can see the scarf pictured in the color insert.

Dimensions: 8 inches x 48 inches

Materials: 3 skeins 50 gram (1 ¾ oz.) Classic Elite Lush, one pair of size 9 needles, one cable needle

Knitting your scarf

Cast on 42 stitches and then follow these steps:

1. **Work Row 1 (right side): K6, beginning with Row 1 of the cable chart, work Row 1 of the chart over the next 6 stitches, k18, work Row 1 of the chart over the next 6 stitches, k6.**

2. **Work Row 2: K6, work Row 2 of the cable chart over the next 6 stitches, k6, p6, k6, work Row 2 of the chart over the next 6 stitches, knit 6.**

3. **Work Row 3: K6, work Row 3 of the cable chart over the next 6 stitches, k6, begin the center cable by working Row 13 of the cable chart over the next 6 stitches, k6, work Row 3 of the chart over the next 6 stitches, k6.**

4. **Work Row 4: K6, work Row 4 of the chart over next 6 stitches, k6, work Row 14 of the chart over next 6 stitches, k6, work Row 4 of the chart over next 6 stitches, k6.**

5. **Work Row 5 (cables): Knit 6, work Row 5 of the chart (follow instructions for 6-st right cable as shown on chart), k6, work Row 15 of the chart over the next 6 stitches, k6, work Row 5 of the chart over the next 6 stitches, knit 6.**

6. **Continue to work the scarf, repeating the 20-row cable chart as established for the outside and center cables until the piece measures approximately 48 inches in length. Continue to work until you're reading to work Row 1 on the side cables. Bind off instead of working Row 1.**

7. **Bind off and block slightly.**

   See Chapter 15 for tips on blocking like a pro.

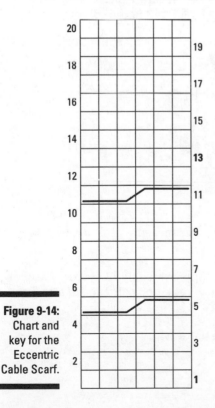

Figure 9-14:
Chart and
key for the
Eccentric
Cable Scarf.

Key

⬜ Knit on right side
Purl on wrong side

6-stitch right cable
Slip 3 stitches to cn, hold in back,
k3, k3 from cn

Varying your scarf

You can change the appearance of your Eccentric Cable Scarf by incorporating any of the following variations:

- ✔ Work the stitches between the cables in another stitch. Seed or moss stitch is attractive and, like garter stitch, is reversible.

- ✔ Work standard cables by turning every 6 rows.

- ✔ Work 8-stitch or 4-stitch cables instead of 6-stitch cables, casting on the appropriate number of stitches accordingly.

- ✔ Work two eccentric cables side to side and crossing in opposite directions in the middle of your scarf. Cast on 6 additional stitches for this version.

Cable Hat with Pompoms

This Cable Hat with Pompoms (see Figure 9-15) is a straightforward hat that uses only one kind of cable: a 6-stitch cable twisting to the right. It begins with a simple knitted rectangle just like the Three-Way Hat presented in Chapter 6. In this version, you make the front and back as separate pieces and seam them along the top and sides. You can see it pictured in the color insert.

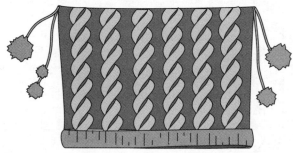

Figure 9-15:
Cable
Hat with
Pompoms.

Dimensions: 21 inches in diameter (each piece measures 10½ inches wide) and 8 inches high

Materials: Two 3.5-ounce/100-gram skein (approximately 132 yards) Cascade Pastaza (50% lama, 50% wool) or equivalent yarn, one pair each of size 7 and 9 needles, a pompom maker.

Gauge: 22 stitches to 4 inches over cable pattern

Knitting the hat pieces

Follow these steps to create the pieces of your hat:

1. **With the smaller needle (the size 7), cast on 50 stitches.**

2. **Work Row 1 (RS): *K1, p1; rep from * to end.**

3. **Work Row 2: *K1, p1; rep from * to end.**

4. **Repeat Rows 1 and 2 once.**

5. **Changing to larger needle (the size 9), work the next row (RS): P2, inc 1, *k2, inc 1, k3, p3; rep from * to end — 57 sts.**

   Cable patterns shrink in width, so to compensate when you move from the rib to the cable pattern, you need to add 1 stitch per cable plus 1 more for symmetry to begin and end on 3 knit stitches.

6. **Work the next row: *K3, p6; rep from *, end k3 (this means knit the last 3 stitches).**

7. **On the next row (RS), begin the cable chart (see Figure 9-16): *P3, work Row 1 of 6-st cable chart; rep from *, end p3.**

Figure 9-16: 6-stitch cable chart with key.

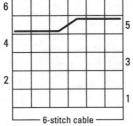

6-stitch cable

Key

☐ Knit on right side
Purl on wrong side

▭ Purl on right side
Knit on wrong side

6-stitch right cable
Slip 3 stitches to cn, hold in back, knit 3, knit 3 from cn

8. **Work the next row: *K3, work Row 2 of cable chart; rep from *, end k3.**

9. **Continue working as established.**

   Begin and end each right-side row with k3, and begin and end each wrong-side row with p3. When you've worked 6 rows of the cable chart, start from Row 1 again.

10. **Work the cable pattern until the piece measures approximately 8 inches in length, ending with Row 4 (WS) of the pattern.**

    When working with cables, try to begin and end on a flat part of the cable, between turning rows.

11. **Work the next row (RS): *P3, k2, k2tog, k2; rep from *, end p3 — 51 stitches.**

    Decreasing 1 stitch in each cable on the final row brings the fabric back to normal width.

12. **Bind off.**

    Or, if you want to seam your pieces together using the three-needle bind-off, run a piece of scrap yarn through the stitches to secure them. (See Chapter 15 for instructions.)

13. **Make a second piece by following Steps 1 through 12.**

Finishing your hat

After you've knitted the pieces of your hat, follow these steps to finish it like a professional:

1. **Gently block the squares.**

   Cables are best blocked by using the wet-blocking method, which allows you to shape and mold the cable pattern.

2. **Seam the top of the hat.**

   Use backstitch or the three-needle bind-off shown in Chapter 15, and then steam the seam.

3. **Sew up the side seams using mattress stitch and steam the seam.**

4. **Add the pompoms.**

   Following the instructions given with your pompom maker, make pompoms. You can make as many or as few as you like, in the same or different sizes. Leave enough of a tail on the pompoms to braid or twist into a cord. Using a tapestry needle, thread the cords to the inside of the hat and secure them in a seam.

Varying your hat

Try any of the following suggestions to create different kinds of fun hats:

- Substitute a column of bobbles for one of the cables. (See Chapter 8 for bobble-making instructions.)

- Use a different kind of 6-stitch cable — for example, the cable from the Eccentric Cable Scarf project or the wave cable from the Cable Sampler, both presented earlier in this section.

- Make the hat longer.

- Use any combination of cable patterns that appeals to you.k

Chapter 10

Let the Sun Shine In: Knitting Lace

*E*ven beginning knitters can make lace. If you can knit and purl, knit 2 stitches together (which I sometimes do inadvertently!), and work a yarn over (explained in Chapter 7), you can make lace. The hardest thing is to keep track of where you are in the pattern (which isn't really a knitting skill . . .).

Knitted lace is versatile. It can be the fabric of an entire garment, the edging on a sleeve, a panel down the front of a sweater, or a single motif in a yoke, to name a few ideas. In a fine yarn on a small needle, it can be intricate and delicate. Worked randomly in a heavy, rustic yarn, it can be minimalist and modern. It can be a small eyelet motif sparsely arranged over an otherwise solid fabric, or it can be light, airy, and full of holes.

Knitted lace makes use of two simple knitting moves — a yarn over (an increase that makes a small hole) and a decrease — to create myriad stitch patterns. Every opening in a lace fabric is made from a yarn-over increase. Every yarn over is paired with a decrease to compensate for the increase. Once you understand the basis of lace's increase/decrease structure, even the most complicated lace patterns become intelligible. Of course, you can follow the instructions for a lace stitch without understanding the underlying structure, but being able to recognize how the pattern manipulates the basic yarn-over/decrease unit is a great confidence builder.

To familiarize yourself with knitted lace, sample the patterns in this chapter and try the Lace Sampler in Appendix B. Look closely at your work. Once you can identify a yarn over (see Chapter 7) on your needle and see the difference between an ssk and a k2tog decrease in your knitting (both explained in detail in Chapter 8), you're on your way to becoming a lace expert.

Recognizing Different Kinds of Lace

Knitted lace is varied enough that different categories have been created to describe (loosely) the different types, such as

- ✔ Eyelet
- ✔ Open lace
- ✔ Faggot lace

The divisions between one kind of lace and another are porous. Better to think of lace patterns as belonging on a continuum — the more solid fabrics with scattered openings (eyelet) at one end, the lacy and open fabrics (allover and faggot patterns) at the other.

Before reading on, you may want to take the time to review how to make a yarn over in Chapter 7 and how to decrease in Chapter 8.

Eyelet patterns

Eyelet patterns generally have fewer openings than out-and-out lace patterns and are characterized by small openwork motifs distributed over a solid stockinette (or other closed stitch pattern) fabric. Figure 10-1 shows a three-eyelet cloverleaf arranged over a stockinette background.

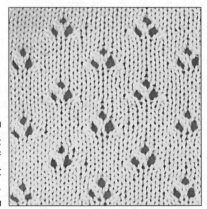

Figure 10-1: Cloverleaf eyelet pattern.

Take a minute to study the detail of the cloverleaf pattern in Figure 10-2. The eyelets are made with yarn over increases. If you look closely, you can see their compensating decreases worked right next to them. The decreases look like slanted stitches and come before and after the two eyelets on the bottom of the cloverleaf and after the eyelet on the top.

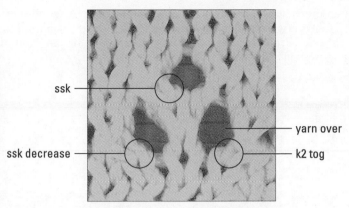

Figure 10-2:
Detail of the cloverleaf eyelet pattern showing yarn overs and corresponding decreases.

ssk

ssk decrease

yarn over

k2 tog

A k2tog (knit 2 stitches together) decrease slants to the right. An ssk (slip slip knit) decrease slants to the left.

Open lace patterns

Out-and-out lace patterns have more openings than solid spaces in their composition. They're frequently used in shawls or any project that cries for a more traditional lace look. Figure 10-3 shows a simple miniature leaf pattern where each little "leaf" is surrounded by lace openings.

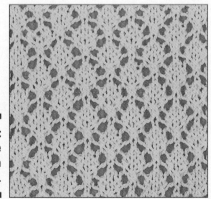

Figure 10-3:
Miniature leaf open lace pattern.

Faggot lace patterns

Faggot patterns (basic lace) are really a category unto themselves. They're composed of nothing but the simplest lace-making unit: a yarn over followed (or preceded) by a decrease. A faggot unit can be worked over and over for a very open mesh-like fabric. Or a faggot grouping can be worked as a vertical panel in an otherwise solid fabric, as shown in Figure 10-4a (and in the scarf in the "Practice Projects" section), or as a vertical panel alternating with other lace or cabled panels, as shown in Figure 10-4b.

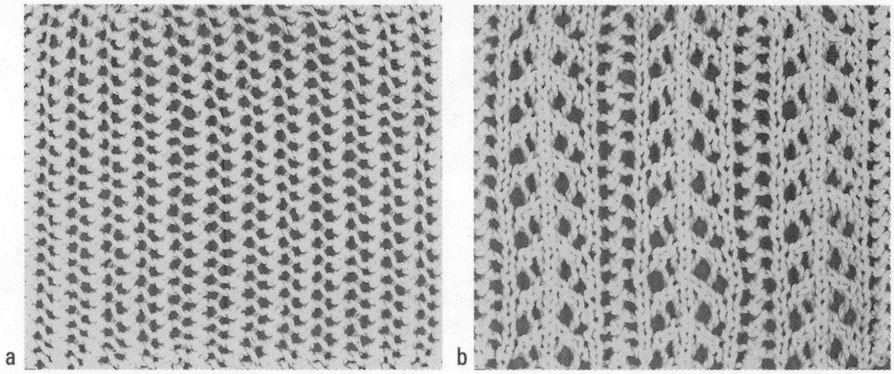

Figure 10-4:
Faggot lace
by itself and
combined
with another
lace pattern.

You can work faggot patterns with a knitted decrease (ssk or k2tog) or a purled decrease. The appearance of faggot lace changes very subtly depending on which decrease you use.

Reading Lace Charts

Like other charts for knitted stitch patterns, charts for knitted lace "picture" the patterns they represent. As you might expect, the two symbols you find most often in lace charts are the one for a yarn-over increase (usually presented as an O) and some kind of slanted line to mimic the direction of a decrease.

Compare the chart for the cloverleaf pattern in Figure 10-5 to the knitted version in Figure 10-2 earlier in this chapter.

The decrease symbol is shown in only one square, even though a decrease involves 2 stitches. Charting the decrease this way allows the yarn-over symbol to occupy the square for the decreased stitch. Sometimes the yarn over shows up adjacent to the decrease as it does in this pattern. Other times, in different patterns, the yarn over isn't placed directly before or after the decrease, but somewhere else entirely in the pattern row. In either case, in most patterns the number of decrease symbols is the same as the number of yarn-over symbols. For every increase there is a decrease.

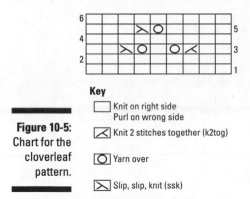

Figure 10-5:
Chart for the cloverleaf pattern.

Key

☐ Knit on right side
Purl on wrong side

▱ Knit 2 stitches together (k2tog)

Ⓞ Yarn over

▰ Slip, slip, knit (ssk)

Keeping up with a changing number of stitches

A lace chart sometimes has to show a changing number of stitches from one row to the next. To keep the stitches lined up on the chart the way they are in the fabric, the chart indicates that a stitch has been eliminated temporarily from the pattern by using the "no stitch" symbol in the square that represents the decreased stitch. The "no stitch" symbol repeats in a vertical row until an increase is made and the stitch is back in play.

The chart in Figure 10-6 shows a pattern in which one stitch is decreased and left out for 10 rows and then created again and left in for the next 10 rows. The take-out/put-back-in pattern repeats every 20 rows. The black squares in the chart hold the place of the disappearing and reappearing stitch. Using the "no stitch" symbol allows the grid to remain uniformly square. Otherwise the edges of the grid would have to go in and out to match the number of stitches in each row.

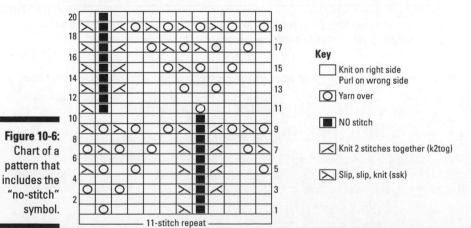

Figure 10-6:
Chart of a pattern that includes the "no-stitch" symbol.

Key

☐ Knit on right side
Purl on wrong side

Ⓞ Yarn over

■ NO stitch

▱ Knit 2 stitches together (k2tog)

▰ Slip, slip, knit (ssk)

11-stitch repeat

Working patterns with the "no stitch" symbol

When you're working from a chart that uses the "no stitch" symbol, skip the symbol when you get to it and work the next stitch on your needle from the chart square just after the "no stitch" symbol.

Choosing Lace Patterns

In general, the simplest lace patterns call for yarn-over/decrease maneuvers on right-side rows only. Others have you make openings on every row. For your first forays into lace knitting, choose patterns that tell you right at the beginning to purl all the wrong-side rows.

Starting with patterns made from vertical panels also helps. You can place a marker after each repeat and keep track of one repeat at a time. It's fairly easy to tell if a pattern is organized as a series of vertical repeats; you'll see "lines" running up and down the fabric.

Some lace patterns maintain the same number of stitches on every row (for every yarn-over increase, there is a decrease on the same row). Other patterns call for a yarn-over increase on one row and the corresponding decrease on another. In these patterns, the stitch count changes from row to row. Often, the pattern alerts you to these changes and tells you which rows you have to look out for.

If you're working a pattern in which the stitch count is consistent on every row, it's easy to track an extra or lost stitch. If you're short a stitch, you've probably neglected to make a yarn over. If you find yourself with an extra stitch, you've probably forgotten to make a decrease. Go to the stitches on your needle and check each repeat for the right number of stitches. This is where it really helps to be able to recognize yarn overs and decreases. See Figure 10-7 for help in recognizing a yarn over, an ssk decrease, or a k2tog decrease.

When you suspect that your stitch count is changing . . .

It probably is! If the stitch pattern doesn't say anything about the stitch count changing on different rows and you suspect that it does, you can figure it out by checking the instructions. Add up the number of yarn overs and decreases (don't forget that double decreases take out two stitches) in each row of a written or charted pattern to see if they're the same.

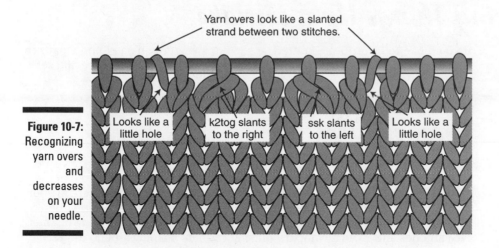

Yarn overs look like a slanted strand between two stitches.

Figure 10-7: Recognizing yarn overs and decreases on your needle.

Looks like a little hole

k2tog slants to the right

ssk slants to the left

Looks like a little hole

Correcting Mistakes When You're Working Lace Patterns

If you make a mistake in a lace pattern and have to rip out stitches, take your time when picking up the recovered stitches. Yarn overs and decreases can be tricky to catch.

When you've ripped out as far back as you need to, slowly take out one more row, pulling the yarn gently from each stitch one at a time and inserting the empty needle into the freed stitch before it has a chance to disappear. (See Chapter 5 for information about ripping out and picking up recovered stitches.) This way, you'll be able to catch all the yarn overs and decreases. Also, if your pattern is purled on all wrong-side rows, try to make the purl row the one you pick up from. In other words, pick up the row with the wrong side facing.

As you go, check that stitches end up in the ready-to-work position (see Chapter 3). Before starting off on your pattern again, read the last pattern row and compare it with the stitches on your needle to make sure that they're all there and all yarn overs and decreases are in the right place.

Always work the edge stitch (or two) in plain stockinette stitch. Doing so stabilizes the sides of your pieces and makes it easier to sew them together. The same is true for cast-on and bound-off edges.

Lacing Things Up a Little

If you'd like to incorporate knitted lace into a sweater and can't find a pattern that appeals to you, you can work in a lace pattern(s) without a specific set of pattern instructions.

Lace insertions

The simplest way to incorporate lace into a knitted project is to work a vertical lace panel or eyelet motif (otherwise known as a lace *insertion*) into a plain stockinette or simple stitch sweater. Place the panel or motif anywhere in your sweater body, far enough away from a shaped edge that the panel won't be involved in any increases or decreases. This way, you can concentrate on the lace stitches and avoid having to work any garment shaping around the yarn overs and decreases of your lace stitch. Figure 10-8 shows two examples of lace insertions.

Figure 10-8:
Designing
with lace
insertions.

If you insert an open lace stitch as a vertical panel, you may want to cast on a few stitches less than the pattern calls for, because lace spreads out more than stockinette. Of course, if you want to be exact, you can work out the gauge of your lace insertion and the gauge of the stitch pattern in the sweater body and do the numbers.

Numerous stitch dictionaries offer a variety of lace patterns to draw from. My favorites are the three books from the Barbara Walker series of stitch patterns. You can find these resources and more listed in the sidebar "Walking through knitting with Barbara Walker" in Chapter 2.

Some stitch pattern books separate lace insertions from allover lace patterns, but if you find a pattern with a vertical orientation (Little Arrowhead, for example), you can isolate a repeat and work it by itself as an insertion.

You can add lace as a horizontal insertion. Fig 10-9 shows Little Arrowhead lace again. This time, several row repeats have been inserted across a piece of stockinette stitch fabric.

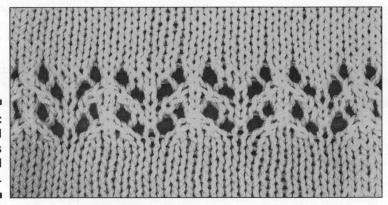

Figure 10-9:
Arrowhead
lace used as
a horizontal
insertion.

Lace edgings

Knitted lace edgings are borders designed with a scalloped or pointed edge. Frequently, they're made in garter stitch to give body to the edging and to ensure that it will lie flat. Some edgings, such as hems and cuffs, are worked horizontally. You cast on the number of stitches required for the width of your piece, work the edging, and then continue on in stockinette or whatever stitch your garment pattern calls for.

Others edgings are worked vertically and then sewn on later. In this case, you simply cast on the number of stitches required for the depth of the lace edging (from 7 to 20, depending on the pattern) and work the edging until its length matches the width of the piece to which you plan to attach it. Then you bind off, turn the edging on its side, and sew it onto the edge of your project. Or, better yet, you can pick up stitches along the border of the edging itself and knit the rest of the piece from there. (See Chapter 15 for details on how to pick up stitches.)

Dress up a sweater by adding a lace border at the bottom of the sweater body or sleeve.

Shaping Up Nicely

Although most lace stitch patterns are easy to master with a little knowledge and concentration, shaping lace pieces — working armholes, necklines, and sleeves — takes a little thought and planning. If you're already keeping track of increases and decreases in your stitch pattern, it's easy to become confused when you also have to keep up with the increases and decreases along the side and neck edges of your lace piece.

The key to shaping is to keep the increase/decrease relationship intact. If you increase a few stitches and begin to work a part of your lace pattern over them, you may shortly find yourself with an unexpected number of stitches.

- ✔ If you work part of your lace repeat that contains a yarn over and not its partner decrease, you will have increased 1 more stitch than you intended.

- ✔ If you decrease and work part of a lace repeat containing a yarn over without its decrease, you will have decreased 1 less stitch than you intended.

Always work increased stitches in stockinette (or whatever background your stitch pattern calls for) until you have enough stitches to include both the yarn over and the decrease for a given lace unit. The further the yarn over is from the decrease, the more stitches you will have to work in stockinette before you can work the lace pattern over your increased stitches.

Working the increases on a sleeve

When you're working on a sleeve and it's time to start shaping, work the first increase, slip a marker onto your needle, knit across to the second increase, slip a second marker onto your needle, work the increase, and finish the row. Work the increased stitch as a knit or purl stitch, depending on what side of the fabric is facing, until you have enough increased stitches that you can include both the yarn over and decrease necessary to maintain the stitch count. If you need to work an entire repeat to catch both yarn over and decrease, work until you have the number of stitches in the repeat on the outsides of your markers before working the pattern over the increased stitches.

Figure 10-10 shows the detail of a chart for a sleeve as it increases along the left side. On Row 21, there are enough stitches for a yarn-over/decrease pair but not enough for the second yarn over and decrease that form the entire repeat. On Row 33, enough stitches have been added that a full repeat with both parts can fit.

Dealing with decreases

When you're decreasing along an edge, if the stitch you eliminate is meant to be a yarn over or a decrease, don't work the other part of the unit (the decrease or yarn over, respectively) for that repeat. Stay in stockinette until you have decreased away both parts of the unit and your pattern has a balance of increases and decreases again.

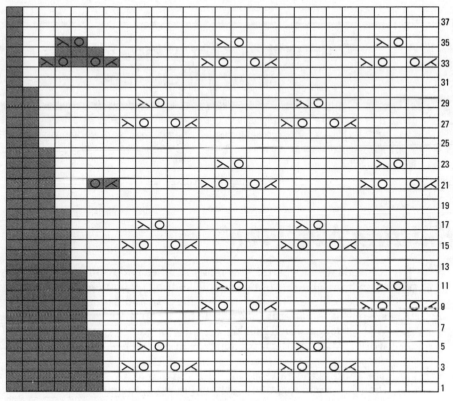

Figure 10-10:
Lace chart
showing
increases.

The sooner you familiarize yourself with the way the yarn-over increases are paired with decreases in your stitch repeat, the easier it will be to shape and manipulate the fabric without adding or losing stitches you hadn't intended to add or lose. When you're shaping the edges of a piece of knitted lace, remember that you're tampering with a repeat that has a balance of increases and decreases. Think in pairs.

Blocking Lace

Lace fabrics need to be blocked for their patterns to show up well. The best way to block a lace piece is to wet-block it by getting it wet and spreading it out in its final shape to dry. (See Chapter 15 for additional tips to get you blocking like a pro.)

Whether you wet-block or steam your piece, spread out the fabric in both directions, using blocking wires if you have them. If the bottom edges are scalloped or pointed, pin these shapes out to define them before blocking.

Getting the effect of lace without actually knitting lace

Knitted lace is a fabric made with yarn overs and decreases, but there are other ways to get lace-type fabrics. Using a very large needle with a fine yarn makes an open and airy piece of knitting. My favorite shawl pattern is a simple garter stitch triangle (with increases worked at either end of every row) made in a fingering- or sport-weight yarn and worked on size 13 needles. Try it!

Knitting Notebook

Knitted lace, no matter how many stitches and rows it takes to make a repeat, is built on a pairing of two simple knitting techniques: a yarn-over increase and a decrease. This marriage of increase and decrease is easy to see in simpler lace patterns, and a little harder to track in more complicated ones. With practice, you'll quickly see how they work together and you'll be able to work any lace pattern you fancy with confidence.

Try knitting the patterns in this section. Make a series of swatches and then sew them together — or simply work one after the other — to create a great scarf.

If you can work the eyelet patterns in this section, there's no reason not to try designing your own. On a sheet of graph paper, plot yarn overs with adjacent decreases in any arrangement you think is attractive. Keep the following in mind:

- ✔ Horizontal eyelets should be spaced 1 stitch apart.
- ✔ Vertical rows should be spaced 4 rows apart.
- ✔ Diagonal eyelets can be spaced every other row.

Eyelet patterns

The increase/decrease structure is usually easy to see in eyelet patterns, making them a good place to begin your lace exploration.

Ridged ribbon eyelet

You can thread a ribbon through these eyelets or use them in a colored stripe pattern. Figure 10-11 shows both a chart and a sample of this pattern. Cast on an odd number of stitches and work this pattern as follows:

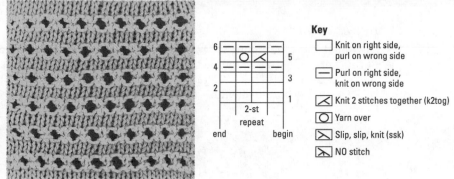

Figure 10-11: Ridged ribbon eyelet and chart.

Key

☐ Knit on right side, purl on wrong side

— Purl on right side, knit on wrong side

◿ Knit 2 stitches together (k2tog)

◯ Yarn over

◺ Slip, slip, knit (ssk)

◹ NO stitch

Rows 1 and 3 (RS): Knit.

Row 2: Purl.

Rows 4 and 6: Knit.

Row 5: *K2tog, yo; rep from *, end k1.

Cloverleaf pattern

The cloverleaf pattern (flip back to Figure 10-1 to see what this pattern looks like) requires a multiple of 10 stitches, plus 5 more. To use it for a scarf, add 2 or three stitches on each side of the pattern. Knit this pattern as follows and see Figure 10-5 for the cloverleaf pattern chart):

Row 1 (RS): Knit.

Row 2 and all ws rows: Purl.

Row 3: K5, k2tog, yo, k1, yo, ssk, k5; rep from *, end k5.

Row 5: K7, *yo, ssk, k8; rep from *, end k6.

Row 7: Knit.

Row 9: *K2tog, yo, k1, yo, ssk, k5; rep from *, end ssk.

Row 11: K2, *yo, ssk, k8; rep from *, end yo, ssk, k1.

Repeat Rows 1–12.

Lace patterns

These patterns are more open — meaning that they have more holes — than the eyelet patterns discussed earlier. Try them as expected in fine yarns on fine needles (think elegant cashmere scarves). Or try them in a chunky yarn on a big needle for the unexpected.

Arrowhead lace

Arrowhead lace (see Figure 10-12) requires a multiple of 6 stitches, plus 1. Row 4 of this pattern uses the double decrease psso, meaning "pass slipped stitch over." "P2sso" means "pass 2 slipped stitches over." (Flip back to Chapter 7 for a refresher on how to make this decrease.) Knit this pattern as follows:

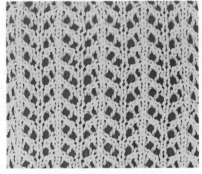

Figure 10-12: Arrowhead lace and chart.

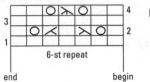

Key

[O] Yarn over

[⟋] Knit 2 stitches together (k2tog)

[⟍] Slip, slip, knit (ssk)

Rows 1 and 3 (ws): Purl.

Row 2: K1, * yo, ssk, k1, k2tog, yo, k1; rep from *.

Row 4: K2, * yo, sl 2 knitwise, k1, p2sso, yo, k3; rep from *, end last repeat k2.

Repeat Rows 1–4.

Miniature leaf pattern

The miniature leaf pattern (see Figure 10-3 to see what this pattern looks like) requires a multiple of 6 stitches, plus 1. Knit this pattern as follows (If you're a visual learner, see the chart in Figure 10-13):

Row 1 and all ws rows: Purl.

Row 2: K1, *k2tog, yo, k1, yo, ssk, k1; rep from *.

Row 4: K2tog, *yo, k3, yo, sl 2 kwise, k1, p2sso; rep from *, end last repeat ssk instead of sl 2, k1, p2sso.

Row 6: K1, *yo, ssk, k1, k2tog, yo, k1; rep from *.

Row 8: K2, *yo, sl 2 kwise, k1, p2sso, yo, k3; rep from *, end last repeat k2.

Repeat Rows 1–8.

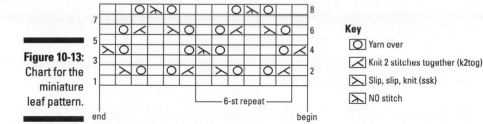

Figure 10-13: Chart for the miniature leaf pattern.

Key

☐○ Yarn over

☐⟋ Knit 2 stitches together (k2tog)

☐⟍ Slip, slip, knit (ssk)

☐⟋ NO stitch

Faggot lace

Faggot lace gives you an allover mesh fabric. Basic faggot is made by alternating a yarn over and an ssk decrease. I find this variation (called purse stitch) faster and easier to work. Cast on an even number of stitches and knit as follows (see the chart in Figure 10-14):

Figure 10-14: Chart for faggot lace.

Key

☐ Knit on right side and wrong side

☐○ yarn over

☐⟋ purl 2 tog

Every row: K1; *yo, p2tog; rep from * , end k1.

To use the faggot repeat as a vertical panel in a garment (whether it's a sweater front or the middle of a scarf), work one repeat between as many stockinette stitches as you like.

Practice Projects

Scarves are natural projects for practicing lace patterns: There's no shaping to consider, and the flat panels really showcase the lace patterns. Try making the scarves in this section. Not only will you improve your lace-making techniques, but you'll also have a terrific scarf or two when you're through!

Scarf with Faggot Lace

This scarf is simple to make. Find yourself a soft, cozy yarn and you'll never want to be without it — except perhaps in the heat of summer. You can see it pictured in the color insert.

Dimensions: The scarf I made measures 9 inches by 52 inches and is worked in one piece. Make your scarf as long as you like.

Materials: Three 50-gram 1 ¾ oz. skeins (124 yards) Classic Elite Lush or similar yarn, one pair of size 9 needles

Making your scarf

To get started, cast on 36 stitches; then knit the pattern as follows:

>Row 1 (RS): K5, *yo, p2tog, k4; rep from * last rep end k5.
>
>Row 2: K2, p3, *yo, p2tog, p4; rep from * end last rep p3, k2.
>
>Repeat Rows 1 and 2 until the scarf reaches the desired length.

Varying your scarf

To make a different scarf on the same theme, try one of the following variations.

- Make the scarf in a different yarn. Use a lightweight yarn for a more delicate scarf or a heavier yarn for an entirely different fabric and feel.
- Add tassels or fringe to the ends of the scarf.
- Instead of stockinette stitch between the faggot panels, work garter or moss stitch.
- Instead of the k4 panel in the pattern, work a cable panel between the faggot patterns. For example, work p2, k4, p2 on the right side and every 4th row, cable the 4 knit stitches. On the wrong sides, work k2, p4, k2.
- To design your own scarf, pick a lace pattern from the Knitting Notebook section earlier in this chapter, add 3 stitches to each side for a garter stitch border, cast on, and go.

Felted Scarf in Horseshoe Lace

This scarf is made from a "lite" version of Icelandic Lopi. A quick spin in the warm cycle of your washing machine will give it a light felting, making it soft and fluffy (see it pictured in the color insert). You make it in two identical sections rather than in one long piece to achieve a pointed edge on either end.

Dimensions: The scarf I made measures 9 inches by 50 inches. Depending on your needle size and how much the fabric contracts in the felting process, your dimensions may vary.

Materials: Four 50-gram skeins (109 yards) of Lite Lopi (100% wool), one pair of size 10 needles

Knitting your scarf

Cast on 43 stitches. Knit 2 rows for a garter stitch border and then knit the following pattern:

Row 1 (RS): K2, * yo, k3, sl 1, k2tog, psso, k3, yo, k1; rep from * end last rep as k2 instead of k1.

Row 2: K2, p 39, k2 (43 sts).

Row 3: K2, *k1, yo, k2, sl 1, k2tog, psso, k2, yo, k1, p1; rep from *, end last rep as k3 instead of k1, p1.

Rows 4, 6, and 8: K2, *p9, k1; repeat from * end last rep as k2 instead of k1.

Row 5: K2, *k2, yo, k1, sl 1, k2tog, psso, k1, yo, k2, p1; rep from *, end last repeat k2 instead of p1.

Row 7: K2, *k3, yo, sl 1, k2tog, psso, yo, k3, p1; rep from *, end k2 instead of p1.

Repeat Rows 1–8 until piece measures approximately 26 inches from the beginning. End by making Row 8 the last row.

With a tapestry needle, thread a piece of scrap yarn through the stitches on the needle while you work a second piece in the same manner as the first one.

Finishing your scarf

When you have two identical scarf halves, you can either sew them together or graft the pieces at the center back for a more knitterly finish. (See Chapter 15 for details on grafting.) Finally, wash your scarf in warm water on the gentle cycle in a washing machine. Lay it flat to dry.

Part III
Color Me Knitting: Working with More than One Color

The 5th Wave By Rich Tennant

"Looks like our trip into the town of Argyll will be delayed while we let one of the local farmers pass with his sheep."

In this part . . .

Part III starts out showing you how to work in more than one color in the easiest manner possible — stripes! This simple technique lends itself to lots of variations and experimentation. I also show you one of my favorite color techniques — slip stitch, which allows you to make complex-looking color patterns without ever having to work with more than one color per row. When you're ready to tackle traditional color work, using two or more colors a row, turn to Chapter 12 for detailed instructions for working repeating Fair Isle patterns and larger intarsia motifs. Check out the color insert for pictures of the simple projects you'll be able to make after you've worked through these chapters.

Chapter 11

Color 101: Earning Your Stripes

In This Chapter

▶ Incorporating colored stripes into your project

▶ Mastering the technical aspects of knitting stripes

▶ Getting creative with stripes

▶ Stitching up a striped scarf

Stitch patterns, cables, and lace are certainly part of knitting's beauty and attraction, but the gorgeous yarn colors are the primary appeal for many knitters. Who, scanning the jewel-colored skeins in a yarn shop, can resist gathering together a palette to take home and knit up? Who can walk by the odd topaz- or hyacinth-colored ball in the sale bin? Who can give away the remaining bit of rose and the tail end of periwinkle from the last project? Not I. But what do you do with a basket of single skeins? You knit in color, that's what!

If you can knit and purl, you already have the skills to knit stripes and slip stitch patterns — quick and easy methods for getting started in color work. Unlike the color techniques in Chapter 12 that require you to go back and forth between colors in a single row, stripes and slip stitch patterns allow you to use as many colors as you please while working with only one color at a time. Read on for pointers and creative ideas to get you going. Be sure to check out Appendix C for more of my thoughts on color.

Now is the time to get out that collection of odd balls of yarn culled from the sale bin of your favorite yarn shop and the bits and pieces of leftovers you've saved. Color patterns in general and stripe and slip-stitch patterns in particular are great ways to incorporate your precious collection into an original project.

Yipes . . . Stripes!

The simplest way to incorporate more than one color in your work, and a great vehicle for exploring color combinations, is to knit stripes. You can look for a striped project pattern and follow the sequence, colors, and spacing given in the design, or you can use the stripe pattern as a template and plug in your own colors and yarns. Better still, take a basic pattern (sweater, scarf, bag, or whatever) and invent your own stripe arrangement. The following sections tell you all you need to know to work in stripes.

Designing with stripes

If you're in a spontaneous mood, gather your yarns together and start knitting, changing yarns as you feel like it. (See the "Joining yarn" sidebar in Chapter 1 to find out how to do so.) If you're in the mood to plot and plan, get out your graph paper, sharpen your colored pencils, and, with the suggestions on designing stripe patterns that follow, get to work.

Never think that stripes are boring. Far from being a single thing, stripes are many-splendored. They offer great variety in scale, balance, sequence, color, and texture. The following list suggests a few ways you can arrange stripes:

- Balanced stripes
- Alternating stripes
- Wide stripes
- Narrow stripes
- One stripe
- Wild stripes

Start a collection of stripe ideas by tearing pages from catalogs and magazines when you see interesting striped patterns or color combinations.

Choosing yarn for striped patterns

Stripes look good in a variety of different yarn types as well as in different colors. You can mix and match smooth and fuzzy, shiny and pebbly. If your stripes are narrow, you can even work with yarns that knit up in different gauges as long as the difference isn't too extreme. To balance the different weights, you can knit the heavier yarns on a smaller needle and the lighter ones on a larger needle.

You can knit stripes in two colors, three colors, or as many colors as you like. You can use color at random or plan for a particular mood in your color combination. Stripes in clean, bright colors with a balance of light and dark are pert and lively; stripes in a few close shades of a single color or colors close to each other on the color wheel (blue, purple, magenta, red) are subtle and sophisticated.

If, before diving in, you want to get an idea of what a stripe pattern might look like knitted in a specific group of yarns, try wrapping samples of the yarns in the proposed pattern around a stiff piece of cardboard for a sneak preview.

Knitting Stripes

Although knitting stripes in stockinette stitch is simple and straightforward, you should know about a couple technical considerations before you get started.

Counting rows

As much as possible, work stripes in an even number of rows. Otherwise, when you come to the end of your stripe in color A and are ready to pick up and work with color B, you'll find B on the opposite edge of your knitting. To keep going, you'll have to cut the yarn, leaving a strand to weave in. (If you do a lot of cutting, you'll have a lot of weaving in to do, but I show you how in Chapter 15.)

If you use three or more colors, you can organize odd- and even-row stripes so that the yarn for the next stripe will be in the right place. You'll have to start some colors on wrong-side rows and carry the yarn colors up both the left and right edges of your work. (Flip to the section "Carrying the yarn up the side as you go," later in this chapter, to find out how to do so.) Changing colors on both sides instead of just one is a good idea anyway if you're using lots of colors — it keeps the side edges from being too bulky.

If you aren't a planner and find yourself unexpectedly ending stripes with no yarn in sight, work on a circular needle. When you're ready to change yarns and the end you need is on the other side, you can slide your knitting to the other end of the needle, pick up your yarn, and carry on.

Changing colors

When you're ready to add a new color in a stripe pattern, secure the new yarn by working the first stitch in the row with the old and new colors held together. To do this, follow these steps:

1. **Insert the RH needle into the first stitch.**

2. **Drape the end of the new yarn behind your work.**

3. **Grab the old and new yarn strands together and work the first stitch.**

4. **Drop the first color and continue on in the new color until it's time to change again.**

When you work back to the edge stitch made with two strands, remember to knit the strands *together*. Otherwise, you'll inadvertently increase a stitch on the edge. When you've worked a few more rows, pull on the strand of the old yarn to tighten up the edge stitch.

You don't need to cut the end of the old color if you'll be using it again in the next few inches. When it's time to change back, simply drop the old color, pick up the new color, and carry on. Be conscious of the tension on the strand you carry up the side of your work: If it's too loose, you'll have sloppy edge stitches, and if it's too taut, your sides will pull in and have no give. Take a stitch or two in the new stripe color and then check the strand carried up the side to make sure that it isn't gaping or pulling.

If you won't be using a color for several inches, it's better to cut the yarn and weave in the end (I tell you how in Chapter 15) than to pick it up and knit with it again. Or you can carry the yarn in along the edge as you go.

Carrying the yarn up the side as you go

To avoid cutting and weaving, you can carry the yarn not in use up the side, tucking it around the working yarn and keeping it close to the edge as you go until you need it again. Here's how:

1. **When you've finished working with color A, work a few rows with color B.**

2. **When you're back at the edge where color A is waiting, and about to start the next row with color B, insert the RH needle into the first stitch.**

3. **With the working strand (A) on the left, bring color B up the side.**

4. **Pick up color A from under color B and make the first stitch.**

   The working strand catches the carried strand. This works the same on the purl side as it does on the knit side. See Figure 11-1.

You can do this every time you're at the beginning of the row if you're making a scarf and want a very tidy edge. If the edge will be enclosed in a seam, you need to catch it only every four to six rows to maintain an even tension on the edge stitches and keep the strand along the side from getting out of hand.

Untwist your yarns periodically for sanity's sake when you're working them around each other up the side edges. And give a gentle tug on the carried strand now and then to make it neat, but not enough to draw up the edge.

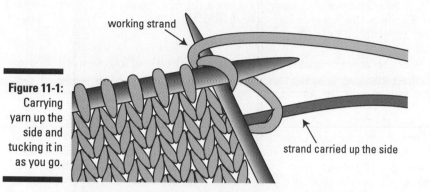

Figure 11-1:
Carrying yarn up the side and tucking it in as you go.

working strand

strand carried up the side

Weaving in ends

When you're obliged to cut the yarn, you can weave the end in vertically along the edge of your knitting, or horizontally along the edge of a stripe.

When you look at your work from the wrong side, you'll see the usual purl bumps. Look below them to see the running threads that connect the stitches. To weave ends horizontally along a stripe, grab a tapestry needle and weave your loose end through 4 or 5 of these running threads. Turn to Chapter 15 for more on tying up loose ends.

Stirring Up Stripes

You can work stripes in flat stockinette stitch, but you can make them more interesting by adding texture to them. You can knit an entire project in a stitch pattern with color stripes running through it or add different textures to different stripes.

If the simplicity and creative pleasure of knitting stripes appeal to you but standard stripes don't inspire you or you'd rather not wear stripes arranged horizontally around your body, don't give up quite yet. The sections that follow introduce some unconventional ways to work stripes into your knitting.

Varying your stitch pattern

Stitch patterns can affect the way your stripe pattern (or color change) looks. In stockinette stitch, if you knit a row in one color and the next row in another color, from the right side the line where the rows meet is sharp and clean. From the wrong side, the line is broken into dots of color by the purl bumps — different effects, different design possibilities. In ribbing or other stitch patterns where purl bumps show on the right side of the fabric, striped patterns show the dots of color unless both the row of the old and the row of the new show a knit face to the right side.

Knit refers to how you make a certain kind of stitch *and* to how a stitch looks from the right side of a fabric. A knit stitch is a smooth V on the right side, even if you make it by purling on a wrong-side row.

If you want a sharp no-dot line between your colors and you're working with a pattern with purls to the right side, simply work "knit" stitches for the first row of the new color. For example, if you're knitting a ribbed pattern, work the last row of the old color in the knit/purl pattern you've established. If the next row is a wrong-side row, purl; if it's a right-side row, knit. Then continue on in your pattern stitch in the new color. Hard as it may be to believe, the misplaced "knit" row is almost invisible. As long as your stripes are several rows deep, the knit row will be almost undetectable in your pattern stitch, and you'll have a distinct transition between stripes.

Making waves

To make wavy stripes, knit a chevron stitch pattern at the same time you work your stripe pattern. (See Chapter 8 for a chevron stitch pattern.) If you've found yourself a good basic sweater pattern and want to add a wavy striped border to the bottom, sample the chevron stitch on different needles until you match the gauge given in your sweater pattern. Then work the border on the body and sleeves as deep as you'd like before going on in stockinette stitch.

Any which way

You can also break up the strong horizontal feel of stripes by knitting randomly striped strips and sewing them together. Or you can work mismatched stripes in vertical panels by using the intarsia method of color knitting. (I cover intarsia in Chapter 12.) Breaking up stripes prevents them from traveling across the width of the entire piece. Finally, you can make patches of stripes (lots of gauge swatches!) and sew them together at 90-degree angles for a patchwork effect.

Slipping Colors

Slip-stitch patterns worked in different colors are a great way to get lots of color and pattern in your knitting with minimal effort. Like knitting stripes, you use only one color in a row, but unlike stripes, slipping stitches in different arrangements creates texture and pattern interest as well.

A slipped stitch is simply a stitch that you transfer *as if to purl*, without actually working it, from the LH needle to the RH needle when you come to it. (If you want to read a little more about slipped stitches, go back to Chapter 7.) If you worked the last row in red and you are working the current row in blue, the stitch you slip will be a red stitch in a blue row.

When you slip stitches repeatedly over a pattern, the fabric draws up a bit as it does in garter stitch making the ratio of rows to stitches almost the same. Like garter stitch, fabrics made from allover repeats of a slipped-stitch pattern tend to be stable and noncurling. Worked in colors, they have a textured tweedy appearance.

Another way to use slip-stitches in color work is to vary the slipping technique from row to row. In most repeating patterns, you slip a stitch for two rows. But, you can also slip them only one row, or for as many as four rows. You can bring the working yarn to the right side between slipped stitches for a woven look. Or, you can purl the stitches in between the slipped stitches, or purl the slipped stitch itself when you bring it back into play. Figure 11-2 shows a couple of ways to manipulate a slip-stitch pattern.

purl stitches   yarn carried in front

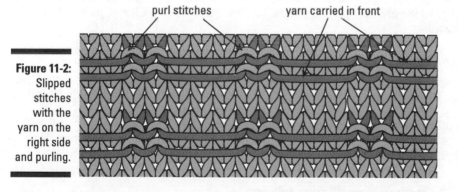

Figure 11-2: Slipped stitches with the yarn on the right side and purling.

Knitting mosaics

Knitting designer Barbara Walker has developed distinctive mosaic patterns that use slipped stitches to create a distinctive square or geometric look — more picture and motif-like than tweedy patterns. Although the results are dramatic, the technique of slipping and working only one color in a row remains the same.

Practice Projects

If you have doubts about your creative abilities or you feel like you wouldn't know where to begin to invent a color pattern, try knitting the projects in this section. Earlier in this chapter, I tell you all you need to know to make these projects: how to change colors and how to carry yarn up the side edge of your knitting. Now, all you need is to relax and indulge in a little color spontaneity. You'll be amazed at the great-looking pieces you can turn out from such simple techniques.

Bold and Bright Scarf

A striped scarf is the classic knitted item par excellence. And the scarf is the classic garment on which to practice stripes! (See it featured in the color insert.) This scarf pattern varies in texture as well as colors. You can follow the pattern given here by using the specific yarns I suggest, or you can substitute yarns from your own collection. Whatever you use will work.

Dimensions: 7 inches by 54 inches

Materials: One 3.5-ounce (100 gram) skein (each approximately 127 yards) of Classic Elite Montera (50% llama/50% wool) each in #3321 sage (A), #3853 red (B), #3881 green (C), 3852 purple (D), and #3898 gold (E); one pair of size 10 needles

Knitting your scarf

Most of the color changes for this scarf occur when the right side is facing. Be on the alert, however, some of the changes begin with the wrong side facing.

Follow these easy steps to a sensational scarf:

1. **Using color A, cast on 30 stitches and work 6 rows of garter stitch (knit every row).**

2. **Begin stripe pattern as follows:**

   With color A, work 8 rows in stockinette stitch (knit on RS rows, purl on WS rows).

   With color B, work 2 rows in stockinette stitch.

   With color C, work 2 rows in stockinette stitch.

   With color D, work 6 rows in stockinette stitch.

   With color E, work 4 rows in stockinette stitch.

With color A, work 7 rows in stockinette and 4 rows in garter stitch.

With color D, beginning with a purl row, work 13 rows in stockinette stitch.

With color C, work 4 rows in stockinette and 6 rows in garter stitch.

With color B, work 2 rows in stockinette stitch.

With color A, work 6 rows in stockinette stitch.

With color E, work 4 rows in stockinette stitch.

With color D, work 6 rows in stockinette stitch.

With color C, work 2 rows in stockinette stitch.

With color B, work 2 rows in stockinette stitch.

With color A, work 6 rows in stockinette stitch.

3. **Repeat the stripe pattern two more times for a total of three repeats.**

4. **End the scarf by working 6 rows of garter stitch in color A.**

5. **Bind off.**

6. **Weave in the ends horizontally along color change lines.**

7. **Block the scarf.**

Varying the stripes

Striped projects are easy to improvise on. The following variations are just a few ideas to get you going.

- ✔ Use yarns in different fibers and textures. They needn't be labeled for the same gauge, but it helps if they can be within half a stitch of each other.

- ✔ Work the scarf by using different stitch patterns in the different stripes. Try seed stitch (see Chapter 2) or one of its variations.

- ✔ Keep the color change sequence, but work the entire scarf in a rib or other single pattern stitch.

- ✔ Play around with scale: For example, double or halve the number of rows in each stripe.

Colorful Garter Slip-Stitch Scarf

Another great scarf to try is a garter slip-stitch scarf. To make this scarf, use the garter slip-stitch pattern presented in the "Knitting Notebook" section of Chapter 7. You can make your scarf as wide and as long as you want — be creative! The following list suggests some ways to jazz up your scarf:

✔ **Color variation 1 — two colors**

Work Rows 1 and 2 with color A.

Work Rows 3 and 4 with color B.

✔ **Color variation 2 — three colors every other row**

Work the four-row pattern, working two rows with color A, the next two rows with color B, and the next two rows with color C. Continue in the pattern, working two rows of each color consecutively.

✔ **Color variation 3 — three colors every row**

Work the four-row pattern, working one row in color A, one row in color B, and one row in color C all the way through.

For more slip-stitch practice, work the Slip-Stitch Sampler in Appendix B.

Chapter 12

Color 201: Advanced Color

• •

In This Chapter

▶ Trying your hand at Fair Isle knitting

▶ Painting with yarn: intarsia

▶ Weaving in ends

▶ Making an Everyday Bag in various patterns

• •

Almost anyone asked to imagine a sweater with color patterns can't help but picture a classic Fair Isle sweater from the Shetland Islands. The traditional XOX patterns developed off the coast of Scotland into subtly changing color designs have become so synonymous with color knitting that the basic technique of knitting repeating color patterns is referred to as Fair Isle knitting and any repeating color pattern as a Fair Isle pattern.

Other kinds of color work — bold picture designs with large color areas — are worked by using a different technique called intarsia.

If you can knit and purl, follow a chart, and drum up a little patience, you can work wonderful color patterns in either technique. All you need to add to what you already know are a few simple techniques for handling the different yarns. Learn and practice these, and you're on your way to painting with yarn.

When you work color patterns using more than one color in a row, you can work with two strands of yarn, carrying them along the back of your work, picking up and dropping them as you need them. This is Fair Isle knitting, or *stranding*, and it's the technique you use for working small repeating color patterns.

For designs involving large areas of color or picture knitting with several colors, it's best to use a different strand of yarn for each color group, a technique called *intarsia*.

Your sweater or project pattern will tell you which method you need to use and may give you some cursory instructions for how to do it.

Knitting Fair Isle

In traditional Fair Isle knitting (sometimes referred to as *stranding* or *jacquard*), you work with two colors per row, knitting or purling with one color for a few stitches and then working with the other color for the next few stitches, according to your pattern. The strand of yarn not in use crosses the stitches on the wrong side of the fabric until it's knitted in again.

Fair Isle patterns have two fairly consistent rules:

- ✔ No more than two colors per row
- ✔ No more than 5 to 7 stitches in any one stretch of color

Within these constraints, you can make what appear to be extraordinarily complex color designs.

The number and variety of the traditional Fair Isle patterns provide a lifetime's worth of exploration. You can work them up in the traditional manner or play with color, arrangement, and scale to make them more contemporary or more your own. Or you can start from scratch. With graph paper and colored pencils or markers, design your own motifs. Just keep in mind the rules for ease and comfort of knitting.

Charting the Fair Isles

Fair Isle charts read like stitch pattern charts. Each square represents a stitch, and the symbol or color given in each square represents the color in which to work the stitch. The pattern chart gives a key listing the symbols used and the colors they represent.

The first row of the chart shows the first right-side row of your knitting and is worked from right to left. The second row of the chart shows the second and wrong side row of your knitting and is worked from left to right. For repeating patterns, the chart shows only one or two repeats and indicates where you are to begin and end the chart for the piece you're working on.

Most color patterns are worked in stockinette stitch. Unless your pattern tells you to do otherwise, knit the pattern on right-side rows and purl it on wrong-side rows. In addition, if a stitch pattern other than stockinette is used in the design, the symbol will represent the color used *and* the type of stitch to make. For example, an *x* may tell you to purl with red on right-side rows and knit with red on wrong-side rows, while the symbol *y* may tell you to knit with red on right-side rows and purl with red on wrong-side rows.

For a black-and-white chart with symbols indicating colors, you may want to make a photocopy of it (enlarged if you like) and color it in. This method eliminates the need to refer frequently to the key to decipher tiny symbols. If you want to experiment with a different color combination, make several copies and color them in with different *colorways* (knitterese for "color combinations") till you find one you like. Knit a little of the pattern in your color choice to see whether it looks as good in yarn as it does in pencil. If you're convinced that it does, you're ready to cast on.

Beginning with the square in the bottom right corner, read and work the chart from right to left. Square one represents the first stitch on your needle. You knit it in whatever color the chart tells you to. Work as many stitches in the first color as the chart shows, and then switch to the next color and work the number of squares given in that color.

If you're knitting in the round, all rounds are right-side rounds. You work the chart from right to left on every round. See Chapter 17 for more on knitting in the round, or *circular knitting*.

Figure 12-1 shows a chart for a repeating triangle pattern 6 stitches wide and four rows high. (You can see it knitted up in the bag shown in the color insert.) This chart doesn't need a key; just pick two yarn colors and plug them in for the different symbols in the chart.

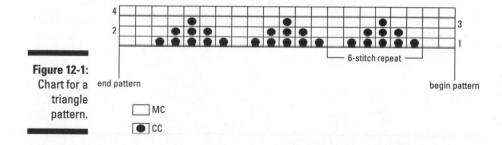

Figure 12-1:
Chart for a
triangle
pattern.

If only two colors are used in a pattern, generally the background is called MC (main color) and the other color is called CC (contrast color). When a pattern includes several colors, they're usually designated by letters — A, B, C, and so on.

Knitting Fair Isle with one hand

Whether you hold the yarn in your right hand or your left hand (English or Continental style), the basic method for working Fair Isle color patterns is the same. You knit and purl as you normally do, dropping and picking up the different yarns as you need them.

To practice this method, choose two colors of yarn: MC and CC. With the MC, cast on 21 stitches and use the charted design in Figure 12-1. You can repeat the two colors throughout, or reverse or change them after every four rows. It's worth trying out the chart both ways to see how a simple color sequence change can completely alter the effect of an easy two-color pattern.

Work with a medium-weight wool yarn if possible. Wool is forgiving. The fuzzy fibers will work themselves together, covering any little holes where color changes don't quite meet up. A shot of steam from your iron will further even out any minor imperfections.

As with stripes, when you start a new color at the end of a row, you can simply work the first stitch with the old and new yarn held together or tie the ends in a temporary knot.

On the knit side

Start your row with the MC and knit the number of stitches called for. (If you're following the chart in Figure 12-1, you'll knit 2 stitches in the MC.) When it's time to switch to the CC, drop the MC, insert your RH needle in the next stitch, wrap, and finish the stitch with the CC. (You don't really need to tie on the new yarn. You'll come back and weave in the end later.) Work the number of stitches your chart tells you to in the CC (5 stitches).

When your chart tells you to switch back to color MC, drop color CC. *Spread out the stitches* just worked in color CC, find the strand of color MC, bring it *over* the strand of CC that is hanging down, and knit the next set of stitches in color MC (see Figure 12-2).

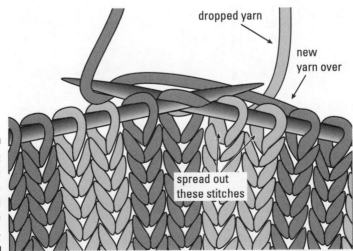

Figure 12-2: Spreading out the stitches and bringing the yarn over.

dropped yarn

new yarn over

spread out these stitches

So far, so good. One more move and you're home free.

When the chart tells you to switch back to the MC, drop the CC. *Spread out the stitches* you just worked in the CC, find the strand of the MC, bring it *under* the strand of the CC left hanging, and then knit the next stitch in the MC (see Figure 12-3).

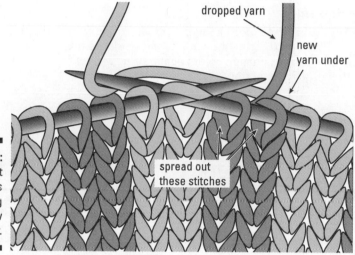

dropped yarn

new yarn under

spread out these stitches

Figure 12-3: Spread out the stitches and bring the new yarn under.

Here are a few tips to help you be successful in Fair Isle knitting:

- You may want to recite a mantra as you work, such as "green over, red under" or something like that. You also might want to add "green 1, red 5" to your mantra if your pattern is a simple repeat — just to keep you on track.

- Designating one yarn as an "over" yarn and one as an "under" will keep your yarns from becoming tangled. It will also give you a very tidy-looking wrong side.

- Always consider the design possibilities of the wrong side in any fabric you're making. I've seen some very handsome sweaters that utilize a few rows of the wrong side of a Fair Isle pattern on the right side of the sweater. If this technique is neatly done, you can read the pattern in the woven-looking carried strands.

- When you've worked back to the first stitch you made in the second color, the loop will be big and sloppy. Give a little tug on the end hanging down, and it will jump right into line.

✔ The key to successful color knitting is maintaining an even and elastic tension over your stitches. If you don't allow enough slack on the new yarn when you change colors in a row, your knitting will gather in and pucker. Too much slack and the stitches at each end of the strand will become loose and sloppy. Spreading out the stitches between colors and gently extending the new yarn over them before you work the next first stitch are usually all you need to do to ensure a flexible and even fabric.

On the purl side

Purl in MC to the first color change, drop MC (don't forget to spread out the stitches!). Pick up CC, bring it *over* MC, and work the next set of stitches in CC. When it's time to change colors again, bring MC *under* CC. Figure 12-4 shows this process in action.

Figure 12-4:
Changing colors on the purl side.

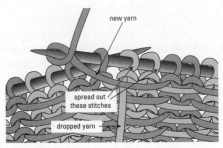

A. Bringing the yarn over.

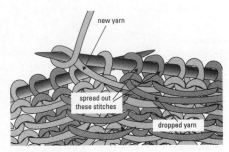

B. Bringing the yarn under.

If, at the first change from the MC to the CC, the strand of the CC is several stitches left of your position, be sure to allow enough slack between the last stitch of the CC in the row before and the first stitch in the CC on the new row. Spread out the just-worked stitches on the RH needle before starting the next color and keep up an under/over rhythm to minimize tangles.

If you find loose or sloppy stitches at the beginning and end of color areas, give a little pull on the strand on the wrong side that connects them (called a float) to tighten up the stitches.

Trying two-handed Fair Isle knitting

Working Fair Isle by alternating one color with the next in one hand is a fine way to work color patterns, but it's slow. If you plan to do a lot of color knitting, invest some time in learning how to knit with your other hand. Pick a quick pattern, like a hat or scarf, and work it up by using the technique for knitting with the yarn held in the opposite hand from the one you've been using (see Chapter 1). Once you've completed the project and you're proficient, if not perfect, at knitting with the other hand, you're ready to try two-handed Fair Isle knitting.

Two-handed knitting isn't that different from traditional Fair Isle knitting. You just carry one yarn in the right hand while you carry the other yarn in the left hand. The benefit is that you never have to drop one color to pick up and work the other color — you have both colors in your hands at all times! Knitting with two hands, you'll really cruise along.

Carry the dominant color in your dominant hand. So if you normally knit English style, carry the main color (MC) in your right hand and the contrasting color (CC) in your left hand. You always use English style to knit the yarn off your right hand, and you use Continental style to knit the yarn off your left hand.

Fixing floats

The strands of yarn carried on along the back are called *floats*. If your pattern has too many stitches between one color change and the next, your floats will be long and sloppy and easily catch on rings and fingers when you take your sweater on and off. You can carry yarn for stretches longer than 5 or 7 stitches, but pushing the traditional limits requires another step: catching the float.

To secure the float in the nonworking yarn (assume that it's the MC) to the wrong side of the fabric, follow these steps:

1. **Work a few stitches with the CC and drop the CC.**
2. **Bring the float color (MC) to the leftover CC and leave it there.**
3. **Pick up the CC again and knit a few more stitches.**

The MC will be caught against the fabric by the working strand of the CC. Repeat if necessary every 5 stitches or so until you begin working with MC again. Be sure that the strand remains relaxed across the back of the fabric and doesn't pull up.

Work the same way to catch the float when you're purling. Figure 12-5 shows how to catch the yarn on a knit row and on a purl row.

Although you can do this routinely every other stitch, you don't need to catch floats this frequently for most projects unless you're deliberately making a very dense and inelastic fabric. Catching the float strand too frequently can distort the stitches, and even if you're using the utmost care, the woven yarn color will peek though on the right side. Catch the yarn only every 5 stitches or so when you're traveling a long distance with your carried yarn.

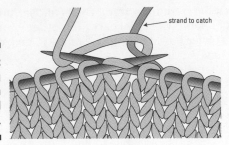
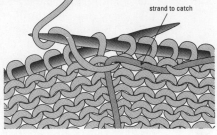

Figure 12-5: Catching the yarn on knit and purl rows.

A. Catching the yarn on a knit row.

B. Catching the yarn on a purl row.

If your design has a lot of long floats and large color areas, you're better off working your colors by using the intarsia method explained in the following section.

Getting into Intarsia

Intarsia is a color technique that lets you paint with yarn. You use this method when you're knitting a bold geometric pattern or an isolated flower or snowflake design.

Intarsia is color knitting without floats. Instead of carrying different colors of yarn across the wrong side of your work so they're at the ready, each color area has its own strand of yarn waiting on a bobbin. When two colors meet, you intertwine the yarns in a way that prevents a gap where one color ends and the next one begins, and then you start working in the next color. Intarsia fabrics stay relaxed and stretchy because no strands are running across the back to stiffen and draw in the fabric.

Charting intarsia

Charts for intarsia patterns generally don't show patterns in repeats. The entire design, whether it's a single rose or a city skyline, is charted. A large intarsia pattern may take a page or more to display.

Follow an intarsia chart just like any other. Start at the bottom right corner and work to the left on the first row, changing yarns as the pattern indicates. Work the next (WS) row to the right. Use a magnetic board and strip (see Chapter 4 for information about these tools) to help you keep your place. If you have a willing friend, she can sit with you and read the chart aloud — "3 red, 12 blue, 7 green . . ." — as you knit.

Doing the duplicate stitch

Duplicate stitch is a simple way of adding a third (or fourth, or fifth) color to your knitting without actually knitting with it. Instead, you embroider the additional color(s) on the fabric, mimicking the stitch it covers.

Thread a tapestry needle with yarn that's the same or a similar weight to the one you've used to knit your piece. Take a good look at your fabric and find the stitches you want to color. Bring your needle up through the center of the V below the one you want to cover. Follow the V up around the base of the stitch above and bring

the needle back through the same stitch where you came out.

Duplicate stitch is best used in small areas. Don't try to avoid two-color knitting by using duplicate stitch for a large motif. Doing so will stiffen the fabric, and the background color will show through. Instead, use this embroidery for tiny motifs and color accents. For example, color the center few stitches of a diamond with it, or use it to paint detail in a knitted leaf or flower.

If you want to create your own design on graph paper, remember that knitted stitches aren't square. If you use square graph paper, your knitted picture will be a somewhat squashed version of your drawing. You can buy special knitter's graph paper with 1-inch segments of 5x7 squares to mimic knitted fabric. If you're comfortable on a computer, you can get software that prints out graph paper in any combination of rows and stitches you'd like. (See Chapter 4.)

Knitting intarsia

Depending on the size of the color area you're knitting, you can use balls, bobbins, or long strands of yarn. If you're working with many colors, your yarns will become entangled, so cut long strands and forget about balls of yarn, which are much harder to sort out. You can use bobbins (see Chapter 4), but I find them a nuisance. You have to take time to wind them, and then you have to stop and unwind them as you knit. And they tangle every bit as much as lengths of yarn or balls. If you're proficient at making butterflies, though (see Chapter 4), they work pretty well.

To practice knitting intarsia, gather yarns in two colors, MC and CC. Cast on 10 stitches in color MC. Then, with color CC, make another slip knot, slide it on the needle, and cast on 10 more stitches — for a total of 20 stitches in all. When you're ready to knit, the stitches in color CC will be the first ones to work on your needle.

To practice intarsia, follow the chart in Figure 12-6.

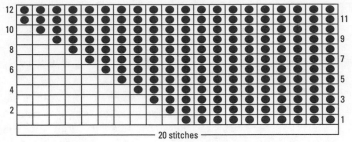

Figure 12-6:
Chart for intarsia practice.

On the knit side

Work in color CC to the first stitch in color MC. Insert your RH needle into the first MC stitch, give a little tug on CC, and bring the CC strand to the left *over* the MC strand. Keep a little tension on CC while you pick up MC from *under* CC. Give a slight tug on A and knit the next stitch. You've just caught the strand you've finished using with the one you're about to use. Figure 12-7 shows how to switch from MC to CC. Continue knitting in CC.

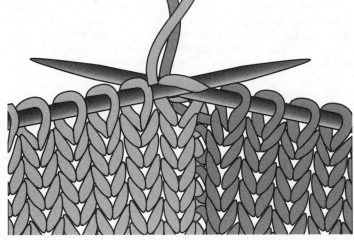

Figure 12-7:
Switching colors on the knit side using intarsia.

On the purl side

Purl the number of stitches given on the chart for color MC. To work the first stitch in color CC, insert the RH needle into the first CC stitch, give a slight tug on MC, and bring it to the left *over* the CC strand. Keeping a little tension on MC, give a slight tug on CC and bring it up from *under* MC to purl the next stitch. You've caught MC with CC to prevent a hole where they meet. See Figure 12-8.

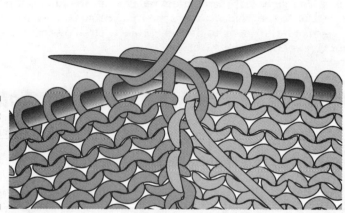

Figure 12-8:
Switching colors on the purl side using intarsia.

Continue purling in CC to the end of the row. Continue to work the chart through Row 12.

Intarsia doesn't work in circular knitting. After the first round, you'll find that all the ends you need to knit in the second round are on the opposite side of the motifs you're working. Of course, you can use a circular needle to work on, but you'll still have to purl.

Using intarsia in motifs

Intarsia is very straightforward and easy when you're working with blocks of color having straight or diagonal edges or when you're making color changes within a few stitches of each other.

If you're knitting a more detailed design in which you need to make a color change that means bringing the new color more than 7 stitches *to the right* to begin knitting, don't try to make the reach with your yarn; the first stitch will pull. Instead, break the yarn and start the color with a fresh end. Yes, you'll have another end to sew in, but your fabric will be smoother. Resolve to be patient.

Ending the Ends

Whether you're working a Fair Isle pattern or an intarsia design, color knitting involves yarn ends that have to be secured somehow or other. They're a nuisance any way you look at it. You can use the quick method and work them in as you go. This gives less-than-perfect results, but sometimes it pays to throw perfection to the winds and do something reasonably well — instead of perfectly — in order to get on to the next project. The slow method can take hours, but gives perfect results. You decide.

Weaving as you go: The quick method

It's possible to work in ends as you go by using the technique for weaving in floats described in the Fair Isle section earlier in this chapter. Doing so saves you enormous amounts of finishing time if you have many ends to finish off. However, this method has its drawbacks. Too frequently, the color you've ended shows through the stitches in the new color field and looks sloppy. The two ends lying together along the wrong side can be bulky and sometimes throw off the tension. But if your design uses many colors, these little glitches will hardly be noticeable from a few feet away — and how many people really get within a few feet of you in a typical day? The busyness of the design will distract from any imperfections.

To weave in the ends where you change colors, drop the old color and work 2 stitches in the new color, leaving the ends at least 3 inches long. After the second stitch, hold both ends together and weave them on the wrong side for several stitches, (look back to Figure 12-5 to see how to catch floats). Later, you can snip the remainder of the ends ½ inch or so from the sweater.

Weaving in later: The slow method

If you decide to weave in the ends with a tapestry needle after you've finished knitting your piece, you have the chance to tweak any misshapen stitches at the color changes. Gently pull and prod the yarn ends and neighboring V legs until the stitches are neat and even. Then you can weave the ends in along the color boundaries in *opposite* directions — yarn on the left weaves to the right, yarn on the right weaves to the left — to better distribute their bulk, directing the colors where they won't peek through.

Knitting Notebook

Figure 12-9 shows some Fair Isle patterns in chart form. Use them in the Everywhere Bag or the Tassel Hat presented in Chapter 6.

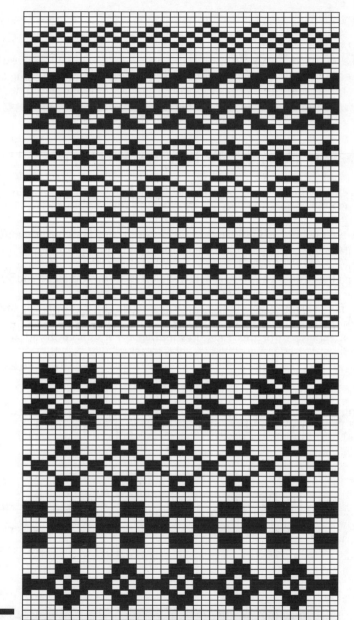

Figure 12-9:
Fair Isle
charts.

Practice Projects

Simple shapes make easy color knitting. The Everyday Bag allows you to try out different patterns and experiment with color combinations while knitting a simple square, and the Intarsia Pillow lets you experiment with knitting a motif using the intarsia technique. Both are featured in the color insert.

Everyday Bag in Triangle Pattern

For this bag, gather up your colored yarns and knit a striped pattern, breaking into the small repeating triangle motif every few stripes.

Dimensions: This bag is made in two pieces about 8½ inches wide and 9½ inches high, seamed together at the bottom and along the sides.

Materials: One 3.5-ounce (100-gram) skein (each approximately 200 yards) of Harrisville Knitting Yarn in each of the following colors: Red (A), Violet (B), Hemlock (C), Magenta (D), Iris (E and CC), Tundra (F), Chianti (G), and Poppy (H and MC) (you can also select another comparable yarn in your favorite eight colors); one pair of size 7 needles; two size 7 double-pointed needles for cord (optional)

Gauge: 18 stitches to 4 inches in Fair Isle pattern (4½ stitches per inch)

Bag: Using A, cast on 39 stitches. Starting with a knit row, work the entire color and chart sequence (see Figure 12-10) in stockinette stitch:

Figure 12-10:
Triangle Fair
Isle chart
for the
Everyday
Bag.

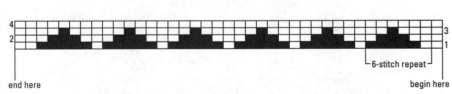

The final row in this chart is worked in one color. Don't try to carry yarn that has ended up on the left edge of your piece all the way across to the right edge to begin knitting with it there. Better to cut the end on the left edge to weave in later and start the color anew on the right edge where you need it.

Rows 1–4: Work in color F.

Rows 5–8: Work in color D.

Rows 9–12: Work chart using H for background (MC) and E for motif (CC).

The photographs presented in this color insert represent the various projects from this book. It is my hope that you'll take a look at the pictures here and use them to inspire creations of your own. A simple scarf can become a stunning accent when you knit it up in a beautiful yarn, rich in color and texture.

Novelty yarns

Button Pillows

A collection of Bags

Everyday Bag and Everywhere Bag
with button

Garter Ridge Scarf

Eccentric Cable
Scarf

Swatch Scarf

Scallop Scarf

Faggot Lace Scarf

A collection of scarves from this book

Felted Horseshoe Lace Scarf

Striped Scarf with Knit-from-the-Top-Down Hat

A collection of knitting samplers

Intarsia Pillow

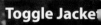

Toggle Jacket

Red Pullover

A collection of Three-Way Hats

Sleeveless Cowl Neck Sweater

Cable Hat

A collection of socks to knit in the round

A collection of the projects in this book

Rows 13–16: Work in color C.

Rows 17–20: Work in color G.

Rows 21–24: Work chart using F for MC and A for CC.

Rows 25–28: Work in color D.

Rows 29–32: Work in color B.

Rows 33–36: Work chart using D for MC and C for CC.

Rows 37–40: Work in color F.

Rows 41–44: Work in color B.

Rows 45–48: Work chart using color E for MC and H for CC.

To finish the piece, work 4 rows garter stitch in D.

Make a second piece the same way. Weave in the ends. Block the pieces. Sew the bottom and side edges.

To avoid having to sew a bottom seam, do the knitterly thing and "pick up" stitches along the bottom edge to work the second piece. With the wrong side facing, look at the cast-on edge. Locate the overlapping strands. Starting at the right edge, go under the first cast-on strand (from wrong side to right side) with the tip of your needle, hook the yarn, and pull it through. You can find more on picking up stitches in Chapter 16.

Do the next stitch the same way and continue to pull stitches through until the end of the row. When you've picked up 39 stitches, turn your work and start Row 1.

Finishing: Weave in loose ends and block gently with steam. If you've picked up stitches, you'll need to seam the bag only along the sides, using the mattress stitch. Otherwise, backstitch the bottom edge of the bag together and then seam the sides. (See Chapter 15 for information on finishing techniques.)

Strap: Using color A, cast on 4 stitches and work in stockinette stitch for 44 inches or the desired length for the strap. Or work the cord on double-pointed needles using the I-cord technique explained in Chapter 6.

Variations:

- ✔ Work the chart throughout the bag every 4 rows instead of working it between stripes. Use the same background color throughout, and change the triangle colors every four rows. Or, work the chart pattern every four rows, changing triangle *and* background colors on each repeat.

- ✔ Try a different pattern from the Knitting Notebook in a stripe instead of the triangle pattern or keep repeating the KN pattern for an all-over treatment.

✔ Turn the bag into a hat by casting on 51 stitches. Work in the triangle pattern until the piece measures 8 inches from the beginning. End with six rows of garter stitch, as in the bag. Work a second piece the same way. Seam the top and sides. Sew tassels or pompoms to the corners.

✔ Turn the bag into a pillow. For a 12-inch pillow, cast on 57 stitches. Work in one or more of the sampler patterns or the triangle pattern until the piece measures 12 inches and bind off. For the back of the pillow, cast on or pick up along the bound off edge another 57 stitches and make another piece. Work until this piece is 8 inches high and bind off. Make a second 8-inch back piece and bind off. Sew the two back pieces along the sides of the front piece, overlapping the back pieces at the center of the square. Insert a 12-inch pillow form.

Intarsia Pillow

This pillow uses a simple Native American motif. I made it in hand-spun and plant-dyed yarn from La Lana Wools in Taos, New Mexico. The pattern and yarn together have the feel of a woven Navajo rug. (You can find out how to order the yarns in the appendix.)

Dimensions: The finished pillow measures 14 inches square.

Materials: Four 2-ounce skeins (each approximately 80 yards) of Obverse Blend Worsted Weight (60% wool, 40% mohair) in Apassionata (MC), 1 skein in Monet (CC); one pair of size 9 needles; one pillow form measuring 14 inches by 14 inches

Pillow front: With the MC, cast on 49 stitches. Work in stockinette stitch for 14 rows. On the next row (RS), begin working the chart in Figure 12-11.

Following the first row of the chart, knit 17 stitches in the MC and 15 stitches in the CC; with another ball of the MC, knit the remaining 17 stitches. Continue in stockinette stitch and work the remaining 43 rows of the chart. Cut the CC after Rows 6, 15, 29, and 38, and start with a fresh strand on the next row. (Otherwise, you'll be carrying the yarn too far, and it may pull between the distant stitches. It's better to weave in the ends later.)

Work the center diamond shape in MC as shown, but work the 6 CC stitches in the center of the diamond (Rows 21, 22, 23, and 24) as duplicate stitch embroidery when you have finished and blocked your pillow piece.

When you've worked through Row 44 of the chart, work 14 more rows with the MC in stockinette stitch.

Figure 12-11:
Intarsia
chart for
pillow.

Pillow back: Cast on (or pick up from edge) 49 stitches. Work in stockinette stitch until the piece measures 9 inches from the beginning. Bind off. Work the second half of the pillow back in the same manner. The back pieces will overlap.

Finishing: Weave in loose ends and block the pieces gently with steam. If you've knit the pieces separately, seam along the bottom edges using the grafting technique or backstitch. Overlap the back pieces along the center back and sew up the sides using the mattress stitch. (See Chapter 15 for information about blocking and seaming techniques.) Insert the pillow form. Voilà!

Part IV
Making Garments: Working with Patterns

The 5th Wave   By Rich Tennant

@RICHTENNANT

"She started knitting oven mitts and toaster cozies. Then one day she saw 'Snowball' shivering next to her drinking bowl and, well, her tail's still wagging in there, so I don't see the harm."

In this part . . .

Once you've mastered the basics of stitches, you'll want to put your skills to work in making more challenging projects. This part guides you through the process of deciphering and working with knitting patterns. It shows you how to finish and assemble the pieces of a project after you've made them. And finally, it takes you through the finishing details: how to pick up neckbands, finish cardigan fronts, and make great-looking buttonholes.

Chapter 13

Knitting Patterns: Helpful Blueprints or Hieroglyphics?

In This Chapter

▶ Understanding knitterese

▶ Making your way through a knitting pattern

▶ Understanding charts

*N*ow that you're handily casting on, knitting, purling, and binding off, you're ready to tackle the intricacies of making projects. To do so requires you to master the art of deciphering knitting patterns.

Pick up any knitting pattern and glance down the page. In the tiniest print, you read things like "sl 1, k1, psso," "ytb," and "ssk." Alas, you think, "This is English?" Not to worry. Everyone who has knitted from a pattern has spent more time than she wants to remember staring in earnest at the page, hoping that the sheer intensity of her gaze will unlock the meaning of the odd "instructions" in front of her.

To say the most in the least amount of space, knitting patterns are written in knitterese — a language full of abbreviations, asterisks, parentheses, and strange ways of spelling out (or rather *not* spelling out) instructions. To the uninitiated, and even to the experienced, these conventions can be daunting. But have no fear; soon you'll be breezing your way through patterns, eager to explain them to anyone who'll listen whether they knit or not, and ignoring everyone at the dinner table while you read through your growing pile of knitting patterns, relishing the pleasure of understanding.

Probably the best way to read this chapter is to gather several knitting patterns and examine each one for the headings and information that I identify and explain.

Deciphering Knitterese

In order to save space, patterns are written in a condensed form with many abbreviations and a lot of shorthand. As you work with patterns, you'll become familiar with the most common abbreviations — for example, RS (right side), WS (wrong side), beg (beginning), and cont (continue). Refer to the Cheat Sheet in the front of this book for a complete list. Pattern instructions explain any unusual abbreviations, or ones that may vary from pattern to pattern.

In addition, knitting patterns use certain phrases that can be confusing until you've had some experience with them. Here are some of the more common phrases that you'll come across in knitting patterns. Others exist, but this list should take care of most patterns that you'll come across as a beginner.

- **as established:** When your instructions set up a series of steps or patterns to work, rather than repeat them row by row, they'll tell you to continue working *as established*. For example, if you're knitting a cardigan with the center front band knitted in, the stitches for center front band may be worked in a different pattern from the rest of the sweater body. Once the pattern tells you how many border stitches to work in the border pattern and how many stitches to work in the sweater body pattern, it will tell you to continue to work the patterns in the front piece *as established*.

- **at same time:** As in "dec 1 st every other row 4 times, *at same time*, when piece measures same length as back to shoulder, work shoulder shaping as for back." This phrase indicates that two things need to happen at the same time. In this example, the neckline shaping (dec 1 st) continues as the shoulder shaping begins. Be on the lookout for this phrase; it's easy to get going on one task and forget to pay attention to the other. When you see this phrase, it's a really good idea to make yourself a chart of the part of the pattern piece you'll be shaping.

- **back of your work:** As in "yarn to the back." The back of your work is the side of your work that faces away from you as you hold your needles. Not to be confused with the right and wrong side of your work, which refers to how you will wear the piece.

- **bind off from each neck edge:** As in "bind off from each neck edge 3 sts once, 2 sts twice, etc." When you shape the neckline on a pullover, you work both edges of the neckline at the same time, but you shape the right side (as you wear it) on right-side rows and the left side on wrong-side rows. Although this instruction may sound tricky, it's quite obvious and simple when you're doing it.

- **end with a WS row:** When you see this phrase, you're to finish the section you're working on by working a WS (wrong-side) row last. The next row you work should be a RS (right-side) row.

- **front of your work:** As in "yarn to the front." The front of your work is the side of your work that faces you as you hold your needles. It could be the wrong side or the right side.

- **inc (or dec) every four (six, eight, or whatever) rows:** Increase or decrease on a (usually) right-side row, and then work three (five, seven, or whatever) rows without shaping. Increase or decrease on the next row. This is how the increases along a sleeve seam are written.

- **inc (or dec) every other row:** Increase or decrease on the (usually) right-side row, and then work the following row without increasing or decreasing. Then, on the next (usually) right side row, work the increase or decrease again.

- **pat rep:** Same as "pattern repeat." When instructions tell you to do something with the stitch repeat, they write it this way. Pattern repeat refers to what's given between an asterisk and a semicolon (* . . . ;) in written patterns and between heavy black lines in a chart.

- **pick up and knit:** As in "with rs facing starting at neck edge, pick up and knit 28 sts along right front edge." Use a separate strand of yarn to create a row of stitches on a needle by pulling loops through along a knitted edge, usually a cardigan front or a neckline. See more on picking up stitches in Chapter 16.

- **place marker (pm):** As in "join, place marker, and begin round." A *marker* is a plastic ring or tied loop of yarn that sits between stitches on your needle to indicate the beginning of a round in circular knitting or to mark pattern repeats. You slip the marker from one needle to the other. Sometimes you use row markers, too. But usually your pattern won't tell you to — your common sense will.

- **preparation row:** Some stitch patterns require a *set-up row*, which is worked only at the beginning of the pattern and is not part of the repeat.

- **reverse shaping:** As in "work to correspond to front, reversing all shaping." When you knit a cardigan, you work two pieces that mirror each other. Most patterns have you work the side that carries the buttons before you work the side that carries the buttonholes. Instead of writing a separate set of instructions for each side, the pattern asks you to work the shaping in the opposite direction on the second piece. This means that you'll be working bind-offs and neck shaping on the reverse side of the fabric as well. If you work the shaping on the wrong side in one piece, you'll work it on the right side when you reverse the shaping.

- **right:** As in "beginning at right front neck edge." Refers to right as opposed to left. When a pattern specifies a right front, it means the front that would be on your right side *as you would wear it*. When in doubt, hold your knitting up to you (wrong side to your body) to determine whether it's the right or left front.

✔ **RS:** As in "with RS facing, pick up and k . . . sts." Refers to the right side as opposed to the wrong side of the fabric. The right side is the side of the piece people will see when you wear it.

✔ **when armhole measures . . . :** Signals that your instructions are about to tell you to do something other than what you've been doing. Measure the armhole *not* from the edge of the piece, but from the marker you've (I hope) put near the middle of the row on which the armhole began.

✔ **work as for . . . :** As in "work as for back until piece measures 21½" from beg." Work the front piece the same as the back. This phrase saves writing out the same instructions twice.

✔ **work even:** Continue in whatever stitch pattern you're using without doing any shaping.

✔ **work to end:** Work in whatever stitch pattern you're using to the end of the row.

✔ **working inc sts into pat:** As in "inc 1 st each side (working inc sts into cable pat) every 4th row." You see this phrase when you're increasing along a sleeve. Whether your pattern is a rib, cable, lace, or color work, as you add stitches, work your stitch pattern over them. For lace and cables, you have to have a certain number of stitches before you can begin to work them in pattern.

✔ **WS:** As in "with WS facing." The wrong side of the garment piece — the one next to your body.

You may run into other phrases that aren't as clear as they could be, but experience will make you familiar with them. Eventually, you'll be surprised at how understandable this language becomes, and you'll wonder that it ever seemed confusing.

For the most part, if you read your instructions carefully, work each step between commas or semi-colons as a complete step, look at your work, and think about what you're doing, you won't have any problems.

To experience some of this knitterese in action, Chapter 14 takes you step by step through the process of working from a sweater pattern — but this time with yarn and needles in hand.

The Anatomy of a Sweater Pattern

Sweater patterns tell you how to make the individual pieces of a sweater and how to put them together. Whether from a book, magazine, or leaflet, sweater patterns are set up in a predictable way. You find information about sizes, materials needed, gauge, and any special pattern stitches or abbreviations listed before the actual piece-by-piece instructions.

Take time to read your pattern before you begin your sweater. Knowing as much as you can about your sweater before you begin to knit will help you anticipate the steps in the instructions and forestall many a mistake. If you find that something in the instructions is confusing in the first read through, don't be alarmed, it may make sense by the time you get to that point in the instructions with needles and yarn in hand.

Picture this

When you sit down with a new sweater pattern — or better yet, when you're choosing one — begin by paying close attention to the picture of the sweater you want to knit. This step may seem obvious, but studying the photograph or drawing and noting the details will clarify parts of the instructions that might otherwise be confusing. Study the picture of your sweater and answer these questions:

- Is it a pullover or a cardigan?

- How is it constructed? Can you tell from the picture whether the sweater is designed with a drop shoulder or a set-in sleeve?

- Does the shoulder slope, or is it worked straight across? (If you can't tell from the photo, check the schematic. The shoulder design will be clear in the little line drawing that often comes with the instructions.)

- Is the body of the sweater shaped in any way, or is it a simple rectangle?

- Is the sweater worked primarily in stockinette stitch? If other pattern stitches are used, can you identify them? Are they knit-and-purl patterns, cables, or something else?

- Is there a color pattern? If so, is it an allover pattern, or is it "placed" along the hem or across the yoke? Does it look like a repeating pattern to knit by using the Fair Isle technique, or is it a pattern with larger color areas to knit in the intarsia method? (See Chapter 12 for details about these methods.)

- Is there ribbing at the bottom edges, or does the sweater begin some other way?

- Does it have a round neckline or a V-neck? Is it finished with a ribbed neckband? A collar? A crocheted edge?

- If the sweater is pictured on a model, study how it fits. Does the collar lie properly around the neck? Does the sleeve cap pull? If the sweater doesn't fit the model well, chances are that it won't look good on you. (Then again, it might.)

The point? Know thy sweater.

How hard is easy?

Many patterns tell you right upfront the level of difficulty the pattern writer has assigned to it.

- ✔ A *beginner* sweater uses basic stitches (knits and purls) and involves minimal shaping and simple finishing.

- ✔ An *intermediate* project uses more challenging stitch patterns and/or shaping and finishing.

- ✔ An *experienced* or *expert* pattern may require all your powers of concentration. It will frequently feature tricky pattern or color work, or may involve complicated shaping or construction details. Work on it only when you're well rested.

It's always a good idea to have more than one project going — something portable and rather brainless to give you a feeling of accomplishment and to keep your hands going while you watch TV or wait for a Web site to load and another more challenging project to work on when you have the time and quiet to concentrate on it.

Sizes

Most patterns begin by listing the sizes given in the instructions. Older patterns may list them in numbered chest sizes — for example, 38 (40, 42, 44, 46). Most current patterns give the sizes in the designations small (medium, large).

This is the first place you see parentheses in a knitting pattern, and it pays to notice where the size you want to make is located: before or inside the parentheses. Every time a number or measurement is given in the pattern, the one for your size will be in the same place in relation to the parentheses. If the pattern is written for small, medium, and large sizes and you're making a small, the numbers for your size will always be written first — outside the parentheses. If you're making a large, your numbers will always be last in the parentheses.

Sweater patterns generally tell you what the finished garment should measure when laid out on a flat surface. Sometimes only the chest/bust width is given. Other times, you also find measurements for overall length, sleeve length, and/or upper arm circumference. Use this info to help you determine what size to knit.

For more information about choosing which size to make, see Chapter 14.

Materials

After "Knitted measurements," the pattern tells you what materials and equipment you need to make your sweater. In this section, the pattern lists the following:

- ✔ **The brand and specific name of the yarn used:** It gives the fiber content of the yarn, the weight and often the number of yards per skein, the color number and name of the yarn, and the number of skeins or balls required for the sweater. If the sweater hasn't been designed for a specific yarn company and isn't a vehicle for selling a particular brand, the pattern may simply call for yarn in a specific weight — for example, worsted weight (see Chapter 4).

- ✔ **The size and type of needles you need:** Often, needles in two sizes are listed — the smaller for cuffs and bottom borders and the larger for the body of the sweater. If the pattern uses double-pointed or a circular needle (say for a neckband or collar), or if the entire sweater is worked in the round, the pattern will tell you which size needle(s) to use and in what length.

  Following the particular needles specified, you always see written in CAPITAL LETTERS or *italics* the following phrase: OR SIZE TO OBTAIN GAUGE. Chapter 5 tells you everything you need to know about gauge and its importance.

- ✔ **Any special equipment or gadgets required:** Constructing some sweaters requires special tools — for example, cable needle, stitch markers, stitch holders, and so on. These tools are listed after the needles.

- ✔ **Buttons or other finishing materials:** If the sweater is a cardigan, the number and size of the buttons called for are listed. If there are pompoms, embroidery, or other embellishments, the materials needed to make them will be listed here.

Check over this list and make sure that you have what you need when you're purchasing yarn and needles for a project. This way, you won't find yourself unable to continue working on your project after the stores have closed because you don't have a particular tool in your supply box.

Gauge

Under the heading "Gauge," you find a formula that reads like this:

14 sts and 21 rows to 4" (10cm) over St st, using larger needles.

This is the gauge formula. It tells you how many stitches and rows are in a 4-inch square of the sweater fabric. If you want to make a sweater that corresponds to the measurements given, you must duplicate this gauge. (I can't say it enough!)

Special pattern stitches

If your sweater has any special pattern stitches or instructions, they may be listed and explained separately and not given again in the body of the instructions. For example, you may see the following:

Seed Stitch

Row 1 (RS): *K1, p1; rep from * to end

Row 2: K the purl sts and p the knits sts. Rep row 2 for pattern.

When you read in the instructions proper, "work seed stitch for 8 rows," come back to this section to find out how to work seed stitch.

Or a special abbreviation may be explained. For example, you may see the following:

C3R (cross 3 right): Sl 1 st to cn and hold to back, k2, p1 from cn.

When you come across C3R in your instructions, don't scratch your head and wonder, "What the heck?" Look in the opening information for an explanation.

The schematic

The *schematic* is a small outline drawing of each sweater piece in the pattern. The pattern usually includes one drawing that shows the body front and back with the neckline sketched in and another drawing of one sleeve. Cardigans usually show a single front, a back, and a sleeve. Listed along the edges of the drawing are the dimensions of the piece in each size — for example, the width and length of the sweater, the distance from the bottom of the sweater to the armhole, the depth of the armhole, and the depth and width of the neck. For examples of schematics, see Chapter 18.

These schematics are a big help. They show you the structure of the sweater at a glance: whether the armhole is straight or shaped and whether the sleeve cap is tall and narrow or short and wide. As you become more familiar with the way actual measurements fit you, you'll know quickly from the schematic whether you want to knit the pattern as is or make changes.

Knitting instructions

After all the introductory information, the instructions for knitting your sweater begin. In general, most patterns for cardigans and pullovers begin with the back piece. Here the pattern tells you how many stitches to cast on and what to do with them. The instructions are sequenced: They describe each step as you work from the bottom border to the shoulder. They tell you what pattern stitches or colors to work, *and* they tell you how to shape (increase or decrease) your piece.

If your sweater has a set-in sleeve and shaped armhole, the pattern will alert you that it's time to begin the shaping by interrupting the text with a boldface heading such as **"Shape armhole"** or **"Armhole shaping."**

After the instructions for the back, the pattern tells you how to make the front (or fronts if you're knitting a cardigan). Generally, the instructions for the front mirror those of the back until it's time to shape the front neckline. Following the front instructions are the instructions for the sleeves.

Finishing

This section of the pattern tells you what to do with your knitted pieces to make them into a sweater. It gives any special blocking instructions and tells the order in which to sew the pieces together. You also find instructions for additional sweater details: how to make the neckband, cardigan bands, collar, crochet edge, and so on.

Reading Charts

Depending on the design of the sweater and the way it's written, a sweater pattern may include a chart to show a stitch, cable, or color pattern. Or it may include a chart to show an unusual feature of a garment, such as a shawl collar.

A chart for a knitted piece uses a grid to represent stitches and rows. It's a picture of the *right* side of the knitted fabric. Every chart comes with a key that tells you how to work each stitch.

When you begin a chart, you start on a right-side row and follow the first row of the chart from right to left. When you work the next wrong-side row, you work the second row of the chart from left to right. Because the chart shows the right side of the fabric, on wrong-side rows you reverse knits and purls.

If the design uses a repeating pattern, the chart generally shows a single or double repeat and not the whole garment piece. Unless the number of stitches in the piece you're making is an exact multiple of the repeat, you'll have to begin and end on a part of the repeat. The chart indicates where you are to begin knitting the repeat.

Figure 13-1 shows a chart for a repeating color motif and indicates how you should use it.

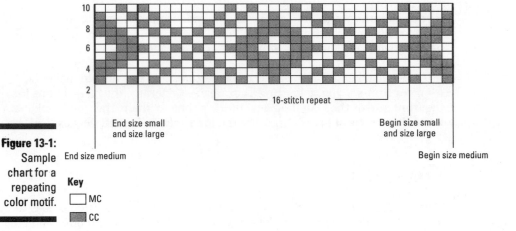

Figure 13-1:
Sample
chart for a
repeating
color motif.

Key

☐ MC

▧ CC

For details on specific kinds of charts, check the chapters that cover the various kinds of knitted stitch patterns.

Buy the longest self-stick notepads you can find and keep them with your knitting project. Use them to keep track of your place on the chart by sticking them along the row *above* the row you're currently working on. It helps you to orient yourself if you can see the rows on the chart that you've already worked.

On right-side rows, work the chart from right to left. On wrong-side rows, work the chart from left to right.

Words and pictures

If you collect vintage knitting patterns, you'll seldom see a chart or schematic. Instead, all the moves are painstakingly written out. Some people who began knitting under the row-by-written-row system regret its demise. Others of us welcome the picture over the written instructions.

The good news is that if you understand better when things are described with words, charts can be written out into word form — and vice versa. If you have a pattern with interminable and obscure directions, read them carefully with graph paper and pencil in hand, and make yourself a chart to better understand the text.

Chapter 14

Following the Blueprint: Knitting Your First Sweater

The moment has finally come. You can knit and purl, shape knitted pieces, manipulate stitches, make cables, and work colorful patterns. You have an idea of how the pieces of a sweater are shaped and fitted together. If you've read Chapter 13, you're now a member of the rarified circle of pattern decipherers. It's time to put yarn to needles and get going on that first sweater. Almost.

A few simple preparatory steps remain before you cast on the first stitch: deciding on the perfect size, determining your gauge, and drawing a quick diagram of your sweater pieces. Of course, you can forget these steps and jump right in, just as you can toss your map in the backseat and drive from Maine to California by following the sun. But your trip is likely to go more smoothly (and your sweater likely to turn out as you imagined) if, before leaving, you check your oil and tires, study your map, and highlight the route to follow. This approach may be less spontaneous, but once you're on the road, you won't hit any dead ends that halt your progress.

Gathering Your Materials

Choosing materials for your first sweater may be daunting if your local knitting store is a yarn and color wonderland. This section gives you some suggestions to help you narrow down the choices.

To knit your first sweater, you need three things: a good pattern, good yarn, and needles. If possible, look for your materials in a knitting shop rather than a department store. People who work in a yarn shop are generally very knowledgeable and can steer you to good pattern choices and quality yarn. If you run into any problems with the pattern or find that something confuses you, they'll most likely be delighted to help you figure it out. Here are some tips to give you a good start:

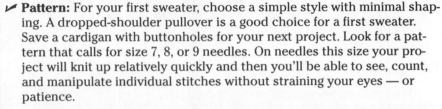

✔ **Pattern:** For your first sweater, choose a simple style with minimal shaping. A dropped-shoulder pullover is a good choice for a first sweater. Save a cardigan with buttonholes for your next project. Look for a pattern that calls for size 7, 8, or 9 needles. On needles this size your project will knit up relatively quickly and then you'll be able to see, count, and manipulate individual stitches without straining your eyes — or patience.

A child's sweater that knits up quickly is a good first sweater. You get to work through all the steps of sweater making in miniature — and little kids look great in anything, whether the sleeves match or not.

✔ **Yarn:** Find a pattern that calls for a medium-weight wool yarn. (If a pattern calls for size 7, 8, or 9 needles, the yarn will be medium weight). Wool is the best choice for a first sweater because it knits up easily, blocks beautifully, and looks wonderful. Choose a color on the lighter side so that it's easy to see individual stitches, and make sure that it's a pretty color.

If you're averse to wool for some reason, look into a blend of other natural fibers before turning to synthetics. Avoid all-cotton yarn for your first project unless you've been working up a lot of the smaller projects in this book and feel that you've had plenty of practice making stitches. Cotton yarn has little give and can be frustrating to work if your hands are new to needles and yarn. If you must use a 100 percent synthetic yarn, make it a yarn of good quality (check with the sales person at your local yarn shop for a recommendation) and resolve to be very careful in the blocking process. (You may want to take a quick look through Chapter 4 before you head to the yarn shop to choose materials for your first sweater.)

✔ **Needles:** If you're using straight needles, make sure that they're 14 inches long. If you have trouble with stitches slipping off your needles, choose wooden or plastic needles for your first project.

Before you leave the store, check the materials list in the pattern to see whether you need to have any other supplies at the ready, such as stitch holders, markers, a pompom maker, or a tapestry needle for sewing up seams or adding buttons.

Supplies to have handy

Keep the following supplies together in a zippered bag with your knitting projects, and you won't have to get up and hunt around for them when you'd rather be knitting. See Chapter 4 for more information about some of these tools.

ߦ Scissors

ߦ Safety pins

ߦ Tape measure and a small ruler

ߦ Ring markers

ߦ Crochet hook

ߦ Spare double-pointed needle

ߦ Scrap yarn (preferably a smooth, white cotton)

ߦ Tapestry needle

ߦ Pencil and paper

ߦ Calculator

It doesn't hurt to include an emery board for a renegade nail that keeps snagging on your yarn.

Before heading home, find a copy machine and photocopy your pattern. You'll want to be able to write on it freely. Keep the copy in a plastic sleeve to carry around with your knitting. The same goes for any charts that come with the pattern.

Preparing to Cast On

Now you're home. You crack open your bag, bring out a ball of yarn, lay your needles in the ready position beside you, and take up your knitting pattern. Sorry, it's time to cool your jets.

Before you put yarn to needles, you have a few small tasks to accomplish: determine the best size to make, check your gauge thoroughly, and if you want to be really thorough, make a diagram as shown in the sidebar "Finding the perfect size" later in this chapter.

Step 1: Be sizewise

Sit down with your materials and take your pattern in hand. Go past the section that says "Sizes" and look for "Knitted Measurements." Don't be tempted to choose a size arbitrarily; one designer's medium is another designer's small. Instead, choose the size in the pattern that most closely matches the size you want your garment to measure. Choose the size according to the bust or chest measurement. If you're not sure how many inches around your sweater should be, check the sidebar "Finding the perfect size" for ideas to help you determine your perfect size for a given style.

Finding the perfect size

If you're wondering whether 21 inches across the chest would fit better than 23 inches, there's an easy way to find out. There's a good chance that you've never measured your favorite sweater. Did you know that it measures 24 inches in width (48 inches in circumference) and 26 inches in length? Probably not. But now's the time to unfold it from the shelf (or dig it out of the pile on the chair), find your tape measure, and see what measurements feel good to you.

Obviously, if your most comfortable sweater is oversized and baggy and the sweater you're planning to knit is short and fitted, you won't use your favorite sweater as a starting point. Look through your closet for something that fits the way you envision your future sweater will fit, measure it, and compare the measurements to those given in the pattern. Or pocket your tape measure and head to your favorite sweater store. Fill your fitting room with sweaters, try them on, measure the ones that fit well, note the numbers in your knitting notebook, neatly refold the sweaters, and return them with a gracious smile to the salesperson. Go home ready to pick the measurements to knit to.

What if you're knitting for someone else and you don't have that person's favorite sweater on hand to measure? Unless you're making a present for this person, you can call and ask. If it's a gift and the person is of average height and build, you're probably safe knitting a medium.

One wonderful thing about knitted fabric is that it's forgiving. It stretches. You can even, in desperation, block it out or block it in — to a point. (See Chapter 15 for information about blocking.) Width is really the only measurement you need to be concerned with when you start your sweater. Length can be adjusted fairly easily once you're underway. It's worth a little (or a lot of) investigation time upfront to ensure that, at the long-awaited moment when the sweater pieces have been knit and blocked and sewn together, you have a masterpiece that fits.

Most patterns are written for more than one size. Generally, instructions for the smallest size are listed first, followed by those for the larger sizes. For example, if the instructions say, "Cast on 100 (112, 120, 128) stitches," you cast on 100 stitches for a size small, 112 stitches for a size medium, 120 for a size large, and 128 for a size extra-large.

When you've determined which set of measurements to make, get out a yellow highlighter or a pencil and carefully go through the pattern, marking every number that refers to your size. If you've made a copy of your pattern, you won't have to mark on the original.

Step 2: Find your gauge

Go to the section in your pattern that gives the required — that's *required* — gauge for the pattern. Check how the gauge in your pattern is measured: what size needles to use and what pattern stitch to work. To brush up on the process of measuring gauge, reread Chapter 5.

Always work your gauge swatch on the exact same needles and the very same yarn you'll use for your project, not just needles of the same size and/or the same yarn in a different color. Facsimiles can be misleading. Needles of the same size, but made out of different material, such as wood or Teflon-coated steel, can make a difference in the size of the stitch you make. After you've worked your swatch to a length of 5 inches or more, thread a piece of scrap yarn through the stitches on the needle. Block your swatch, ideally in the same manner you'll use to block your sweater (see Chapter 15). And then let it rest.

The big picture: Keeping track of where you are

Sweaters aren't knit in one sitting. No matter how much you love to knit, eventually you're going to have to put it down. For this reason, I highly recommend that you develop a system to remind yourself of where you're going and to help you keep track of where you are at the moment as you put down your knitting and pick it up again later.

My favorite method for tracking a sweater in progress involves making a diagram of whatever I'm working on. I'm indebted to Gertrude Taylor's book *America's Knitting Book* for the idea for this system. I read her book when I was in high school and have been diagramming sweaters ever since. What follows is my version of her system. A *diagram* is a quick outline drawing you make of your sweater piece. On it, you can show all the knitting information embedded in the text of your pattern. If your sweater pattern is a map of your entire sweater, the diagram you make is a map of the piece you're working on at the moment. It gives you an instant visual picture of where you are, where you're headed, and the steps you have to take to get there. (See the accompanying figure for an example.)

I usually work from a general diagram on plain white paper when I begin and move to graph paper when I get to the shaping area so I can chart out every stitch. Because most sweater patterns have you begin with the back, draw a

diagram for that piece first and enter the information that will remind you of the steps en route to the finished piece, such as the following:

- How many stitches to cast on
- How many inches to work in the border stitch
- Where to begin the armhole bind-off
- How many stitches to bind off
- How many stitches to decrease

As you work through the sweater, you can mark off your route as you go (doing so is helpful if you put your work down for a few days) and make notes on things you want to remember. If I'm working on a sweater with armhole shaping, for example, I note on my diagram the number of rows I've worked to the first shaping row. This way, when I'm working on the front, I know exactly how many rows to work for my piece to be the same as the back.

As I work through shaping, I can mark off my progress by checking off the decreases as I make them. When I reach the shoulder, I count the rows between the beginning of the armhole shaping and the shoulder and note it on my diagram, and then I finish any shoulder and neck shaping the pattern calls for. Now I have a map that I can use to make the front, up to the point of the neckline. Using my diagram, I can work the front as I did the back, following my notes.

(continued)

(continued)

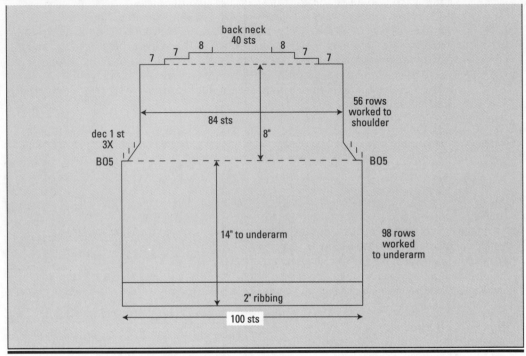

After the swatch has rested, it's time to measure it to determine your gauge. (See Chapter 5 for instructions on measuring a gauge swatch.)

✔ If you have more stitches per inch than the pattern calls for, go up one needle size.

✔ If you have fewer stitches per inch than the pattern calls for, go down one needle size.

Re-knit the swatch to ensure that the needle change has corrected your gauge for the pattern.

Tinker with your needle size until you come as close to the *stitch* gauge required by the pattern as you can. Stitch gauge determines how wide a sweater is. If you're off on stitch gauge, your sweater will be off widthwise. Once you've cast on and started knitting, you can't do much to make your sweater wider or narrower.

Row gauge *will* affect your sleeve shaping, raglan shaping, and the placement of a cable or other distinctive vertical pattern that might be interrupted in an awkward place if your row gauge is off. But there are ways to work around a not-so-perfect row gauge with a little diagramming and planning.

Knitting . . . at Last!

When you've read through the instructions and established your gauge, it's time to cast on and launch your sweater.

Knitting the back

Most sweater patterns instruct you to begin with the back. They tell you which needles to use to get started, how many stitches to cast on, and what stitches to begin with.

Here are some tips for getting started with this piece:

✔ For the two-strand cast-on method (see Chapter 1), allow 1 to 1½ inches for each stitch to be cast on, and add an extra 12 inches or so for a tail that you can later use to seam up the sweater. If the end gets in your way as you knit, make a butterfly with it. (See Chapter 4.)

✔ If you're working a rib, check that the pattern has the right number of stitches to give you a ribbing that meets up at the sides in a continuous fashion once it's seamed. For a 1 x 1 rib, you should have an even number of stitches; for a 2 x 2 rib, you should have a multiple of 4 plus 2 more.

✔ Cast-on edges take a lot of wear, and a well-worn and loved sweater can begin to fray or even break along the bottom edge. You can discourage this wear by casting on with a double strand of yarn (work the cast-on with two balls of yarn) and then continuing with a single strand.

After you've worked a few rows, take a look at the cast-on edge. You'll see that it looks different from each side: One side shows small neat bumps, and the other shows overlapping diagonal stitches. It's up to you to decide which side you prefer for the right side. If you use the two-strand cast-on and make the first row a right-side row, the little bumps will show on the right side. If you'd rather use the other side of the cast-on as the right side, make the first row of your knitting a wrong-side row.

If you're supposed to work the border of your sweater on smaller needles than the body of the sweater, your instructions will tell you when to change to larger ones. At the change row, simply knit the next row with one of the larger needles. When you come to the end of the row, use the other larger needle and put the smaller needles aside for the time being. Continue on in the stitch pattern(s) given in your pattern.

Measuring your piece

As accurate as your gauge swatch may be, knitting a piece so much larger than a swatch can throw off your careful measurements. For peace of mind, take a gauge reading after you've worked a good 4 inches or so. Work to the halfway point in your row so that you can spread out the stitches along both needles to the width of the fabric. Lay out your piece on a flat surface and measure it. If it's supposed to measure 22 inches across, check to see that it does.

When it's time to measure the length of your piece, work to the center of the row, lay the piece flat, and measure it from the very bottom — the first row — to the knitting needle. Take your measurement somewhere in the middle, not on the edge. Your edges will be more stretched and wobbly and not as stable as the center knitting.

Using a row marker when shaping an armhole

If your sweater has a shaped armhole, the instructions will tell you when to begin the armhole shaping. Before starting any decreasing, put a safety pin into one of the stitches on the needle to mark the beginning of the armhole. You'll measure from that mark when you're determining the depth of the armhole.

Continue to work the back until you've worked the number of inches given in your pattern to the shoulder. If the shoulder is shaped, work the shoulder shaping. If not, bind off the shoulders and back neck or leave the shoulder stitches on a holder for the three-needle bind-off (see Chapter 15). If your pattern has a straight shoulder bind-off and you'd prefer it with shaped shoulders, see the sidebar "Sloping the shoulders."

At this point, you have completed your sweater back. You're a quarter of the way to a finished sweater — and you have a useful tool. You now have a *very accurate* gauge swatch. Block the back (see Chapter 15) and have it at the ready. You may need to measure the gauge one more time.

Knitting the front

The front of a pullover is generally worked in the same way as the back as far as the neckline.

If you took the trouble to count rows as you knitted up the back and you make the front the exact same number of rows, you can use the nearly invisible and fun-to-do mattress stitch to seam them together (see Chapter 15). If, on the other hand, you rely on measuring your pieces to check their sameness, you won't necessarily have the *exact* same number of rows in both front and back pieces, and you'll have to seam up your sweater by using the less-than-wonderful back stitch (again, see Chapter 15). Ah, well.

Safety pins can help you keep track of the number of rows you've worked. Pin the first stitch from which you want to count. Then, as you knit, stop every once in a while, count 20 rows, and pin the next stitch. If you pin a stitch every 20 rows, it's easy to keep track of the row number, and you won't have to count from the very beginning each time.

Sloping the shoulders

If your pattern is designed with a straight shoulder and you want it to angle up slightly from shoulder edge to neck, changing your pattern is easy. Instead of binding off all the shoulder stitches at once, bind off several groups of stitches over several rows in stair-step fashion.

For an average gauge of 4 to 6 stitches an inch, three steps will make a good slope. Divide the number of stitches for one shoulder by three to determine how many stitches to bind off for each shoulder step. If the number of stitches in the shoulder isn't evenly divisible by three, make the first two steps the same number of stitches and the third step at the neckline the odd one.

On a piece of graph paper, mark off enough squares in a horizontal line to represent the right shoulder and fill in the steps. (If you have enough room on your graph paper, map out enough squares to represent the back neck and both shoulders, too.) See the accompanying figure.

When you reach the shoulder and are ready to bind off, with the right side facing, bind off the number of stitches for the first "step" at the beginning of the next two rows. Then bind off the number of stitches for the second step at the beginning of the next two rows. Then bind off the remaining shoulder stitches at the beginning of the next two rows. Finally, bind off the back neck stitches.

Some patterns with straight shoulders tell you to bind off all the stitches on the last row of the back piece and don't distinguish shoulder stitches from back-neck stitches. If the instructions don't give specific numbers for shoulder stitches, look at the final line in the instructions for the front. There you should be able to find the number of stitches remaining for each shoulder after you've worked the neckline shaping.

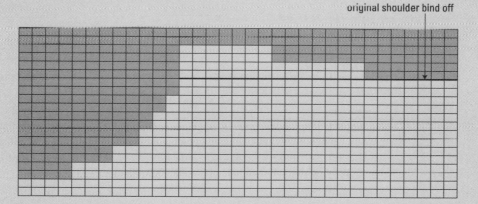

original shoulder bind off

Your pattern will tell you to work the front until it measures a certain length and to "end with a WS (wrong-side) row." You'll begin the neckline on the next (right-side) row.

To shape a neckline, you begin by binding off a group of stitches at the center of your sweater piece. Your pattern will tell you "join a 2nd ball of yarn" before you begin to bind them off. You'll need 2 balls of yarn to work the remainder of the neckline, one for each side. To join the second ball of yarn, simply start knitting and binding off with the strand from the second ball. When you return to shape the left side of your neckline, pick up and use the yarn from the first ball.

At this point, get out the graph paper again. It's helpful to chart the neckline shaping stitch by stitch, especially if the shoulders are shaped as well. Often, the shoulder shaping begins while the neckline is still being worked (your pattern will read "at the same time"), and having a chart in front of you will make it clear what you should be doing and when. See the sidebar "Charting neckline and shoulder shaping" for an example.

Knitting sleeves

When you've worked your way to the sleeves, you're almost home free. Sleeves are smaller than body parts and go quickly. And shaping makes them interesting to do.

In general, sleeves begin at the cuff, are worked in the same stitch patterns as the back and front, and are shaped by regular increases along the sides. Your pattern will tell you how many stitches to cast on, what stitch to work, when to change needles to a larger size if required, when to begin increasing, and how often to increase. In general, patterns instruct you to increase at regular row intervals, although sometimes they tell you to increase at intervals measured in inches.

Here are some tips for knitting sleeves:

- ✔ If you work the increases two stitches in from the edges, seaming your sleeve will be a breeze. You'll have a straight line of undistorted stitches to work with. Here's how to work the increase row: k2, m1 (using your favorite increase), work across to the last 2 stitches, m1, k2.

- ✔ Using two balls of yarn and one needle, cast on for two sleeves and work them both at the same time. Doing so ensures that you'll end up with identical pieces. Cast on the number of stitches required for one sleeve. With the second ball of yarn, cast on the same number of stitches on the same needle. Work each sleeve with its own ball of yarn.

- ✔ If you're working a sweater with a dropped shoulder, you can pick up stitches along the armhole edge of the body and knit down, saving yourself from having to sew the sleeve to the body. (Find out about picking up stitches in Chapter 16.) You'll have to check to see how many stitches your sleeve is supposed to have when you've worked all the increases. This is the number to pick up. Work a good inch before you begin decreasing.

Once in a while, you may run into a glitch in sleeve making if the pattern tells you to increase every so many rows and your row gauge is different from the designer's. Your sleeve may measure the correct length before you have worked all the necessary increases. You'll have a sleeve that's the right *length* but the wrong *width* at the armhole.

Charting neckline and shoulder shaping

Here's a set of sample instructions for front neck and shoulder shaping and a chart drawn from them:

> Next row (RS): Work 27 sts, join 2nd ball of yarn and bind off center 15 sts, work to end. Working both sides at once, bind off from each neck edge 3 sts once, 2 sts twice, then dec 1 st every other row twice AT SAME TIME when piece measures same length as back to shoulder, shape shoulder as for back.

The instructions given for the shoulder shaping for the back are as follows: Bind off 9 sts at beg of next 6 rows. The accompanying figure shows this pattern charted.

You'll be shaping the right and left sides of your piece on different rows. Your shaping will be symmetrical but off by one row. You can see this by checking the bind offs at either side of the center front neck edge.

where back shoulder bind offs begin

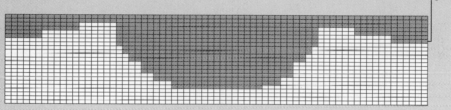

If you're working an angled or shaped-sleeve cap, the top of your sleeve needs to fit *exactly* into the carved-out shape in the sweater body. To ensure that your sleeve will be the correct length *and* width when you reach the armhole, graph it. (You can buy large sheets of graph paper at an artist's supply store or simply tape two pieces together lengthwise.) If you're working a cable or lace pattern that requires a certain number of stitches, graphing your sleeve offers the further advantage of helping you see when you will have increased enough stitches to begin working the pattern over them.

To graph a sleeve, follow these steps:

1. **Draw a line at the bottom of your graph paper to represent the first row after the bottom rib or border of the cuff has been completed. Mark the center.**

2. **Go to the sweater back you've finished and blocked and take a new and improved gauge reading. Subtract the cuff measurement from the length your sleeve should measure to the armhole. Multiply the row gauge per inch by the length your sleeve should measure from the end of the rib or border to the underarm.**

3. **Count this number of rows from your bottom line and mark the top row to represent the underarm. At the underarm mark, count out a horizontal line of squares to represent the width your sleeve should be at this point, making sure that the centers of top and bottom rows are aligned.**

4. **Mark a row about 1 inch below the underarm. Then check your pattern for the first increase row and mark it.**

   The rows of squares between the marked rows represent the number of rows you have in which to make your increases.

5. **Draw in the rest of the increases.**

   If you get them all in *before* reaching the top line, you're all set. If not, reconfigure the increases so that they're closer together, and you can be sure of ending up with the correct number of stitches when your sleeve measures the right length.

Figure 14-1 shows a chart of a sleeve with increases.

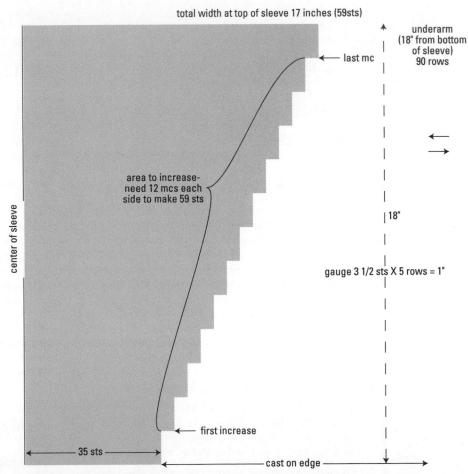

total width at top of sleeve 17 inches (59sts)

last mc

underarm
(18" from bottom
of sleeve)
90 rows

area to increase-
need 12 mcs each
side to make 59 sts

18"

gauge 3 1/2 sts X 5 rows = 1"

center of sleeve

first increase

35 sts

cast on edge

Figure 14-1:
Charting a
sleeve with
increases
(looking at
the right half
of the
sleeve).

When you've completed your back, front, and sleeves, you're ready to finish your sweater. Turn to Chapter 15 for instructions.

Chapter 15

Fearless Finishing: Putting It All Together

In This Chapter
▶ Knowing what to do with loose ends
▶ Blocking (shaping and smoothing) your sweater pieces
▶ Seaming your pieces together

*W*hen you've finished making the various pieces of your project, whether the back and front panels of a pillow or the sleeves of a sweater, you've reached the Cinderella moment. Time to turn those crumpled, curling, lumpy knitted pieces sprouting the odd end of yarn into smooth, flat, even pieces waiting to be joined into a beautifully crafted item. No matter what's gone before, the finishing is what makes or breaks the final product.

For people who love to knit, weaving in ends, blocking, and seaming aren't exciting because they aren't knitting. However, once you know how to finish your pieces neatly, you'll have the expertise necessary to make the finishing process, if not exactly a pleasure, at least a manageable interval between the end of knitting one project and the beginning of a new one. And the pleasure that comes from seeing your Fairy Godmother powers at work will inspire kinder feelings toward this part of the process.

To properly finish your knitting projects, you need to know how to do three basic things:

✔ Weave in the loose ends of yarn that you left hanging when you changed colors or when you had to start a new ball of yarn.

✔ Block your knitting to smooth out your stitches and to set the shapes of your pieces.

✔ Join your knitted pieces together if you're making anything more complicated than a scarf or a potholder.

The purpose of this chapter is to introduce you to the techniques you need to know so that you can finish your knitting like a pro.

Tying Up Loose Ends

The first step in the finishing process is taking care of all the loose ends hanging about. If you've managed to make all the yarn changes at the side edges, that's where you'll find most of the ends. Otherwise, you'll have loose ends scattered here and there that require different techniques for successfully making them disappear.

Although there are various techniques for weaving in ends (and weave you must; there's no getting around it), keep in mind that your goal is a nice smooth fabric without glitches or an unattractive ridge in the middle of your knitting. You can hide your loose ends by doing the following:

- Weaving them vertically up the side edges
- Weaving them in sideways on the wrong side of the fabric
- Weaving them in along a bound-off edge

Use whichever method will safely tuck in your ends *and* result in a smooth, unblemished right side. Every situation (thickness of yarn, location of join) is different. Try the techniques in this section, and if you discover something that works better in a given circumstance, use it.

Don't try to weave in 6-inch yarn ends. With wool yarn, running a yarn end in over 3 or 4 stitches is enough to secure it. The fuzzy nature of the fibers helps the woven ends "stick" to the back of the fabric. With slick yarns, such as rayon and polished cotton, you need to weave in longer ends to prevent them from working their way out. But five to six ins and outs should be sufficient.

Weaving them up the sides

If you have joined yarns at the side edges by knotting the two ends together, follow these steps to weave in the ends:

1. **Untie the knot.**

    Don't worry. Your knitting won't unravel.

2. **Thread one end through the tapestry needle and weave it down the side loops at the edge of your knitting.**

3. **Thread the second end through the tapestry needle and weave it up the side loops at the edge of your knitting. (See Figure 15-1.)**

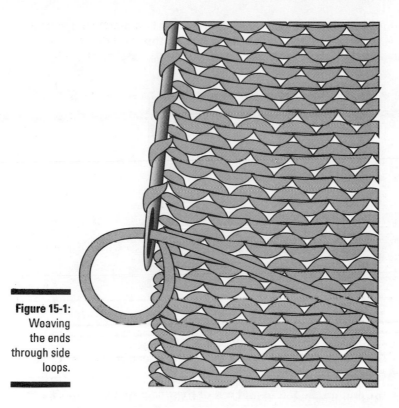

Figure 15-1:
Weaving
the ends
through side
loops.

If rather than knotting your two ends together, you've joined them by working the two strands together for the edge stitch, use a tapestry needle to pick out one of the ends and then weave it up the side as outlined in the preceding steps. Weave the other end in the opposite direction. However, if the two strands are thin and won't add much bulk to the edge stitch, don't bother to pick out the extra thread. Just weave each end in up and down the sides in opposite directions.

If for some reason you've left an end that's too short to comfortably thread through a needle, run your needle through the appropriate nearby loops as if it were threaded. With the eye of the needle at the short yarn end, finagle the yarn end through the eye of the tapestry needle and pull the needle through the loops. The end will be woven in and secured.

Weaving the ends horizontally

If you switched yarns in the middle of a row and have loose ends dangling there, you need to weave the ends in horizontally. Untie the knot or pick out one of the stitches if you've worked a stitch with a double strand of yarn.

Take a careful look at those by-now very familiar purl bumps. You'll notice that the tops of the purl stitches look like "over" bumps and the running threads between the stitches look like "under" bumps. See Figure 15-2.

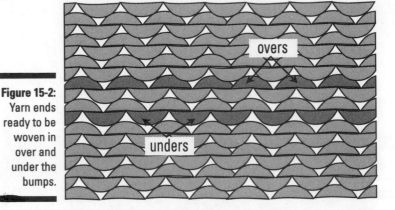

Figure 15-2:
Yarn ends ready to be woven in over and under the bumps.

Using a tapestry needle, weave the ends in as follows:

1. **Weave the end on the right in and out of the *under* bumps, working to the left.**

2. **Weave the end on the left in and out of the *under* bumps, working to the right.**

   The ends will cross each other, filling in the gap between the old yarn and the new. See Figure 15-3.

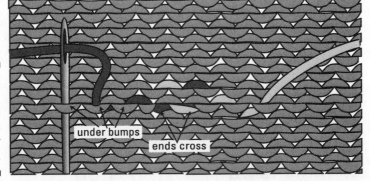

Figure 15-3:
Threading the strand through the under bumps.

Work fairly loosely so as not to pull the fabric in any way. Check the right side of the fabric to make sure that it looks smooth.

Tweaking Vs

As you're weaving in ends, keep an eye out for loose or misshapen stitches on the right (front) side of your fabric. While you're holding the tapestry needle, you can tweak them back into line by using the tip of your needle to adjust the legs of the stitch, as shown in the following figure.

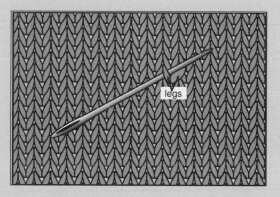

Remember that a row of stitches is connected. If you have a loose or sloppy stitch, you can pull on the legs of the neighboring Vs in either direction for as many stitches as you need to in order to redistribute the extra yarn. If one side of the V is distorted or larger than the other, you can pull slightly on the other side or tweak the stitch in whatever way is necessary to even it out.

You don't need to get too fussy about this. Blocking straightens any general and minor unevenness, but sometimes, especially in color work, the stitches around the color changes can use a little extra help.

If your yarn is particularly slippery, weave in the end following the path of the neighboring stitches around the under and over bumps, as shown in Figure 15-4. This creates a little extra bulk, but it completely secures the strand.

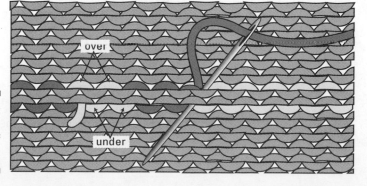

Figure 15-4:
Following the path of the stitch.

Once your ends are worked into the fabric, snip them about ½ inch from the surface and gently stretch and release the fabric to pull the tail into the fabric.

Weaving ends into a bound-off edge

When you're weaving in an end at a bound-off edge that forms a curve, you can weave in the end in a way that creates an uninterrupted line of bound off stitches. For example, you can use this technique where you've joined a second ball of yarn at the start of neckline shaping or on the final bound off stitch of a neckband worked on a circular needle. Follow these steps:

1. **Thread a tapestry needle with the yarn end.**

2. **Notice the chain of interconnected Vs that form the bound off edge and go under the legs of the first V next to the loose end and back through the initial stitch, mimicking the path of a bound-off stitch. (See Figure 15-5.)**

3. **Finish weaving in the end by running the needle under the series of V-legs along one side of the bound-off edge.**

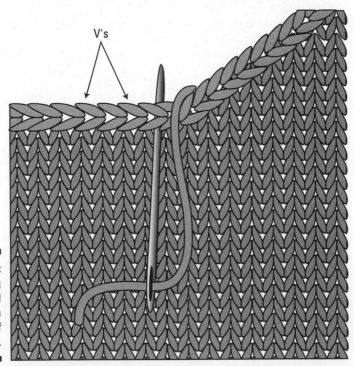

Figure 15-5: Weaving in an end along a bound-off edge.

When you knit pieces to be sewn together later, leave a tail that's long enough to use for joining the pieces smoothly.

One final thing to check before you're ready to block are any stitches left "open" to be sewn or grafted together later. If you've put them on a pin-type stitch holder, re-thread them, using a tapestry needle, onto a colorfast piece of scrap yarn long enough that you can knot it without bunching up the stitches. When you're blocking, you want your pieces to lie nice and flat.

Better Blocking

When you *block* a piece of knitting, you wet it down or steam it to coax it into its final shape, letting the moisture and/or heat smooth out all the uneven stitches and straighten out wavy rolling edges. Blocking is crucial to the final look of your work. All those long hours of careful stitch creation deserve your best efforts now.

Don't try and seam up your sweater before you block the pieces. Curling edges make it hard to see what you're doing. If you're ready to block something you've knit in the round, move on to the section on three-dimensional blocking presented later in this chapter to find out what to do next.

Getting your blocking equipment together

You can block any knitted fabric as long as you have a tape measure and a large, flat surface on which to spread out your pieces — such as a bed or a spot on the floor that pets or children won't disturb. But you'll find the job more pleasant to undertake and get better results if you invest in a bit of blocking equipment. See Chapter 4 for more information on any of the specialized equipment presented in this section. You need the following whether you wet-block or steam your pieces:

- A large, flat, preferably padded surface for laying out your pieces — at least a little larger than the knitted piece itself
- Blocking wires (You can block your pieces without these. But you'll have much nicer results if you invest in a set.)
- Pins (preferably T-pins) to hold your knitted fabric to the blocking board. Don't use pins with colorful plastic heads, the steam will melt them.
- A tape measure so that you can block your pieces to the correct size
- A steam iron or spray bottle for water

✔ A large towel if you're wet blocking

✔ Schematic drawings of your pieces so that you can determine the exact shape you need

Steam, dunk, or spray? Deciding which blocking method to use

There are different methods for blocking, and the best one to use depends on the fiber of your yarn, the amount of time you have, and the stitch pattern you've used. You can wet block just about anything that's colorfast with superb results. Steam blocking is faster than wet blocking and is fine for sweaters in stockinette stitch and not susceptible to steam damage. But don't use it on acrylics or for stitch patterns with texture you want to highlight. Read through this list to identify the type of knitting you need to block and then go on to the appropriate sections later in this chapter to find out exactly how to steam or wet-block.

✔ **Noncolorfast yarns:** You can wet- or spray-block just about anything with superior results — *except* yarn that you suspect may be less than colorfast. Before blocking a striped or color-patterned sweater, wet a 20-inch sample of each color and wrap the strands around a paper towel. Let them dry. If any of the colors bleed onto the paper, forget wet blocking. Steam the pieces and send the completed sweater to the dry cleaner when it needs a wash.

✔ **Mohair and other fuzzy yarns:** Wet-block fuzzy yarns such as mohair. Steam will flatten them. When they dry, you can gently run a special mohair brush, or your own hairbrush, over them. Use a light touch.

✔ **Wool, cotton, and blended yarns:** You can steam-block wool, cotton, and many blends with great success. Steaming is quicker and easier than wet blocking but requires care and attention.

✔ **Synthetic yarns:** *Don't* steam a synthetic yarn. It will die before your eyes. Too much steam-heat destroys a synthetic yarn's resilience. Talk about Cinderella — too much steam-heat is like the clock striking midnight for synthetics.

✔ **Cabled and/or richly textured sweaters**: No matter the fiber, these are best wet blocked with the right side facing up. While the sweater pieces are damp, you can mold and sculpt the 3-D patterns. Steaming will flatten them somewhat.

With so many blended yarns on the market and new kinds of fibers in novelty yarns, caution is critical. If you have any doubts about the fiber of your yarn and how it will respond to heat, experiment on your gauge swatch before working on your sweater. You'll quickly know whether steam enhances or ruins your yarn.

Wet blocking

When you wet-block a knitted piece, you get it completely wet in a sink or basin of water. (You can take this opportunity to add a little gentle soap to the water and swish out whatever dirt and grime your piece may have picked up while you worked on it. Just be sure to give it several good rinses.) Then follow these steps:

1. **Drain the water from the sink, press on the piece to eliminate a little of the water, and lift it out as a piece without letting any part of it stretch down. Press the piece between your palms to squeeze a little more water out of it, but don't wring it.**

   Have a large towel at the ready.

2. **Spread out your piece on the towel without stretching it, fold the ends of the towel over it, and gently and loosely roll up the towel to absorb a little more water.**

   You don't want to get the piece too dry. It should be more wet than damp — just not dripping wet — when you lay it out to block. If you roll too tightly, you'll have creases in your knitted piece.

3. **If you're using blocking wires, unroll the piece and weave in the wires along the edges.**

   Blocking wires come with instructions on how best to do this.

4. **Gently lay your piece out on the blocking board.**

   For a stockinette piece, lay it face down on the blocking board; for a textured or cabled sweater, lay it right side up. If your board has a cover with a grid, line up the centerlines of your pieces with the grid.

5. **Using your schematic for reference and the grid as a guide, starting at the center, spread your piece out to the correct dimensions without distorting the direction of the stitches.**

   If you're blocking a sweater, check that your piece is the right width and the correct length from the bottom edge to the beginning of the armhole and from the beginning of the armhole to the shoulder. (See Figure 15-6.) Pin all pieces in a few places to keep them flat. Run your palms lightly over the piece to help keep everything smooth and even.

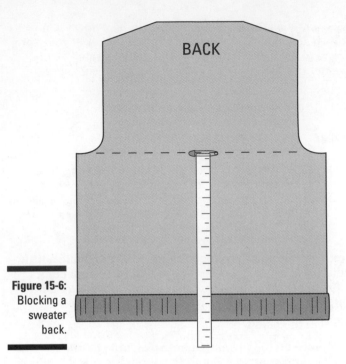

BACK

Figure 15-6:
Blocking a
sweater
back.

6. **Sculpt your piece while it's wet.**

   • If your design has a ribbed border, decide how much you want the rib to hug you. If you want it to pull in as much as possible, keep the rib compressed. If you want it to pull in only slightly or to hang fairly straight, pin it out completely to the width of the piece.

   • If you're blocking a cabled or highly textured piece, pinch and mold the contours of the cable crossings to highlight their three-dimensional qualities.

   • If your piece is lace, spread out the fabric so that the openings are really open.

   • If the bottom edge of your piece is scalloped or pointed, pin out the waves or points.

7. **Go away and start another sweater while this one dries.**

   Drying may take a day or so.

If you're in a hurry, you can get your piece to dry in a matter of hours by placing a fan in front of it. The bigger the fan, the quicker it dries. A window fan will do the trick in no time.

Wet-blocking identical pieces

When you're blocking two pieces that should be identical — cardigan fronts and sleeves, for example — lay them out side by side if you have enough space and measure back and forth or line them up on symmetrical gridlines for comparison. Figure 15-7 shows you how to line up cardigan fronts.

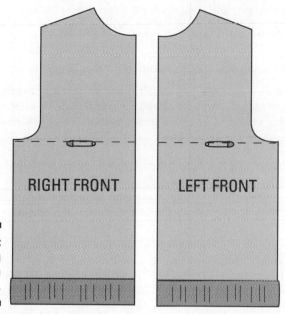

RIGHT FRONT   LEFT FRONT

Figure 15-7:
Blocking
cardigan
fronts.

If you're short on blocking space, you can lay out fronts and sleeves one at a time on top of each other to ensure that they'll be identical when dry. When they're still damp, but not dry, you can move the top piece off and lay it down gently to the side for the last stages of drying.

If you decide to block one piece at a time, you can still ensure that your pieces will be blocked to identical dimensions. Block the first piece according to the dimensions on your diagram. When it's dry, but before taking it off the board, stick straight pins into the blocking board to mark the outline of the piece you're removing. Put them in at strategic points (bottom right and left corners, top right and left corners) to show the corners of the outline. Then lay down the next piece within the parameter of the pins.

Spray blocking

Spray blocking is much like wet blocking. (Read the preceding two sections for a few more details.) Just follow these steps:

1. **If you're using blocking wires, thread them along the side edges.**

2. **Spread out your knitted piece(s) on your blocking board, wrong side up for stockinette or right side up for texture and cables.**

3. **Align and measure until you have everything straight.**

4. **Pin the edges every few inches (if you're not using blocking wires), or closer together if you see that the edge is rolling severely between pins.**

5. **With a clean spray bottle filled with room-temperature water, spray and spray your piece. Press gently with your hands to even out the fabric, pinching and molding any three-dimensional details.**

6. **Let the sweater dry.**

   This usually takes a day or two depending on the thickness of the project, general humidity, and so on.

7. **When your piece is dry, remove it from the blocking board.**

Steam blocking

Follow these steps to steam-block a piece:

1. **Lay out your knitted piece as described in the "Wet blocking" section.**

2. **With a steam iron, hover over the piece about ½ inch away from the surface.**

   You want the steam to penetrate the piece without the weight of the iron pressing down on it. If your knitting is cotton, you can let the iron touch the fabric very lightly, but keep it moving and don't let the full weight of the iron lay on the surface.

3. **After steaming, let your pieces rest and dry for at least half an hour.**

Three-dimensional blocking

Not all knitting is flat. Still, all knitting needs to be blocked.

For sweaters worked in the round, you can use wet blocking, spray blocking, or steam blocking. Lay out the completed sweater, arranging it according to the dimensions of your schematic. If you plan to make most of your sweaters in the round, consider investing in a *wooly board* — an adjustable wooden frame with arms that you can dress in your wet sweater. After the sweater dries, take it off the frame and — voilà! — your sweater is flat, smooth, and even.

Hats can be steamed while they lie flat, one side at a time. Or find a mixing bowl that's the right size, wet your hat, and drape it over the upside-down bowl to dry. If you've made a tam or beret, you can block it over a dinner plate. Be inventive!

If you plan to knit a lot of socks and mittens, add blockers to your next Christmas or birthday list. Blockers are wooden sock and mitten-shaped templates with biscuit-type holes cut out to aid air circulation. They come in various sizes for your different projects. Simply wet down your socks or mittens, pull them on over the forms, and let them dry to smooth perfection.

Assembling the Pieces

After you've blocked your sweater or project, it's time to put them together. You can choose between techniques that mimic and work with knitted stitches or traditional sewing methods.

- ✔ If you opt for the sewing method, turn to the end of this section for an explanation of the backstitch and how to use it to sew sweater pieces together.
- ✔ If you choose the more knitterly techniques, the ones you use will be determined by how the stitches are coming together: head to head, side to side, or head to side. See Figure 15-8.

When you've completed seaming your sweater pieces together, no matter what method you use, steam all the seams, pressing down on them with your fingertips to encourage them to lie flat.

Understanding the basic techniques

The techniques in this section help you join your pieces together in ways becoming to knitting. These techniques work with the structure of the stitches creating 'seams' that are smooth and flexible.

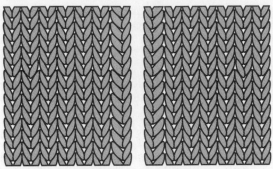

Stitches side-to-side

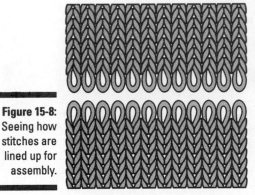

Figure 15-8:
Seeing how
stitches are
lined up for
assembly.

Stitches head-to-head

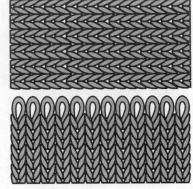

Stitches head-to-side

Joining stitches head to head

The two techniques in this section show you how to join sets of stitches that meet head to head. The *three-needle bind-off* is the quickest and easiest method and creates a stable — and visible — seam. It's great for shoulders. *Grafting* stitches head to head creates a very stretchy and almost invisible join. It's a good technique to use when you want to give the illusion of uninterrupted fabric, say when joining the center back seam of a scarf you've worked in two pieces.

Three-needle bind-off

Use this quick technique when you're joining stitches head to head. You get to do two things at once: bind off and join two pieces together — perfect for joining shoulder seams. To do the three-needle bind-off, you need three needles: one each to hold the shoulder stitches and one for working the actual bind-off. If you don't have three needles of the same size, use a smaller one for holding the stitches of one or both of the pieces to be bound off, and use the regular-size needle for binding off.

To work the three-needle bind-off, thread the open stitches of your pieces onto a needle — one for each piece. If you've left a long tail end (about four times the width of the stitches to be joined), you can use it to work the bind off. Thread your first needle through the stitches on the first piece so the point comes out where the tail is. When you're threading the second needle through the second piece, make sure your needle tips will point in the same direction when your pieces are arranged right sides together as shown in Figure 15-9. If you haven't left a tail end for this maneuver, you can start working with a fresh strand and weave in the end later.

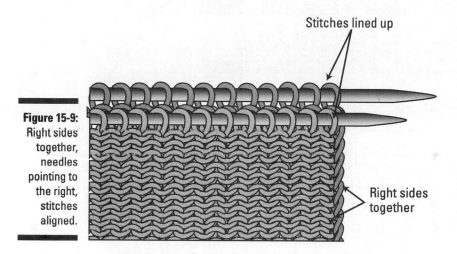

Stitches lined up

Figure 15-9:
Right sides together, needles pointing to the right, stitches aligned.

Right sides together

You will be knitting and binding off the same way you usually would, but working stitches from two LH needles at the same time instead of one. Follow these steps:

1. **Insert the third needle knitwise (as if you were knitting) into the first stitch on *both* needles, as shown in Figure 15-10.**

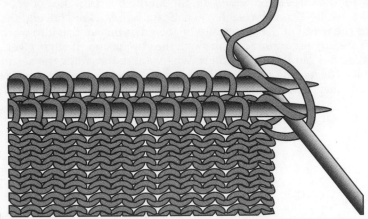

Figure 15-10: Inserting the RH needle into the first stitch on both needles.

2. **Wrap the yarn around the RH needle as if to knit, and draw the loop through both stitches.**

3. **Knit the next pair of stitches together in the same way.**

4. **Using the tip of either LH needle, go into the first stitch knitted on the RH needle and lift it over the second stitch and off the needle, as shown in Figure 15-11.**

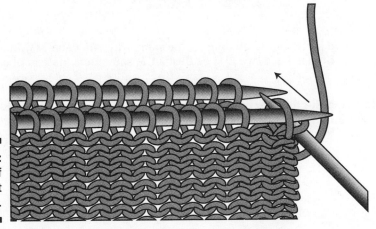

Figure 15-11: Binding off the first stitch.

5. **Continue to knit 2 stitches together from the LH needles and bind off one.**

Grafting stitches head to head

Grafting (also known as the Kitchener stitch) is another way to join two knitted pieces when their stitches meet head to head. It's a way to "mock" knitting by using a tapestry needle — grafting creates an essentially invisible seam. The smoothest join — and also the stretchiest — is made by grafting "live" stitches (stitches that haven't been bound off yet) together. But you can also graft two bound-off edges if you want more stability. Just work the same steps for grafting live stitches, working in and out of the stitches just below the bound-off row.

If you plan to graft live stitches, don't bind off on the final row. Instead, leave a yarn tail for grafting about four times the width of the piece and, with a tapestry needle, run a piece of scrap yarn through the live stitches to secure them while you block your pieces. Blocking "sets" the stitches, enabling you to pull out the scrap yarn without fear of the stitches unraveling. If you're working with a slippery yarn and the stitches want to pull out of their loops even after blocking, leave the scrap yarn in the loops and pull it out one or two stitches at a time as you graft them.

Follow these steps to graft your pieces:

1. **Line up the pieces right sides up with the stitches head to head.**

2. **Thread a tapestry needle with the working yarn.**

   If you've left a tail on the side you'll begin grafting from, use it. If not, start a fresh strand and weave in the end later. You'll be grafting the stitches from right to left. If you're more comfortable working left to right, or your yarn tail is at the other end, you can reverse direction.

   Use a tapestry needle with a blunt tip for any kind of seaming on knits. Sharp points can too easily pierce the yarn. Always aim to go in and out and around stitches when you sew pieces together.

3. **Starting in the bottom piece, insert the needle *up* through the first loop on the right and pull the yarn through.**

4. **Insert the needle *up* through the first loop on the right of the upper piece and pull the yarn through (Steps 3 and 4 are pictured in Figure 15-12).**

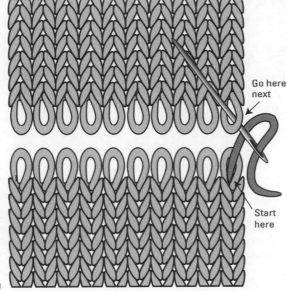

Go here
next

Start
here

Figure 15-12:
Inserting the
needle up
through the
edge
stitches.

5. **Insert the needle *down* into the first loop on the bottom piece (the same loop you began in) and come *up* through the loop next to it. Pull the yarn through.**

6. **Insert the needle *down* into the first loop on the upper piece (the same one you came up from before) and *up* through the stitch next to it. Pull the yarn through.**

   See Steps 5 and 6 pictured in Figure 15-13.

7. **Repeat Steps 5 and 6.**

   Follow the rhythm down and up, down and up, as you move from one piece to the other. Once you get going, you'll be able to see the mock stitches you're making, as shown in Figure 15-14.

8. **When you come to the last stitches, insert the needle *down* into the last stitch on the bottom piece and then *down* into the last stitch on the top piece. Run the end along the side loops and snip.**

Except for the first step, you will go through two stitches on each piece — the stitch you've already come up through and the new stitch right next to it — before changing to the other piece. Work at an even tension, trying to match the size of the stitches you're marrying. If you find any grafted stitches that look out of kilter with the rest, you can go back with the tip of your needle and tweak them, working out any unevenness.

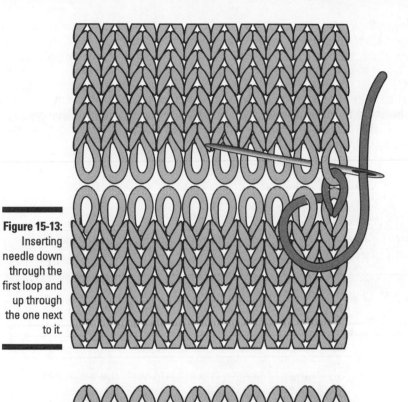

Figure 15-13:
Inserting needle down through the first loop and up through the one next to it.

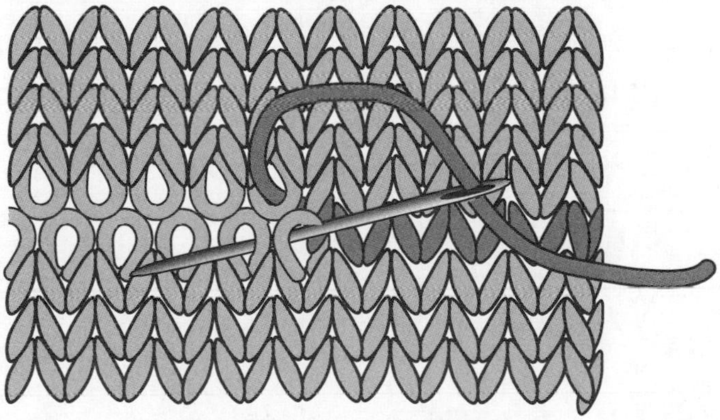

Figure 15-14:
Completed grafting stitches.

Joining stitches side to side with mattress stitch

Mattress stitch makes a practically invisible and nicely flexible seam. You can't use it successfully, however, on pieces that don't have the same number — within one or two — of rows. It's worth keeping track of your rows when working backs and fronts to be able to join them at the sides using this wonderful technique.

To join knitted pieces with the mattress stitch, lay out your pieces side to side next to each other, right sides facing up, bottom edges toward you. You seam from the bottom edge up. If you've left a tail of yarn at the cast-on edge, you can use it to get started.

To work mattress stitch, you need to be able to recognize the running threads between the first 2 edge stitches. If you gently pull these stitches apart, you'll see the series of little horizontal — running — threads connecting them, as shown in Figure 15-15.

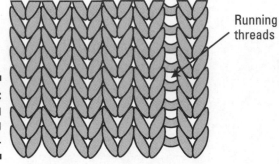

Running threads

Figure 15-15: Identifying the running threads.

Thread the strand on a tapestry needle. Working through the two threads on the cast-on row, join the bottom edge of the pieces using a figure eight, as shown in Figure 15-16. The direction you work the figure eight depends on which piece your yarn is coming from.

Figure 15-16: Joining the bottom edge with a figure 8 for mattress stitch.

To work the mattress stitch, follow these steps:

1. **Locate the running thread (look back to Figure 15-15) between the first and second stitch on the bottom row of one piece.**

2. **Bring your needle under the thread; then pick up the running thread between the first and second stitch on the opposing piece, as shown in Figure 15-17.**

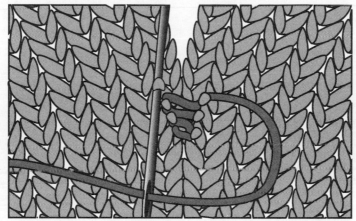

Figure 15-17:
Picking up the running thread in mattress stitch.

3. **Work back and forth from running thread to running thread to running thread, keeping the tension easy but firm.**

    Check by pulling laterally on the seam from time to time. The amount of give should be the same as between 2 stitches.

When you've finished your seam, take a moment to admire it.

Grafting stitches head to side

This method makes a smooth and weightless seam. As in head-to-head grafting, you make a mock knit stitch, but instead of going in and out of stitches lined up head to head, you graft the heads of stitches on one piece to the *sides* of stitches on the other piece. (Actually, as in mattress stitch, you'll be picking up running threads when you're joining to the sides of the stitches.) It's a great method for joining a sleeve top to a sweater body on a dropped shoulder sweater — no shaped armhole or sleeve cap.

Before working this graft, make sure that you can recognize the running thread between the 2 "side" stitches. (Flip back to Figure 15-15 for help identifying running threads.) Then line up your pieces, heads on the bottom, sides above as shown in Figure 15-18 later in this section.

Mattress stitch on other stitches

As long as you can find the running threads between the first 2 edge stitches, you can use the mattress stitch invisibly on a variety of knitted fabrics.

- **Reverse stockinette:** By now, you're probably familiar with purl bumps. If you look closely at the back of stockinette fabric, you see that the purl (or "over") bumps are separated by "under" bumps. The under bumps are the running threads between stitches. Locate the under bump between the two edge purl bumps and alternate picking them up on each piece.

- **Garter stitch:** For garter stitch, you need to pick up only one running thread every other row — the one that's easy to see. The rows in garter stitch are so condensed that the fabric will actually stretch along the seam if you try to pick up the running stitch on every row. So give yourself a break.

- **Ribbed borders:** Working the mattress stitch on a ribbed border is no different from working it on stockinette or reverse stockinette. Study the stitches until you can recognize the column of running threads between the first 2 stitches (knit or purl). Then pick up one running thread at a time as you go back and forth between pieces.

Always take the time to figure out how your ribs will come together where they meet so that your rib pattern will circle around unbroken. If you're working a knit 2, purl 2 rib, begin and end each piece with 2 knit stitches. When you seam them by using the mattress stitch, you'll have a single 2-stitch rib. For a knit 1, purl 1 rib, as long as you begin with a knit stitch and end with a purl stitch, you'll have an unbroken sequence when you seam them.

Keep in mind that in 1 square inch of stockinette fabric, there are more vertical rows of stitches than there are stitches across. For every one inch worth of *heads*, you'll need to pick up one inch worth of *sides* (running threads). This is easy. If your gauge is 5 stitches to the inch and 7 rows to the inch, you'll want to pick up 5 running threads out of every 7 as follows: pick up one running thread, then 2 running threads together, 1 running thread, then 2 together, then 1 running thread. Then start over. If you look closely at Figure 15-18, you'll be able to see that 2 running threads have been picked up every few stitches to compensate for the difference in vertical and horizontal stitches per inch.

Follow these steps to graft heads of stitches to sides of stitches:

1. **With needle and yarn, come *up* through the first "head" stitch on the right or left end of your work. Fig 15-18 shows working from right to left, but you can work in either direction.**

2. **Go around the running thread between the first 2 stitches in the sweater body (see Figure 15-18).**

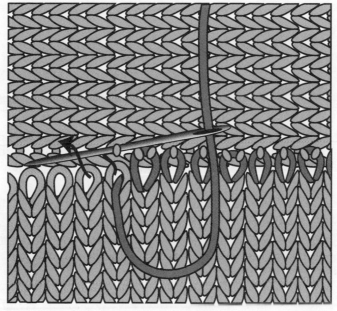

Figure 15-18:
Grafting heads of stitches to sides of stitches.

3. **Go back down into the same stitch you came out of and up through the next stitch — the stitch to the right if you're traveling in that direction or to the left if you're going that way.**

4. **Repeat Steps 2 and 3.**

The best version of this seam is made by grafting "live" stitches to the armhole edge, but you can use it with a bound-off edge as well. Just go into the stitches (heads) directly below the bound off edge.

Sewing seams with backstitch

When you join knitted pieces by using the backstitch, you sew them together in the conventional manner, *right* sides together, tapestry needle moving in and out along the seam line. Try to maintain a knitterly frame of mind and, when possible, work the stitches consistently — either in the trough of running threads between the first two stitches when you're working vertically or along the same row of stitches when you're working with a horizontal edge.

To help you keep your needle going in and out of the right slot between stitches, run a few strands of sewing thread in a bright color along the seam line — in and out of running threads or in and out of a row of stitches. Pull it out when you've completed your seam.

Follow these steps to complete the backstitch:

1. **Pin the pieces right sides together.**

   If you haven't counted rows and one piece is slightly longer or wider than the other, you'll have to ease in the extra fabric so the pieces begin and end in the same place. If you've blocked the front and back to the same dimensions, they should line up fairly well even if one piece has more rows than the other.

2. **With tapestry needle and yarn, bring the needle from the bottom up through both layers one stitch in from each edge. Go around the edge, come out in the same spot to secure the end of the yarn, and bring the bottom edges of the pieces together.**

3. **Go around again and come out 1 stitch farther up from the initial stitch, as shown in Figure 15-19a.**

4. **Insert the needle back through the initial stitch and bring the tip out through both layers again, a few stitches from where it last came out, as shown in Figure 15-19b.**

Keep needle going in and out along running stitches (under bumps) between first two stitches

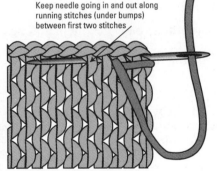
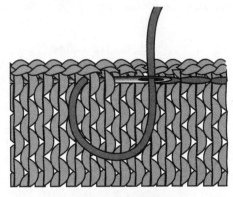

Figure 15-19: Working a backstitch seam.

a. Beginning a backstitch seam.

b. Continuing the backstitch.

5. **Continue in this manner going forward, coming back, and keeping an even tension. Bring your needle in and out in the spaces between stitches and avoid splitting the working yarn as well. Give your knitting a gentle stretch to keep it flexible.**

Determining the order of sweater assembly

Sweaters are usually put together in the following order:

1. Tack down any pockets and work pocket trims or embroidery details on sweater pieces before seaming them together.

2. Sew the shoulder seams. Sew both shoulders for a cardigan or a pullover with a neckband picked up and worked on a circular needle. Sew only one shoulder if you want to work the neckband on straight needles, and then seam the second shoulder and neckband together.

3. Work the neckband and front bands on cardigans.

4. Sew the tops of sleeves to the sweater front and back.

5. Sew the side seams.

6. Sew the sleeve seams.

7. Sew on buttons if you're making a cardigan.

If you've worked your sweater in a medium or lightweight plied yarn, you can use the same yarn for seaming the parts. If the yarn is heavy or a single ply that shreds, use a finer yarn *in the same fiber* in a similar color.

Joining backs to fronts at the shoulder

The first pieces to join after blocking are the front and back at the shoulders (stitches head to head). You have three choices:

- ✔ Use the three-needle bind-off, which makes it possible to bind off the edges of two pieces and seam them together at the same time.
- ✔ Graft the shoulder stitches together.
- ✔ Use the backstitch to seam the pieces together.

Because most knitters would rather knit than sew, the first option is a good one to learn as you start developing your finishing repertoire. Turn back to the previous section "Understanding the basic techniques" for instructions on how to work any of these joins.

When you've joined your front and back pieces at the shoulder, work the neckband of the collar before adding the sleeves or seaming the sides — less bulk to contend with. See Chapter 16 for information about neckline details.

Attaching a sleeve to a sweater body

How you attach the sleeves to your sweater body depends on the design of your sleeve cap and armhole. If you're making a dropped-shoulder sweater or one with an angled armhole and straight cap, you can use the heads-to-sides grafting technique explained in the "Understanding the basic techniques" section earlier in this chapter. If you're making a sweater with a set-in sleeve, you need to use the backstitch for seaming.

Attaching set-in sleeves

To attach a set-in sleeve to a sweater body, follow these steps:

1. **Mark the center of the sleeve cap at the top edge and align it with the shoulder seam on the sweater body, as shown in Figure 15-20.**

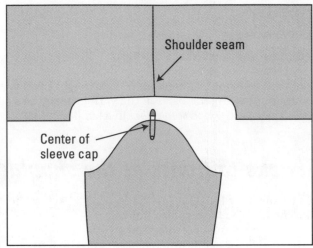

Figure 15-20:
Set-in
sleeve and
armhole.

2. **With the right sides together, pin the center top of the sleeve cap to the shoulder seam.**

3. **Working on only one side at a time, line up the bound-off stitches at the beginning of the armhole, shaping on both the sleeve and sweater body, and pin the pieces together there.**

4. **Pin the sleeve cap edge to the armhole every inch or so between the bound-off stitches and the shoulder, as shown in Figure 15-21.**

5. **Use the backstitch or chain stitch, and with an even tension, sew the pieces together along the edge from the bound-off stitches to the shoulder.**

   Once you've come to the vertical section of the armhole in the sweater body, keep your stitches in the trough between the first 2 stitches.

6. **When you reach the shoulder, pin the other half of the armhole and sleeve in the same manner and sew from the shoulder to the bound-off stitches.**

7. **Steam your seam well, pressing down on it with your fingertips as the moisture penetrates.**

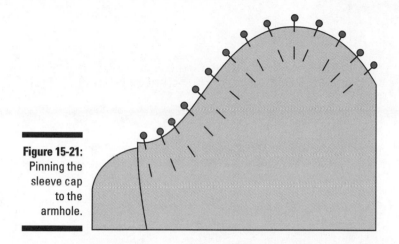

Figure 15-21:
Pinning the
sleeve cap
to the
armhole.

Making side and sleeve seams

Once you've completed the shoulder seams and neckband and attached the
sleeves to your sweater body, the rest is all downhill. If you counted rows and
you have the same number (almost) on the front and back pieces, you can
use the mattress stitch to seam your pieces together — and you won't
believe how good they look.

If your front(s) and back have a different number of rows (off by more than 2),
use the back stitch technique to seam them together.

Chapter 16

Defining Details

• •

In This Chapter

▶ Picking up stitches to create bands

▶ Working neckbands and cardigan borders

▶ Figuring out where to place buttons and buttonholes

• •

Most knitting patterns give you the absolute most basic plan for making a sweater. A generic plan, so to speak. After you work the pieces, block them, and seam the shoulders, you must bring your own expertise to the finishing details — neckbands, edgings, buttonholes, and cardigan bands. This chapter takes you on a beginner's tour of techniques for picking up stitches evenly, making cardigan bands, and installing buttonholes. The procedures shown here by no means exhaust the possibilities, but they're a great place to start.

Pick Up and Go

The cast-on edges of knitted garments are generally very presentable and need no finishing. Not true for the other edges of a knitted piece. Edges not encased in a seam — necklines, the center front edges of a cardigan, and the armholes on a vest, for example — require some kind of finishing or edging. Usually, a neckline is finished with a neckband or collar, a cardigan with bands along the front edges for buttons and buttonholes.

Picking up stitches is a knitter's way to avoid sewing on these extra edgings. Instead of knitting a collar or button band separately and sewing it onto a knitted garment, you can use needle and yarn to pull up new loops along a knitted edge and knit up a border right then and there. Some knitters are so enamored of picking up stitches that they make sleeves for garments by picking up stitches around the armholes and knitting the sleeves upside down to the cuffs. (Knitters are very ingenious.) Follow the instructions in this section to see how to pick up a row of completely new stitches and knit up from there.

You can pick up stitches from three kinds of edges:

- **Horizontal:** Such as the bound-off stitches along a back neck
- **Vertical:** Such as the center front of a cardigan
- **Diagonal or curved:** Such as the shaped section of a front neckline

To pick up stitches, you need the yarn for your project and a needle in the size you plan to use for your band or collar — usually one or two sizes smaller than the one you use for the main part of your knitting.

Be sure to block your sweater back and fronts before picking up stitches. (See Chapter 15 for the details on blocking.) Instead of having to cope with edges that want to curl in or out, your edges to be picked up will lie nice and flat and be easy to work.

Picking up stitches along a horizontal edge

This is the easiest, most straightforward form of picking up stitches — you pick up 1 stitch in each bound-off stitch. When you're done, you should barely see a transition between the stitches you picked up from the new set of stitches. You use this method when picking up stitches along a back neck edge and for the center front group of stitches that form the base of a round neckline. Follow these simple steps:

1. **With the right side facing, starting at the right end of the work, insert the needle into the first stitch (the V) just below the bound-off edge.**

    Make sure that your needle isn't just going under the threads of the bound-off stitches but into the entire stitch below (the one you can see clearly), as shown in Figure 16-1.

Pick up the next loop from
the center of the stitch

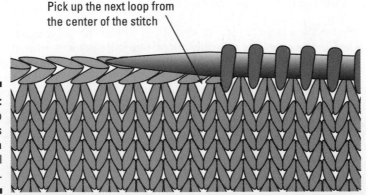

Figure 16-1:
Picking up
stitches
along a
horizontal
edge.

2. **Wrap the yarn around the needle just as if you were knitting and then pull a loop through.**

   You can secure the loose yarn end temporarily by tying it onto your knitting, or you can just start picking up stitches and secure it later. After you pick up the first stitch, the yarn will be taut.

3. **Continue pulling through one loop in each stitch across the row.**

   After you've finished picking up all the stitches you need to, turn your work around (so that the wrong side is facing you) and work the first wrong side row in your stitch pattern. That's all there is to it!

Picking up stitches on a vertical edge

To pick up stitches along a vertical edge — a cardigan front, for example, use the same pull-through-a-stitch procedure that you used to pick up stitches along a horizontal edge. This time, however, bring the loop up between the running threads connecting the first 2 stitches along the edge, as shown in Figure 16-2. Here's how to do it:

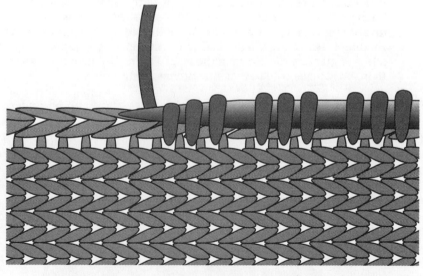

Figure 16-2: Picking up stitches along a vertical edge.

1. **With the right side facing, starting at the right end of your work, insert your needle between the running threads of the first 2 stitches.**

2. **Wrap and pull the new loop through.**

3. **Continue pulling stitches up through the column of running threads until you've picked up the number of stitches you need.**

There are more vertical rows of stitches per inch than there are stitches across. When you pick up stitches along a vertical edge, you match stitches to rows. To keep the correct ratio of stitches to rows, you need to skip a running thread interval every few stitches. You can find more information about this in the section "Bring on the Bands," later in this chapter.

Picking up stitches on a diagonal or curved edge

Most curved edges are made by a series of stepped bind-offs followed by decreases that give a far-from-smooth curved line. Not to worry. Making an attractive continuous curve is the job of the picked-up band.

When you pick up stitches along a curved edge, avoid working in the very edge stitch. Instead, work into a stitch or between stitches at least 1 full stitch in from the edge. Your aim is to make a nice-looking line for your border to begin on, not to see how close you can work to the uneven edge of your knitting.

Pick up stitches on the bound off edges of the back neck and the center front bound off section as shown in the sections earlier in this chapter on picking up stitches on horizontal edges. Along the side neck edges, pick up between running threads, then in the center of stitches as you follow the line of stitches marking the curve of the neck. Figure 16-3 gives you an idea of where to insert your needle to pick up stitches along a curve.

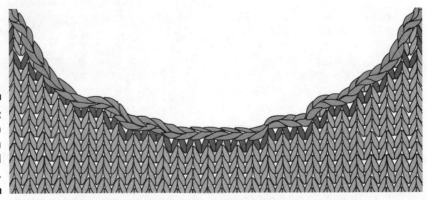

Figure 16-3:
Picking up
stitches on
a curved
neckline.

Picking up: A reality check

Picking up stitches is relatively simple once you get the hang of it. The rub comes when you painstakingly pick up a cardigan border or neckband according to your pattern instructions. You pick up the exact number of stitches called for, knit the correct number of rows given in the stitch pattern, and bind off the last stitch. Then, after all your effort, you find that your otherwise lovely cardigan has a stretched and droopy button band or that you can't squeeze your pullover over your head.

Your pattern will tell you how many stitches to pick up around the neck. It may or may not tell you how to distribute them: so many along the back neck, so many along the left and right front neck edges. It may be up to you to figure out

how many stitches to pick up where. Also, if the gauge on your border pattern is different from the sweater designer's, or if you alter the pattern in any way, your border may not fit as planned. Use your pattern as a guide, but keep a critical eye on your own work. At the first sign that your band is starting to gape or your neckband is shrinking the neck opening, be prepared to toss your sweater map in the backseat. Resolve to pick up stitches according to your knitted pieces, *not* according to your pattern. Just remember that if you're changing the number of stitches to pick up, you must come out with a number that works as a multiple of your stitch pattern.

Bring on the Bands

Cardigan sweaters usually have bands that border the center front. Cardigan bands keep the center edge from stretching, add a neat trim to an otherwise rough-looking edge, and create a place for fastenings — usually buttons. You can knit a cardigan band in two ways: knit them from the bottom up or pick up stitches along the edge and knit them out.

- ✔ **Vertically knit bands** are knitted *in the same direction* as the sweater body, from bottom to top. They can be knitted as part of the front (usually in a noncurling stitch like rib, seed, or garter) or made separately and sewn on later.

- ✔ **Horizontally knit bands** are usually made by picking up stitches along the center front edge and knitting *at a right angle* to the sweater body for an inch or so. Like vertical bands, they can be made separately and sewn on later if, unlike most knitters, you'd rather sew than knit.

It's a good idea to have some understanding of how these bands work — how to plan and make them. Once you're familiar with both types, you just might want to turn your perfectly fitting pullover pattern into a cardigan.

Whenever you're making a vertical or horizontal band in a ribbed stitch (1 x 1 or 2 x 2), end your band on a knit rib and add an extra knit stitch at the outside edge. Edge stitches are never great looking and tend to curl and disappear. If you work an extra knit stitch, it will tuck itself in and become an unobtrusive facing. What you'll notice is a symmetrical band with a tidy edge. Try it!

Bottoms up! Vertical bands

On a vertical band, the stitches in the band are worked in the same direction as the body of the sweater. A vertical band allows you to have a ribbed band that matches the bottom ribbed edge of your sweater.

Knitted-in vertical bands

Vertical cardigan bands knitted in at the same time as the sweater are convenient and easy. No need for further finishing — you just knit to the end of the row for your front panel and continue to knit the stitches for the band. Their drawback is their lack of stability. Worked on the same-size needle as the sweater body, they don't always make a taut edge. If you find your band less than successful, try one of the following remedies:

- Work the band in a stitch pattern with a shorter row gauge, such as a garter stitch band on a stockinette stitch body.

- Work short rows in the band at regular intervals. With short rows you can work 8 rows of border for every 10 rows of sweater, preventing the border from stretching out. Once you figure out which ratio will give you a good match, you can work along confident that your band will sit nicely on your sweater front. (Knitting short rows is a method of decreasing rows. See Chapter 8 for more on short rows.)

- Work the band on separate double-pointed needles in a smaller size (slightly awkward but doable). Just work the band on the smaller short needle, then work the body on the larger needles. When you come back to the band, pick up the other double-pointed needle, work back and forth on the band, leave the smaller needle suspended in the band, and return to the larger needle.

Vertical bands knitted separately

You work these bands as separate pieces and later join them to the front of the cardigan. You just cast on the number of stitches you need to achieve the width of your band and then knit it up — be prepared for a lot of turning! Generally, you make the band on a smaller needle than the sweater body to give it more stability. Sew the band to the sweater edge by using the mattress stitch, which you can find in Chapter 15.

Horizontal picked-up bands

The key to knitting attractive horizontal picked-up bands is to find the right number of stitches to pick up along the front edges of your sweater. Too many and you have a droopy band that stretches the sweater front; too few and the band will draw up the sweater at the center front. Sweater patterns tell you how many stitches to pick up along a cardigan edge in one of two ways: They give you a total number of stitches to pick up or give you a pick-up rhythm, telling you something like, "Pick up 3 out of every 4 stitches."

When you pick up stitches along a vertical edge and knit the band from there, you're working at a right angle to your knitted piece — stitches to rows. One inch worth of rows on the vertical edge has to match one inch worth of stitches on the band you're knitting. Most of the time, this means picking up a few stitches and then skipping one at regular intervals — a pick-up rhythm.

The rhythm method

Be grateful when instructions give you the pick-up rhythm. You don't have to worry about getting a particular number of stitches into a band. You're concerned instead with a ratio of rows to stitches.

Rhythm instructions are easy to test. Along the cardigan edge (or along your gauge swatch), pick up 32 stitches and work in the rhythm your pattern gives you and work them for 1 inch. (See Figure 16-4.) Then check the edge you've made. Be honest. If the band lies nice and flat and doesn't pucker, stretch, or distort the front edge in any way, you're on. Rip out those test stitches and pick up the stitches in the same way all along the edge.

If the band puckers and draws in, you're skipping too many stitches. Instead of 3 out of 4 stitches, try 4 out of 5 or 5 out of 6. And if the band stretches the edge of your sweater, you aren't skipping enough stitches. Try picking up 2 out of 3. Keep experimenting until you get the right ratio.

The section method

If your pattern gives you a total number of stitches to pick up, you have to ration the total out in equal sections along the front edge and pick up stitches evenly along the edge. The following steps tell you how to do this:

1. **Divide the front edge into equal sections about 2 inches long.**

   You can measure out sections with a ruler, but it's better to count rows. Use safety pins to mark them.

2. **Count the number of sections you've made.**

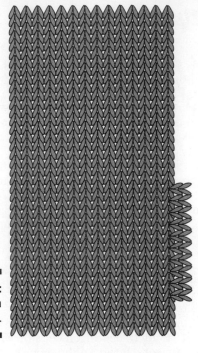

Knitting a test band to see
if you have the correct ratio
of stitches to rows.

Figure 16-4:
Knitting a
test band.

3. **Divide the number of stitches to pick up by the number of sections and pick up that number of stitches between pins.**

   For example, if you are to pick up 120 stitches and you've made 12 sections, pick up 10 stitches in each section.

You might want to test your band by picking up stitches in a few sections (about 6 inches or so) and knitting a band from them to ensure that the band doesn't distort the edge.

Hole in One: Buttonholes

Unless you plan to tie it, snap it, or leave it hanging open, you need to add buttons and buttonholes to a cardigan. Knitted buttonholes are rarely gorgeous, but with a little thought and planning you can make buttonholes that don't sacrifice good looks to workaday function.

The appearance of a buttonhole has a lot to do with how it fits into the background stitch on which it's worked. A buttonhole that looks great on stockinette fabric may look clumsy on a ribbed band, for example. Take the time to work a practice buttonhole in the stitch pattern you're using. Aim to make the buttonhole and stitch pattern work together. If you plan ahead and buy your buttons before working your buttonholes, you can test your buttons in your practice buttonholes to guarantee a good fit.

Horizontal and *vertical* describe how a buttonhole is worked — between rows or between stitches — and/or how they look in a finished band. Keep in mind that a vertical buttonhole lies horizontally on a picked-up cardigan band.

All-purpose horizontal buttonhole

Most knitting patterns give instructions for a generic cast-off/cast-on 2-row buttonhole that read like this: "Bind off 3 stitches, cast on 3 stitches over bound-off stitches on next row." Although this method works, it makes a loose and unattractive buttonhole. The following technique creates a more durable buttonhole, and it looks better, too! (See Figure 16-5.)

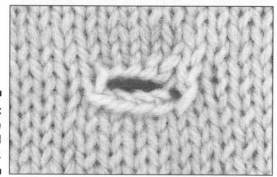

Figure 16-5:
All-purpose horizontal buttonhole.

These instructions are for a 4-stitch buttonhole. This buttonhole takes two rows to complete. To make it, you need to know how to cast on by using the thumb or cable method (see Chapter 8).

To knit Row 1 (a right-side row), follow these steps:

1. **Work to the position of the buttonhole.**

2. **Bind off 4 stitches.**

Before you begin to bind off the buttonhole stitches, you need to knit 2 more stitches after you've reached the buttonhole site. If your instructions tell you to knit 3 and bind off 4, you'll need to knit the 3 stitches and then knit 2 more before you can begin to bind off.

When you've bound off the last stitch, you'll have 1 stitch on the right-hand needle at the end of the buttonhole.

3. **Get ready to knit the next stitch on the left-hand needle by inserting the right-hand needle into it.**

4. **Give the yarn a good tug and then wrap and pull the new loop through.**

5. **Continue working to the end of the row.**

    If you count your stitches, you should have 4 fewer stitches on your needle for each buttonhole you've worked on the row.

To work Row 2, follow these steps:

1. **Work to the bound-off stitches.**

2. **Using the thumb or cable cast on method, *firmly* cast on 4 stitches.**

3. **Before continuing on, with the tip of the LH needle, pick up the outer edge of the loop from the first bound-off stitch (see Figure 16-6) and purl it together with the next stitch. Buttonhole complete.**

4. **Continue to purl or work in pattern to the end of the row.**

    All done!

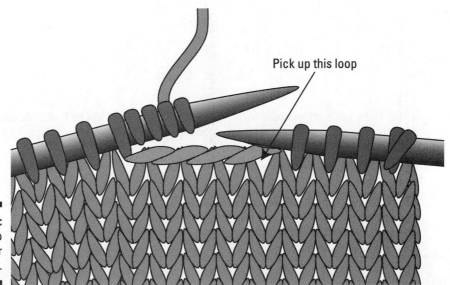

Pick up this loop

Figure 16-6:
Picking up
the outer
loop.

Fitting in

When you sample a horizontal buttonhole, keep in mind that it must work with your button choice *and* with the stitch pattern of your fabric. Whether you make your buttonhole over an odd or even number of stitches helps determine how it fits into its background. If possible, use the following pointers to ensure that your buttonholes blend neatly into their setting.

✔ In a 1 x 1 rib, seed stitch, or moss stitch pattern, make the buttonhole over an odd number of stitches so that you can center it between 2 knit ribs.

✔ In a 2 x 2 rib pattern or double seed stitch, make the buttonhole over an even number of stitches so that you can plant it symmetrically between knit stitches.

Simple vertical buttonhole

A vertical buttonhole (see Figure 16-7) is stretchier than a cast-off horizontal buttonhole. You work each side of the buttonhole with a separate ball of yarn. Test it with your buttons to know how many rows to work. The instructions that follow are for working this buttonhole in 1 x 1 ribbing. Place the buttonhole in the purl trough to camouflage it.

Figure 16-7:
Vertical
buttonhole.

1. **Work Row 1 (right side):**

   1. Work in rib pattern to the spot for the buttonhole, ending with a knit stitch.

   2. Purl into the front and the back of the next (purl) stitch. (See the bar increase in Chapter 8 if you don't remember how to do this. Increasing 1 stitch in the purl trough allows for symmetry — both sides of the buttonhole will be bordered by a purl stitch.)

   3. Continue in the rib pattern to the end of the row.

2. **Work Row 2:**

   1. Work in the rib pattern to the increased stitch (you can recognize it by finding a stray stitch between a knit and a purl), and knit the increased stitch.

   2. Drop the yarn and, with another ball of yarn, beginning with k1, rib in pattern to the end of the row.

3. **Work Row 3: Rib to the buttonhole. Pick up the yarn from the other side and work in rib to the end of the row.**

4. **Repeat Rows 2 and 3 as many times as needed for the buttonhole.**

5. **Close the buttonhole.**

   - On a right-side row, purl the 2 stitches at the top of the hole together.

   - On a wrong-side row, knit them together.

6. **To finish, cut the separate strand and weave in the ends.**

   Weaving the ends in along the edges of the buttonhole helps keep it from stretching.

To work a vertical button in a 2 x 2 rib (k2, p2, k2, p2), work the slit between 2 purl stitches.

Round (eyelet) buttonhole

The eyelet buttonhole (see Figure 16-8) may not appeal to you if you're a seamstress because it doesn't look like a sewn buttonhole — it's round, not slit-like. But I love this buttonhole. It's easy to remember, simple to execute, and adjusts to fit whatever button is appropriate for the yarn and needle size you're using.

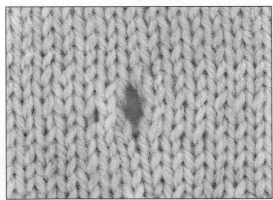

Figure 16-8:
Eyelet
buttonhole.

I give instructions for working this buttonhole in a stockinette fabric, but it also sits discreetly in the purl troughs of ribbing and is all but invisible in garter stitch, which is more than can be said for a lot of knitted slit-like buttonholes. You work this eyelet buttonhole over 1 stitch, and it takes 3 rows to complete. You may want to review how to make the different kinds of yarn overs in Chapter 7 before you get started.

Always pair a decrease with the yarn over when you work an eyelet buttonhole.

To work the buttonhole in stockinette stitch, follow these steps:

1. **Work Row 1 (RS):** Knit to 2 stitches before the buttonhole stitch. Make a double yarn over by bringing the yarn through the needles to the front, then over the RH needle to the back, then to the front between the needles again. Knit the next 2 stitches together. Knit to the end of the row.

2. **Work Row 2:** Purl to the yarn over. Purl into the yarn over letting the second wrap drop from the left needle. Purl to the end of the row.

3. **Work Row 3:** Knit to the stitch above the buttonhole. Knit into the hole (not the stitch above) and carry on.

You can make a slightly smaller buttonhole by making a *single* yarn over instead of a double one. (Wrap only once instead of twice.)

If you're using the eyelet buttonhole in place of a horizontal buttonhole, work it in what would be the second bound-off stitch of a horizontal buttonhole. Use graph paper if need be to figure out where to place the eyelet.

Button Up!

Never underestimate the power of a button to make or break a sweater. The perfect button can enhance the theme of a sweater, such as a shimmery pearl button on a dressy sweater or a rustic bone button on an outdoorsy sweater. On the other hand, the contrast of a rugged button on a dressy sweater or a shell button on a bulky sweater might make an otherwise ho-hum garment really sing. You can even design a whole sweater around a single spectacular button or sew on several buttons that share a theme but don't necessarily match. Be brave and experiment.

Still, you need to keep in mind that buttons, buttonholes, and cardigan bands need to work together; otherwise, you may find that your cardigan refuses to stay buttoned.

Plotting button placement

Knit up the front panel of your sweater (if you're planning a knit-in band) or the band that will carry the buttons before you work the piece with the buttonholes. This way, you can use safety pins or ties of contrasting yarn to mark where the buttons should go and plan where to make the corresponding buttonholes. Make sure to use enough buttons to prevent gaps.

For a woman's sweater, buttons generally go on the left front panel. For a man's sweater, they go on the right.

Begin by positioning the top and bottom buttons on your band. Use your eyes to determine the best distance from the edge for the top and bottom buttons. The top button generally should start ½ inch to 1 inch from the top of the sweater. (For a delicate or medium-weight sweater, place the top button closer to the neck.) The bottom button on a standard cardigan should be ½ inch to 1 inch from the bottom edge. If you're working a jacket-type cardigan, you may want to place the bottom button farther up for freedom of movement.

After you've placed the top and bottom buttons, count the rows (or stitches for a picked-up band) between these buttons to determine where to place the others evenly between them. Don't rely on measuring with a ruler. For greater accuracy, chart your button placement on graph paper.

So happy together: Keeping your buttons buttoned

Cardigan instructions simply tell you to sew on your buttons opposite the buttonholes. But a couple of refinements will help your buttons stay snuggly in their holes and keep your bands lined up neatly.

- ✔ **To place a button for a vertical buttonhole:** Center both the button and the buttonhole along the center line of the front bands. Then plot your button/buttonhole pair so that the center of the button lines up with the top corner of the buttonhole. This will discourage the button from sneaking free.

- ✔ **To place a button for a horizontal buttonhole:** Don't center both the buttons and buttonholes in the center of their respective bands. When you button your sweater, the button won't stay centered in the hole. Instead, the bands will pull apart until the button catches in the corner of the buttonhole. Avoid this sliding problem by moving the button away from the center toward the outer edge of the band. When you button up, your bands will remain aligned one on top of the other.

Sewing on buttons

If you've used a plied yarn for your sweater or project, you can unply a small strand and use it to sew on your buttons. You also can use embroidery thread or simple sewing thread.

As you sew your buttons on, don't be afraid to go into the yarn strand itself. If you try to secure a button by going around the strand and only in and out of the holes between stitches, your button will be unstable and will pull the stitch out of shape.

Most knitted fabric is dense enough to require a button with a shank — a small metal or plastic loop on the back of the button to sew through. If you use a button with holes in it instead, you can make a thread shank to allow room for the depth of the band fabric. The following steps tell you how:

1. **Position a toothpick or skinny double-pointed needle between the holes on the top of the button and sew the button on around it, as in Figure 16-9.**

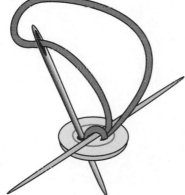

Figure 16-9:
Sewing a button over a toothpick.

2. **Before knotting off, take out the toothpick, lift the button to take up the slack, and wind the thread several times around the "shank" under the button.**

3. **Bring the thread to the wrong side, knot off, and weave in the end.**

Chapter 17

Knitting in Circles

• •

In This Chapter

▶ Selecting circular and double-pointed needles

▶ Discovering how to cast on in circular knitting

▶ Figuring out your gauge

▶ Getting around to making a hat and socks

• •

*W*hen you knit back and forth on straight needles, you make flat pieces that have to be sewn together. When you knit in the round (often called circular knitting), you work on a continuous circular needle or double-pointed needles to knit a seamless tube — great for sweater bodies, sleeves, hats, socks, and mittens. You knit round and round spiral-like with the right side always facing. Intrepid circular knitters have devised ways of making an entire sweater from bottom to top (or top to bottom) without having a single seam to sew up when the last stitch has been bound off.

Knitting in the round makes it easy to work repeating color patterns because the right side of the fabric is all you ever see. You don't need to peer over the edge of your knitting to check what color the next stitch should be. If you're averse to purling for some reason, knitting in the round allows you to skip it entirely — as long as you stick to stockinette stitch.

Choosing Needles for Knitting in the Round

Circular and double-pointed needles are designed for knitting in the round and come in the same sizes that regular knitting needles do. A circular needle consists of two needle tips joined by a flexible cable. Double-pointed needles have points at both ends that allow you to knit around creating a continuous tube. They come in sets of four or five needles of the same size and length. See Chapter 4 for information about needles.

Circular needles

Circular needles come in lengths (measured tip to tip) from 11 to 36 inches. The needle length you choose for your project must have a smaller circumference than the tube you plan to knit. You won't be able to comfortably stretch your stitches around a needle that's longer than the required circumference of the item you're knitting. For example, to knit a hat that measures 21 inches around, you need a 16-inch needle because 21 inches worth of stitches won't stretch around 24 inches of needle. The same goes for working neckbands and collars in the round. The most useful lengths to collect are 16 inches and 24 or 29 inches. 16-inch needles are handy for smaller projects like hats and baby sweaters and work well for neckbands. 24-inch and 29-inch needles work for larger sweaters.

Even if you never knit in the round, you can still use circular needles to work back and forth, turning your work at the end of each row. A 39-inch circular needle makes a good choice for afghans and other large, unwieldy projects. And some knitters like to keep the center of gravity in their lap and not at the ends of straight needles. Circular needles also are a better choice for knitting in tight places (such as automobiles), and you never have to worry about keeping track of two needles rather than one.

When you first take a circular needle from its package, it will be tightly coiled. Run the coil under hot water or immerse it in a sink of hot water for a few moments to relax the kinks. If you want to store circular needles in a way that keeps them straightened out, you can buy a special canvas holder that sorts them by size and allows them to hang uncurled. (See the appendix for a list of sources.) Keep a needle gauge somewhere in the vicinity of your collection of circular needles because the size is rarely marked on them.

Double-pointed needles

Depending on their length, double-pointed needles can accommodate a variety of circumferences. Lengths vary from 5 to 10 inches. The shorter ones are great for socks and mittens, the longer ones for hats and sleeves. Aim for an inch or so of empty needle at each end. If you leave more than an inch, you'll spend too much time sliding stitches down to the tip so that you can knit them; if you leave less than an inch, you'll lose stitches off the ends. (Most diehard knitters-in-the-round use a circular needle for any project larger around than 16 inches. Circular needles are like driving on the interstate — no stop signs. Double-pointed needles require you to slow down a bit where they intersect.)

If you're buying double-pointed needles to make socks or mittens, or if you're getting ready to knit up a neckband for the first time, choose wooden or bamboo needles. Their slight grip on the stitches will keep the ones on the waiting needles from sliding off to oblivion when you're not looking.

Casting On for Circular Knitting

To knit on circular needles, cast your stitches directly onto the needle as you would on a straight needle. (For a refresher on how to cast on, see Chapter 1.) Before you start to knit, make sure that the cast-on edge hasn't twisted around the needle — if you have stitches that spiral around the needle, you'll feel like a cat chasing its tail when it comes time to find the bottom edge. The yarn end should be coming from the RH needle tip, as shown in Figure 17-1.

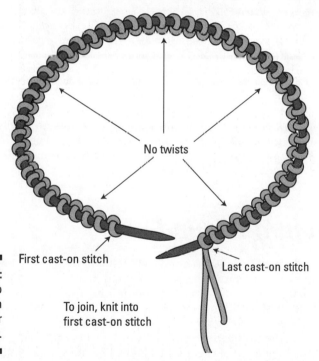

No twists

First cast-on stitch

Last cast-on stitch

Figure 17-1:
Ready to
knit on
circular
needles.

To join, knit into
first cast-on stitch

Casting on and getting started on a set of double-pointed needles can be a little trickier than using single-pointed needles. Instead of trying to cast all your stitches onto one small needle or several separate needles, cast the total number of stitches needed onto a straight needle of the correct size. Then slide them purlwise onto your double-pointed needles, distributing them in equal or close-to-equal amounts. Leave one of the needles free to start knitting with.

If you're using a set of four double-pointed needles, use three needles for your stitches — form them into a triangle (see Figure17-2a), yarn end at the bottom point. Save the fourth (empty) needle for knitting. If you're using a set of five needles, put your stitches on four needles, making a square (see Figure 17-2b), and knit with the fifth (empty) needle. Make sure that the stitches aren't twisted around any of the needles, and you're ready to go.

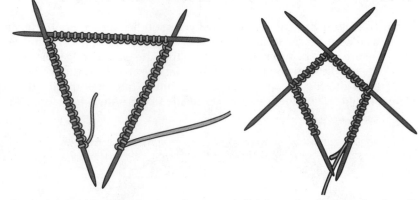

Figure 17-2:
Dividing stitches among double-pointed needles.

a. Knitting on three double-pointed needles   b. Knitting on four double-pointed needles

If you lay your work on a table while transferring your cast-on stitches and arranging your needles, you can keep things steady *and* pay attention to what you're doing at the same time. Trying to focus on one of your needles while the others are flopping around is most annoying.

Up and Running Around

After you've cast on, pattern instructions will tell you to *join* and begin knitting. This simply means that when you work the first stitch you will be bringing the first and last cast on stitches together joining the circle of stitches. To work the first stitch of the round, insert the tip of the RH needle into the first stitch on the LH needle (the first cast-on stitch) and knit or purl as usual. Place a marker on the RH needle before making this first stitch if you want to keep track of the beginning of the round. Figure 17-3 shows the first stitch being made with a marker in place. For more information about markers, see Chapter 4.

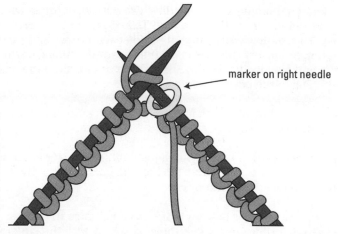

marker on right needle

Figure 17-3:
The first
stitch in a
round on a
circular
needle.

Whether you're working on a circular needle or double-pointed needles, the first and last cast-on stitches rarely make a neat join. To tighten up the connection, you can do one of the following:

✔ Cast on an extra stitch at the end, transfer it to the LH needle, and make your first stitch a k2tog, working the increased stitch with the first stitch on the LH needle.

✔ Before working the first stitch, wrap the yarn around the first and last cast-on stitches as follows: Transfer the first stitch on the LH needle to the RH needle. Bring the ball yarn from front to back between the needles and transfer the first 2 stitches on the RH needle to the LH needle. Bring the yarn forward between the needles and transfer the first stitch on the LH needle back to the RH needle. Bring the yarn back between the stitches, give a little tug on the yarn, and you're ready to knit the first stitch.

For double-pointed needles, use the empty needle to begin working the first round. If the first stitch is a knit stitch, make sure that the yarn is in back of your work. If the first stitch is a purl stitch, bring the yarn to the front between the needles, bring the empty needle *under* the yarn, and insert it to purl into the first stitch on the LH needle. After the first couple of stitches, arrange the back ends of the two working needles on top of the other needles. (Do you feel like you have a spider by one leg?) The first round or two may feel awkward, but as your piece begins to grow, the weight of your knitting will keep the needles nicely in place, and soon you'll be cruising along.

When you knit on double-pointed needles, the stitches worked where the needles meet can be looser than the rest. To keep them neat, give an extra tug on the yarn as you work the first stitch on each needle and remember to tug again after you insert the needle into the second stitch. Or, when you come to the end of a needle, knit the first stitch or two from the next one before switching to the empty needle.

Rounds (rnds) are what you work in circular knitting. *Rows* are what you work in flat (back and forth) knitting.

To work stockinette stitch in the round, just knit. For garter stitch in the round, alternate a knit round with a purl round. For ribs, knit over the knit stitches and purl over the purl ones.

If you're working a sweater pattern that has you change to a larger needle after the bottom border, simply knit the next round with the larger needle. You don't need to slide the stitches from a smaller to a larger needle.

Measuring Gauge in the Round

Although you can knit stockinette stitch back and forth and in the round, your gauge for these two methods may differ. (See Chapter 5 for more on gauge.)

A purl stitch is very slightly larger than a knit stitch. When you work stockinette stitch on straight needles, every other row is a purl row, and the difference in the sizes of your knits and purls averages out. However, when working stockinette stitch in the round, you're always making *knit* stitches, so a knitted piece with the same number of stitches as that same piece done on straight needles will be slightly smaller. Depending on how you knit and the difference in size between your knit and purl stitches, your gauge in stockinette may vary from circular to straight knitting.

If you take your gauge for a project worked on circular needles and you must be exact, make your gauge swatch as follows. Using the same needle you plan to use in your project, cast on 24 stitches or so. Work one row. Break (cut) the yarn, slide your knitting, with the right side facing back to the knitting end of the needle, and knit another row. Break the yarn and repeat. In other words, work all the rows from the right side. Then measure your gauge.

Practice Projects

Although you can make sweaters in the round, the quintessential knit-in-the-round projects are socks, hats, and mittens. These garments hug your ankles, head, and hands, respectively, so making them seamless prevents the potential discomfort of a seam rubbing on skin. (Imagine hiking in socks with seams over the heel and up the back of the ankle!) Plus, knitting these things in the round is a little like knitting sculpture: While you work, you mold the piece to the body part it will cover. The color insert features both of the projects in this section.

Easy Knit-from-the-Top-Down Hat

The beauty of this hat is that you don't have to know how many inches around you want it to be before you start to knit. Start at the top with an inch or so of 4-stitch I-cord (see Chapter 6) and then increase at regular intervals (8 intervals in the round) until the circumference of what you're knitting fits around your head. (Picture a pie cut into 8 pieces — the increases fall along the lines of the wedges. In this case, the pie wedges curve around spiral-like because you'll be increasing on only one side of the wedge.) Then stop increasing and continue to knit round and round for the length you desire from crown to edge. In this version of the hat, you knit in stockinette stitch to the very edge and bind off. The last inch or so rolls up for a brim.

If you're knitting a hat as a gift and you don't know the circumference of the recipient's head, you can use the following numbers and you'll probably be close to the target. In general, hats measure anywhere from 18 inches for a baby, 21 inches for a child, to 22 inches for a woman, to 23½ inches for a man. From crown to brim, count on 7 inches for a baby hat and 9 to 11 inches for an adult hat.

Dimensions: This hat measures 17¾ (19, 20¾, 22½) inches around and 7 (8, 10, 11½) inches from crown tip to brim. The final inch of stitches rolls up. The hat will fit a baby, child, woman, or man, respectively.

Materials: Two 3.5 oz. (50g) skeins (each approximately 99 yards) of Classic Elite Maya 50% lama/50% wool; one set of 5 size 8 double-pointed needles (I strongly recommend wooden needles); one size 8 circular needle, 16 inches; one size 7 circular needle, 16 inches (optional). (When you make a rolled hem, your roll will be a little neater and tighter if you work it on a smaller needle.)

Note: You can work the entire hat on double-pointed needles if you like. If so, choose 8-inch needles. If you plan to switch to a 16-inch needle when you have enough stitches to go around, you can use shorter double-points at the start.

Gauge: 20 stitches make 4 inches. For this project, you can get by with working a gauge swatch back and forth on your needle. A hat is small enough and the fit is flexible enough, that if your gauge is off a little, you'll still have a great hat.

Note: When the pattern tells you to increase, work the next stitch by knitting into the front and then the back of it. See Chapter 7 for more on knitting into the fronts and backs of stitches.

Hat

The hat begins with I-cord (see Chapter 6 if you need a review) on two needles as explained in the following section.

Make I-cord

On double-pointed needles, cast on 4 stitches. With the yarn at the *left* end of the stitches, * insert your RH needle into the first stitch, give a gentle tug on the yarn, and knit the 4 stitches. Don't turn your work around as you normally would. Instead, slide the stitches down to the right end of the same needle so that the yarn is at the left end. Repeat from *. Continue working I-cord until the little tail you're making measures 1 inch (4 inches if you want to tie it into a knot).

Begin circular knitting

Next round (increase round): Increase in the first stitch (2 stitches on RH needle); with an empty needle, increase in the next stitch, (2 stitches); with a third needle, increase in the next stitch (2 stitches); and with the fourth needle, increase in the last stitch — 8 stitches on 4 needles. Pin a small safety pin on the running thread between the first and last stitches of the round to help you keep track of the beginnings of the rounds.

Next round: * Knit the 2 stitches on the first needle. *With the freed needle, knit the two stitches on the next needle; repeat from * 2 more times — another round completed.

As you continue working in the round, always knit the stitches of one needle onto a freed needle, then work the next needle's stitches onto the just freed needle, and so on. Move the safety pin up to the running thread between rounds from time to time so you can keep track of where they begin and end.

> Next round (inc round): Knit, working an inc in every stitch — 16 stitches (4 on each needle).
>
> Next round: Knit.
>
> Next round (inc round): * K1, inc in next stitch; rep from * to end of round — 24 stitches (6 stitches on each needle).
>
> Next round: Knit.
>
> Next round: * K2, inc in next stitch; rep from * to end of round — 32 stitches (8 stitches on each needle).
>
> Next round: Knit.
>
> Next round (inc round): * K3, inc in next stitch; rep from * to end of round — 40 stitches (10 on each needle).

Are you beginning to see the pattern? You're working 8 sections and increasing 1 stitch on the last stitch of each section every other round. If it helps you can place a marker *after* each increase and work your increases in each stitch just before your markers. Continue in this pattern. After a few more rounds, take a good look at your knitting. You'll see a pinwheel pattern of little bumps curving to the right. The bumps are the increased stitches. If you lose track of whether you're working an increase row or a plain knit row, you can tell by looking at your knitting. If you see a bump at the base of the increased stitch on the needle, you've just increased in the last round and are ready to work a plain row. If you see a full V stitch above an increased bump, you've just finished a plain knit row and are ready for an increase row.

Continue in this pattern, increasing at the end of each of the 8 sections until you have 80 stitches on the needles — 10 in each section.

When you have 80 stitches on your needle, you can start the next round with the size 8 circular needle, but place a marker at the beginning of the round to keep your place. Continue in pattern until you have 88 (96, 104, 112) stitches. Continue to knit every round without increasing until the hat measures 6 (7½, 8½, 9½) inches from the beginning. Work another 4 rows on the smaller needle and bind off.

Varying the hat

You can vary this hat in the following ways:

- End the hat with a 1 x 1 rib.

- Work the hat in stripes.

- Work the hat by using a different kind of increase.

- Work the hat according to the instructions, but work in reverse stockinette stripes or garter stitch stripes (see Chapter 2) after you finish the increase pattern.

- Work a Fair Isle color pattern between the end of the increases and the beginning of the roll.

- Work the increases in 6 sections instead of 8 (increase to 6 stitches instead of 8 on the first increase row, and then follow the same procedure).

- Attach a braid, pompom, tassel, beads, or shells to the I-cord handle.

- Embroider the hat.

- Work the hat in the reverse direction. Measure around your head, multiply the number of inches around your head by the gauge of your knitting, add or subtract a few numbers from the answer to get a number divisible by 8, and cast on that many stitches. Knit or work a pattern stitch for 4 inches. Then work a k2tog decrease spaced evenly 8 times around your needle. These decreases will mark the 8 sections you'll be decreasing in. Continue to decrease every other round in the 8-section pattern until you have 8 stitches left. K2tog (4 times) in the next round. Work I-cord on the remaining 4 stitches for as long as you like.

Basic Socks

Socks are one of the most satisfying things to make — easy enough to be fun to work, but tricky enough to be interesting. And they're relatively quick to make. The pattern I offer here is very basic. If you can knit in the round and decrease and you know how to pick up stitches, you can make them.

Sizes: For a baby, child, woman, and man

Materials: 1 (1, 2, 2) 3.5-ounce (100-gram) skeins (each approximately 200 yards) of Harrisville Highland-Style Knitting Yarn; one set of 5 size 7 double-pointed needles

Gauge: Approximately 20 sts = 4". A little difference either way won't matter too much with socks.

Note: You can make these socks in a solid color or work stripes in the leg and the heel sections and the toe in a different color.

Leg: Cast on 28 (32, 40, 44) stitches. Divide the stitches on the 4 needles as follows:

- **Needle #1:** 8 (8, 10, 12) stitches
- **Needle #2:** 6 (8, 10, 10) stitches
- **Needle #3:** 8 (8, 10, 12) stitches
- **Needle #4:** 6 (8, 10, 10) stitches

Arrange them as shown in Figure 17-2b, making sure that the stitches aren't twisted around the needle. (Needle #1 is the first on the left.) Insert the free needle knitwise into the first stitch on needle #1. Holding needle #4 close to #1, wrap and knit the stitch. You've joined the circle. Place a marker on the needle and knit the next stitch. Purl the next 2 stitches. Continue in k2, p2 rib to the end of the needle. With the free needle, work in k2, p2 rib to the end of the next needle. Repeat on needles #3 and #4.

Starting with needle #1, continue to work in 2 x 2 rib until the piece measures 4½ (6, 8½, 10) inches from the beginning. End at the marker (1 stitch on RH needle). Leave the marker in place while you work the heel flap.

Heel flap: Knit 7 (7, 9, 11) stitches. Turn your work. Purl to the end of the needle and then, with the *same* needle, continue to purl the 6 (8, 10, 10) stitches from needle #4. You'll have 14 (16, 20, 22) stitches on the needle with the marker. These are your heel flap stitches. (The remaining stitches are instep stitches and aren't worked until the heel is complete. Just leave them on needles #2 and #3 for the time being.)

Starting with the right side facing: * Slip 1, knit 1; repeat from * to end of row. The slip 1, knit 1 pattern makes a durable stitch for the heel.

Next row: Slip 1, purl to end. Repeat these 2 rows 6 (7, 9, 11) times more. End ready to start a right-side row.

Turn the heel: (In this section, you make your heel flap curve up toward the leg at a right angle — very exciting.) On your heel flap stitches, knit to the marker. Transfer the marker to the RH needle and then knit 2, slip slip knit, knit 1. Turn your work — 2 (3, 5, 7) sts left on the LH needle.

Next row (rs): Slip 1, purl 5 (2 stitches past marker), purl 2 together, purl 1, and then turn your work.

Next row: Slip 1, knit across to within 1 stitch of the gap made when you turned your work, slip slip knit (working the stitches on either side of the gap together), knit 1, and turn your work.

Next row: Slip 1, purl to within 1 stitch of the gap, purl 2 together, purl 1, and turn your work.

Continue in this manner until all the stitches have been used up, ending with a wrong-side row; you now have 10 (10, 12, 14) stitches. Heel turned!

Heel gusset: Next row (rs): Knit to the marker. Take out the marker and put a safety pin between the 2 stitches to show you the beginning of the round.

With an empty needle, knit the second half of the heel stitches. With the same needle, pick up 7 (8, 10, 11) stitches along the left side of the heel flap.

If you've slipped the first stitch of each row when working the heel flap, you'll have a series of large loops to pick up from along the edge. To pick up the first stitch, insert your needle into the edge loop and draw a loop (stitch) through. Continue to insert and draw a loop through for the number of stitches you need to pick up. You will have to skip a stitch here or there to come out with the right number — you've worked more rows than you'll need for stitches.

With an empty needle, knit across the first half of the instep stitches. With an empty needle, work across the second half of the instep stitches. With the freed needle, pick up 7 (8, 10, 11) stitches along the heel flap and knit across the remaining heel stitches to the safety pin at the center back.

Starting at center back, you should have half the heel stitches plus the 7 (8, 10, 11) stitches picked up along the heel flap on needle #1, half the instep stitches on needle #2, the other half of the instep stitches on needle #3, and the other 7 (8, 10, 11) picked-up stitches and remaining heel stitches on needle #4.

Shape the gusset: Starting at the marker, work to the last 3 stitches on needle #1, knit 2 together, knit 1, and work across the instep stitches. On needle #4, knit 1, slip slip knit, and work to the end of the round.

Next round: Knit the round without decreasing.

Repeat these two rounds, decreasing at the end of needle #1 and the beginning of needle #4 until you have a total of 28 (32, 40, 44) stitches — 7 (8, 10, 11) stitches on each needle. Continue in stockinette stitch until the foot measures 4½ (6½, 7, 7½) inches from the back of the heel.

Shape the toe: Knit to last 3 stitches of needle #1, slip slip knit, knit 1; knit 1, knit 2 together at the beginning of needle #2; knit to the last 3 stitches of needle #3; slip slip knit, knit 1, knit 1, knit 2 together at the beginning of needle #4.

Next round: Work 1 round plain in stockinette stitch. Repeat these 2 rounds until 3 stitches remain on each needle. Break off the yarn, leaving an 8-inch tail. With a tapestry needle, draw the end through the stitches on the needles and pull snug.

Chapter 18

Working from the Blueprint: Starter Garments

Making accessories is a great way to develop your knitting skills and become familiar with their creative possibilities, but making a soft, attractive garment to wrap yourself in is another kind of satisfaction entirely.

The sweaters in this chapter use simple shapes and garment construction to introduce you to sweater-making and enable you to apply the techniques and skills you've learned in this part of the book. You can see them photographed in the color insert.

The sweaters are basic with detailed instructions. You can knit up all three quickly on relatively big needles. Make them as they are or as a springboard for trying ideas from earlier chapters. Or you can work up one of the variations listed at the end of each pattern.

In the materials sections, I list the specific yarns used in the sweaters you see photographed, but feel free to substitute any other yarn that meets the gauge. Or you can take what you've learned about gauge and dimensions and apply it to these patterns, writing in your own numbers to achieve the fit you want.

Sleeveless Cowl Neck Sweater in the Round

This sweater knits up in no time in a wonderful bulky tweed blend from Classic Elite. Any other yarn with the same gauge will work as well. Because the yarn is heavy, you could even try holding two finer yarns together to create your own yarn blend. Just make sure that you arrive at the correct gauge. You can see this sweater featured in the color insert.

The shape of this sweater is as straightforward as you can get — the body is a rectangular tube with a few stitches taken out at the armholes. It's worked in the round, so all you do is cast on, knit up, and bind off. If you need a reminder on circular knitting, turn back to Chapter 17 for specifics. See the shape of the sweater in the schematic in Figure 18-1.

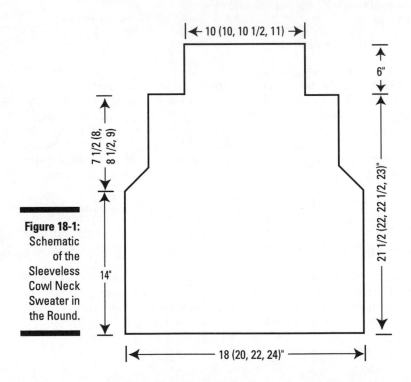

Figure 18-1: Schematic of the Sleeveless Cowl Neck Sweater in the Round.

Sizes: To fit small (medium, large, extra-large). Directions are for size small, with the larger sizes in parentheses. If only one figure is given, it applies to all sizes.

Knitted measurements: Bust 36 (40, 44, 48) inches; length 21½ (22, 22½, 23) inches

Materials:

- Seven 3.5-ounce/100-gram skeins (each approximately 99 yards) of Classic Elite Gatsby (70% wool, 15% viscose, 15% nylon) in French Blue or a color you like
- One size 11 circular needle (24 inches long)
- One size 11 circular needle (16 inches long)
- One set of 4 or 5 size 11 double-pointed needles (optional — for detachable sleeves)

Gauge: 12 stitches and 18 rows to 4 inches over stockinette stitch on circular needle

When you work in the round, you make stockinette fabric by knitting every round.

Knitting the body

With the longer, 24-inch circular needle, cast on 108 (120, 132, 144) stitches. Then do the following:

> Place marker on tip of RH needle to mark beg of round and bring tips of needles together to work the first stitch (called joining the round). Knit 54 (60, 66, 72) sts for the front of the sweater.
>
> Place a second marker and k54 (60, 66, 72) sts for the back, ending at the first marker.
>
> Continue in St st (knit every rnd) until piece measures 14 inches from beg (the cast-on rnd), ending at the first marker.

When knitting in the round, you can make a neat join between the first and last cast-on stitches by casting on 1 extra stitch. With your needles poised to knit, but before working the first stitch, transfer the first stitch on the RH needle (the extra stitch) to the LH needle. Place the marker on the RH needle, k2tog from the LH needle, and continue the round.

Shaping the armholes

When your piece measures 14 inches, it's time to start shaping the armholes. When you knit the body of a sweater in the round, you have to switch to flat knitting when you get to the armhole. From this point on, you can still work on your circular needle, but you have to work in the flat style — back and forth, right-side *rows* alternating with wrong-side *rows*.

Before you start to shape the armhole, use a safety pin or tie a small piece of yarn on a stitch on the needle to mark the first shaping row. Place it somewhere near the center front. You can measure from this marker when you need to know the depth of the armhole.

Shape the armhole for the front yoke as follows:

> Next row (RS): Bind off 2 (2, 3, 3) sts, work to 2nd marker. Place rem 54 (60, 66, 72) sts on holder or draw a piece of scrap yarn through sts with tapestry needle. Turn your work so the WS is facing.

> Next row (WS): Bind off 2 (2, 3, 3) sts, work to end of row — 50 (56, 60, 66) sts. Cont in St st and bind off 1 st at each edge every other row 4 (5, 5, 6) more times — 42 (46, 50, 54) sts.

After you complete the shaping, work the stitches on your needle evenly in stockinette stitch (knit RS rows, purl WS rows) until the piece measures 7½ (8, 8½, 9) inches from the beginning of the armhole shaping, ending with a wrong-side row (the last row you work is a wrong-side row). Measure from your marker, not along the edge of the armhole.

When you finish shaping the armhole, start binding off the shoulder stitches as follows:

> Next row (RS): Bind off 6 (8, 9, 10) sts for shoulder, work to end.

> Next row: Bind off 6 (8, 9, 10) sts. Place remaining 30 (30, 32, 34) sts on holder or scrap yarn.

Instead of binding off the shoulder stitches, you can leave them on a holder or piece of scrap yarn (use a different holder or scrap yarn for each shoulder and the neck stitches), and when you've completed the back yoke, you can work the 3-needle bind-off to seam the shoulders. (You can find instructions for the 3-needle bind-off in Chapter 15.)

Repeat the shaping instructions for the front yoke.

Finishing and making the collar

Sew (or knit together) the shoulder seams. Then make the collar:

> Starting at right shoulder seam, with RS facing and smaller circular needle, transfer 30 (30, 32, 34) sts from back neck and 30 (30, 32, 34) sts from front neck to needle — 60 (60, 64, 68) sts.

Join (bring tips of needles together), place marker, and work in rnds St st until collar measures 6 inches. Bind off loosely and weave in ends.

Most knitting instructions tell you to 'bind off loosely' for a good reason. Bound off edges tend to be inelastic and frequently draw the fabric in. This isn't an issue on a cowl neck as in this sweater, but if you're working a fitted neckband and your bind off row is tight, there's a good chance you may not be able to get your sweater over your head. The easiest way to remedy this is to work the bind off row on a size or two larger needle.

Adding detachable sleeves

If it gets chilly, you can pull these ribbed sleeves on over your arms and you'll stay as warm as toast.

Note: As you work the sleeve, you increase stitches along a center "seam" (this isn't a true seam, just a designated couple of stitches. To maintain the rib pattern, work the new stitches on the first two increase rounds as knit stitches. After the third increase round, work the new stitches as purls to follow the rib pattern. As you continue to increase, work the increased stitches as knits or purls, depending on how they fall in the rib. See Figure 18-2. If you want a refresher on how to make increases, see Chapter 8.

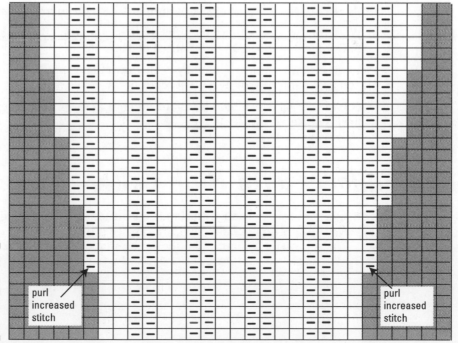

Figure 18-2: Working increases into the rib pattern.

purl increased stitch

purl increased stitch

Cast on 28 (32, 32, 32) stitches on a regular needle.

Transfer sts to 3 or 4 double-pointed needles, dividing sts evenly on each needle and leaving one needle free. Place marker on RH needle and with free needle, begin first rnd: Work in k2, p2 rib to end of round. Continue in rib for 2¼ inches.

Next round (inc round): K1, m1, work in rib to last st before marker, m1, k1. Continue to work in rib pattern, working increase round every 12 (12, 12, 10) rnds 5 (5, 5, 7) times more — 40 (44, 44, 48) sts now on needles. As you make these increases, notice that they always happen on either side of the 2 center back "seam" stitches.

Continue in pattern until sleeve measures 19 (19, 19½, 19½) inches or desired length when you're wearing it on your arm. Bind off *loosely*.

Varying your sweater

You can alter this basic sweater pattern in any of the following ways:

- Go down two needle sizes and work the sweater in a 2 x 2 or 3 x 3 rib for a clingy fit.

- Work the sweater in a striped pattern using lots of different colors and textures of yarn.

- Work the sweater in an eyelet pattern or lace pattern from Chapter 10.

- Work the sweater with a 3-inch ribbed or garter stitch border along the bottom and a ribbed or garter stitch collar.

- Work the sweater with a chunky cable down the front. (Remember to add 1 or 2 stitches for every 4 stitches of the cable.)

- Forget the collar and bind off all the stitches at the shoulder for a boat-neck sweater.

Red Pullover with High Collar

Here's another basic sweater with simple construction — an angled armhole, flat sleeve top, and no neck shaping. You can see it pictured in the color insert. The schematic in Figure 18-3 shows the shapes of the pieces.

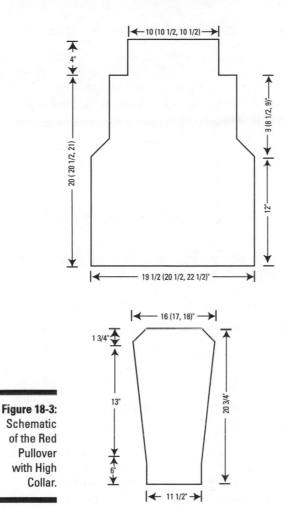

Figure 18-3:
Schematic
of the Red
Pullover
with High
Collar.

I've given this sweater a contemporary feeling by using a long ribbed border on the sleeve cuffs and body and then blocking out the rib for a relaxed shape that doesn't cling. You can knit this sweater quickly on size 9 needles. You'll want to make one in each of your favorite colors.

Notice that I've worked the shaping (increases and decreases) 2 stitches in from the edges instead of right at the edge. I think it's easier to seam this way, and I like the way it looks. The line of shaping stitches is clearly delineated. If you prefer to hide your shaping, by all means work your increases and decreases on the 2 stitches at each edge.

Sizes: To fit small (medium, large). Directions are for size small, with the larger sizes in parentheses. If only one figure is given, it applies to all sizes.

Knitted measurements: Bust 39 (41, 45) inches; length 20 (20½, 21) inches; width at upper arm 16 (17, 18) inches

Materials:

- Eight 3.5-ounce (100-gram) skeins (each approximately 132 yards) of Cascade Yarns Pastaza in #19 (red)
- One pair size 9 needles
- One size 9 circular needle
- 16-inch stitch holders

Gauge: 16 stitches and 21 rows to 4 inches in stockinette stitch on larger needles

Note: You'll need to know how to decrease and increase to make this sweater. If you need to review these techniques, turn to Chapter 8.

Knitting the back

Cast on 78 (82, 90) sts, and then follow these steps.

> Row 1: * K2, p2; rep from *, end k2.
>
> Row 2: * P2, k2; rep from *, end p2. Cont in k2, p2 rib until piece measures 6 inches from beg, end with ws row.

Ribbing looks the same on both sides. Take a look at the very bottom cast on edge. It looks different from each side — small bumps on one side, overlapping strands on the other. Decide which you want to be the right side, and pin a safety pin to that side to remind you which is which.

After you finish the ribbing, work in stockinette stitch until the piece measures 12 inches in length. End with a wrong-side row.

Before you start to shape the armhole, pin a safety pin or tie a small piece of yarn on a stitch on the needle to mark the first shaping row. Place it somewhere near the center front. You can measure from this marker when you need to know the depth of the armhole. Then do the following:

> Next row (RS): Bind off 2 sts, knit to end of row.
>
> Next row: Bind off 2 sts, purl to end of row — 74 (78, 86) sts.

Because you can bind off only at the beginning of a row, the bind-off for the right armhole is one row lower than the bind-off for the left armhole. But no one will ever notice the one-row difference.

Next row (RS) *dec row:* K2, k2tog, knit to last 4 sts, ssk, k2 — 72 (76, 84) sts.

Knitters use k2tog and ssk decreases at either end of a piece when they are shaping to make the shaping stitches symmetrical. In this case, the decreases slant away from each other. If you want them to slant in the other direction, just work ssk on the right side of your piece and k2tog on the left side. Your shaping stitches will still mirror each other.

Next row: Purl. Cont to work in St st, working the dec row given above every other row 3 (3, 5) times more — 66 (70, 74) sts. Cont in St st until piece measures 8 (8½, 9) inches from beg of armhole, end with a WS row.

Next row (RS): Bind off 14 (14, 16) sts, work 38 (42, 42) sts, bind off rem 13 (14, 16) sts. Place neck sts on scrap yarn.

Instead of binding off the shoulder stitches, you can leave them on a holder or piece of scrap yarn, and when you've completed the front, you can work the 3-needle bind-off to seam the shoulders. (See Chapter 15 for instructions for the 3-needle bind-off.)

Knitting the front

Work the front exactly the same as the back.

Knitting the sleeves

Cast on 46 sts; then follow these steps:

Next row (RS): *K2, p2; rep from *, end k2.

Next row: *P2, k2; rep from *, end p2. Cont to work in k2, p2 rib until piece measures 6 inches from beg.

Next row (RS): Knit.

Next row: Purl.

Next row (RS) *inc row:* K2, m1, knit to end of row, m1, k2 — 48 sts. Cont in St st, working inc row every 8 rows 2 (1, 0) times, then every 6 rows 6 (7, 5) times, and then every 4 rows 0 (2, 7) times — 64 (68, 72) sts now on needle. Work in St st until piece measures 19 inches from beg, end with ws row.

Shape the sleeve cap (the top of the sleeve) as follows:

Next row (RS): Bind off 2 sts, knit to end.

Next row: Bind off 2 sts, purl to end — 60 (64, 68) sts.

Next row *dec row:* K2, k2tog, work to last 4 sts, ssk, k2. Cont in St st, working dec row 3 (3, 5) times more — 52 (56, 56) sts.

Finishing and making the collar

Block the pieces gently. (Either wet block or steam gently. See Chapter 15 for blocking instructions.) If you've left the shoulder stitches open on scrap yarn, you can seam them using the 3-needle bind off or graft them. Otherwise, use the backstitch to seam the shoulders. See Chapter 15.

Use the circular needle to make the collar. Starting at the right shoulder seam, with the right side (and back piece) facing you, transfer 38 (42, 42) stitches from the back neck and 38 (42, 42) stitches from the front neck to the needle. Place a marker, join (bring tips of circular needle together to work the first stitch), and work rounds in stockinette stitch for 4 inches. Bind off loosely.

Sew the side and sleeve seams.

Varying your sweater

You can alter this pattern in a number of ways. Here are some ideas:

- ✔ Work the entire sweater in k2, p2 rib.
- ✔ Work a different stitch pattern above the ribbing or for the entire sweater. Don't forget to check your gauge.
- ✔ Work the ribbed borders in a different color.
- ✔ Work a chevron or scalloped border. Add stripes to it.

Toggle Jacket

This is a cozy jacket to wear on autumn walks or when the thermostat doesn't kick in (see it featured in the color insert). You can forget the pockets if you don't want to bother with them.

I've given the instructions in the standard way, with lengths measured in inches. But I've also given you the number of rows to knit for each piece. If you knit by the row method, you won't have to figure out where to put the buttonholes — I've already done that for you. (Of course, if your row gauge is different from mine, your sweater and sleeves may be a bit shorter or longer than the length given in the pattern.)

I've also included a chart of the left neckline shaping. If you find it comforting to work from a graph, you may want to chart out the right front piece so that you can track where you are and when to work each buttonhole. Figure 18-4 shows the schematic of the pieces you'll be making.

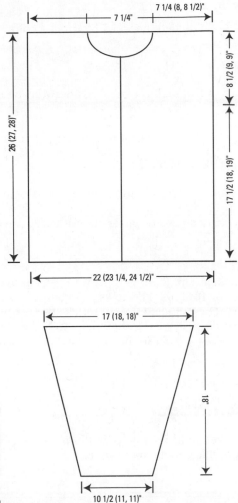

Figure 18-4:
Schematic
of the
Toggle
Jacket.

Sizes: To fit small (medium, large). Directions are for size small, with the larger sizes in parentheses. If only one figure is given, it applies to all sizes.

Knitted measurements: Bust 44 (46½, 49) inches; length 26 (27, 28) inches; width at upper arm 17 (18, 18) inches

Materials:

- ✔ Eight (eight, nine) 3.5-ounce/100-gram skeins (each approximately 110 yards) Tahki Soho Bulky Tweed in #373

- ✔ One pair each of sizes 10 and 10½ needles

- ✔ Several yarn holders or scrap yarn to hold stitches

✔ Stitch markers or scrap yarn

✔ One skein or part of a skein of medium-weight yarn in a color close to the main color for seaming

✔ Five toggle buttons

Gauge: 12 stitches and 16 rows to 4 inches over stockinette stitch using the larger needles

Working the back panel

With the smaller needle, cast on 66 (70, 74) stitches; then do the following:

Starting with a RS row, work 8 rows of garter st (knit every row). Change to larger needle.

Next row (RS): Knit.

Next row: Purl. Cont in St st (knit RS rows, purl WS rows) until back measures 26 (27, 28) inches or 104 (108, 112) rows from beg, end with a WS row. Work 22 (24, 26) stitches, bind off the center 22 stitches, and knit the remaining 22 (24, 26) stitches. Place the shoulder stitches on holders or thread the stitches on to scrap yarn so they're ready for the 3-needle bind-off.

Making pocket linings

You'll need to have your pocket linings ready to go when you work the front panels of the sweater. Best to make them in advance.

A note on counting your rows

The easiest way to count rows in stockinette stitch is to count the purl bumps on the wrong side. They're clearer to see than the Vs on the right side. When you're counting rows on the Toggle Jacket, you can easily identify the first 8 rows of garter stitch border. Start counting the stockinette rows beginning with Row 9.

Use safety pins to help you keep track of the number of rows you've worked. Pin the first stitch you want to count from; then, as you knit, stop every once in a while and count 20 rows. Place a safety pin every 20 rows. That way you won't have to count from the very beginning each time.

With the larger needle, cast on 23 stitches. Then do the following:

> Work in St st until pocket measures 7 inches (28 rows) from beg, end with ws row.
>
> Next row (RS): Bind off 1 st, work to end.
>
> Next row (WS): Bind off 1 st, work to end — 21 sts remaining. Place sts on holder.
>
> Make another pocket the same way.

Working the left front panel

With the smaller needle, cast on 36 (38, 40) sts, and then proceed as follows:

> Starting with RS row, work 8 rows of garter st. Change to larger needles.
>
> Next row (RS): Knit.
>
> Next row: K6, place marker, purl to end of row. The 6 sts between the edge and the marker make the front border. While you work the rest of the sweater front in St st, you'll be working these 6 stitches in garter stitch.
>
> Cont as established (working 6 border stitches in garter stitch and the rest of the stitches in St st) until piece measures approximately 9 inches (38 rows) from beg, end with WS row.

To add a pocket, follow these steps:

> Next row (RS): K5 (6, 7), place next 21 sts on holder (you'll finish them off later), slide the 21 pocket sts from holder to LH needle with RS facing. Knit across the 21 pocket sts, then knit the remaining 10 (11, 12) sts in the established patterns.
>
> Continue as established until piece measures 23¼ (23¾, 24¾) inches or 93 (95, 99) rows from beg, end with RS row.

Count garter stitch ridges up the center front border right side facing. You're ready to start the neck shaping when you have 46 (47, 49) ridges up the center front (not counting the cast on ridge at the very bottom edge).

Left front neck shaping (decreases) always takes place on the *wrong* side of the piece. Right front neck shaping always takes place on the *right* side of the piece.

To shape the neck, do the following:

Next row (WS): Bind off 10 (9,9) sts, purl to end.

Next row: Knit.

Next row (WS) *dec row:* Purl 2, p2tbl (purl 2 sts through back of loop (see Chapter 8 if you need to be reminded how to do this), purl to end. Cont to dec at neck edge on WS rows 3 (4.4) more times — 22 (24, 26) sts. Cont in St st until front is same number of rows as back.

Thread the 22 (24, 26) shoulder sts onto a piece of scrap yarn to secure them.

Figure 18-5 shows the chart for the left front neck shaping. Make your own chart for the right front.

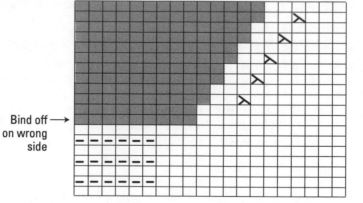

Figure 18-5: Chart of the Toggle Jacket's left front neck shaping.

Bind off → on wrong side

Working the right front panel

You work the right front panel the same as the left front panel with these changes: You work buttonholes along the center front border as you go and work the neckline shaping on RS rows instead of WS rows.

To make an eyelet buttonhole, you need to remember how to work a double yarn over. Bring the yarn to the front through the needles, wrap the yarn over the top and under to the front again. When you knit the next 2 stitches together, the yarn crosses the needle, and there will be two wraps on the needle. On the following row, knit into the wraps. As you knit into the wraps, you'll catch one yarn over and the other will simply slide off the needle. (You need a double wrap to make the buttonhole large enough to accommodate the buttons.) Then carry on with the rest of the row.

With the smaller needle, cast on 36 (38, 40) sts. Then do the following:

Beginning with a RS row, work 8 rows of garter st. Change to larger needles.

Next row (RS): Knit.

Next row: P30 (32, 34) sts, place marker, k6 (these 6 stitches make the front border).

Cont as established (6 border stitches in garter stitch, the rest of the sweater front in St st) until piece measures approximately 4½ (5, 6) inches or 18 (21, 25) rows [9 (10, 12) garter st ridges from beg], end with a WS row.

Next row (RS) *beg buttonhole:* K2, make double yo, k2tog, knit to end of row.

Next row: Purl to marker, knit next 6 sts, including yo.

Next row (RS): K2, knit into *hole* (go into the hole as if it were a stitch) made by yo, knit to end of row.

As you continue to work the right front panel, work the buttonholes as follows:

- ✔ **Size small:** On rows 37, 55, 73, 91
- ✔ **Size medium:** On rows 39, 57, 75, 93
- ✔ **Size large:** On rows 43, 61, 79, 97

For all sizes, continue as established until the piece measures approximately 9½ inches or 38 rows, ending with a wrong-side row.

To add a pocket, follow these steps:

Next row (RS): K10 (11, 12) sts, place next 21 sts on holder, slide the 21 pocket sts to LH needle with RS facing, knit the 21 pocket sts, knit the remaining 5 (6, 7) sts.

Cont in St st and garter st patterns as established until piece measures 23¼ (23¾, 24¾) inches or 94 (96, 100) rows from beg, end with a ws row.

You're ready to start the neck shaping when you have 47 (48, 50) garter ridges up the front. To shape the neck, do the following:

Next row (RS): Bind off 10 (9, 9) sts, knit to end.

Next row: Purl.

Next row (RS): K2, k2tog, knit to end of row. Cont to dec at neck edge on RS rows 3 (4, 4) more times — 22, 24, 26 sts. Cont in St st until front is same number of rows as back. Thread the 22 (24, 26) shoulder stitches onto a piece of scrap yarn.

Making the sleeves

With smaller needles, cast on 32 (34, 34) stitches. Then do the following:

> Beginning with RS row, work 8 rows in garter st. Change to larger needles.
>
> Next row (RS): Knit.
>
> Next row: Purl.
>
> Next row (RS) *inc row:* K2, m1, knit to last 2 sts, m1, k2 — 34 (36, 36) sts.
>
> Small size: Cont to work in St st, working inc row every 6 rows 9 more times — 52 sts.
>
> Medium and large sizes: Cont to work in St st, working inc row every 6 rows 7 more times, and then every 4 rows 3 more times — 56 sts.

Regardless of the size of your garment, after you finish making the increases, work the stitches on your needle evenly until the piece measures 18 inches from the beginning.

Bind off stitches if you'd like to sew the tops of the sleeves to the sweater. Or, if you'd like to graft the sleeve stitches to the sweater body for a smoother join, thread the stitches onto a piece of scrap yarn instead of binding off. See Chapter 15 for information about grafting sleeve tops to sweater bodies.

Finishing your sweater

Block the sweater pieces. Steaming is the quickest method and for this simple project without a lot of textured stitches, steaming will work just fine.

Join the shoulders using the 3-needle bind off shown in Chapter 15.

Adding the collar

With the smaller needles and the right side of the jacket facing you, starting at the *center* of the front band, do the following:

> Pick up 18 sts to shoulder, pick up 22 sts along back neck, pick up 18 sts to center of front band — 58 sts. (Need a refresher on picking up stitches? Turn to Chapter 16.)
>
> Work in garter st for 12 rows (6 ridges), change to larger needles, and continue in garter st for 12 more rows.
>
> Work 1 more RS row. Then bind off loosely.

Adding pocket trim

Do the following to finish off the pocket stitches on each front:

> Slide the 21 pocket stitches resting on a holder to the LH needle from left to right with the RS facing.

> Turn your work so the WS is facing. With the yarn you'll be using to knit the trim, make a slip knot on the RH needle, knit the 21 sts, turn work, and cast on 1 more st as follows: Insert RH needle into first st, wrap and pull through a loop, leaving old loop on LH needle. Bring new loop to the right and put it on the LH needle — 23 sts. (This is the cable cast on. You can see pictures to illustrate the steps in Chapter 8.)

> Work in garter st for 5 more rows (3 ridges). Bind off in knit sts from the WS for a final garter ridge.

> Using your knitting yarn, or a smooth medium weight yarn in a similar color, sew the sides of the pocket trim to the jacket front using mattress stitch.

> Do the same to the pocket stitches on the other front.

Sew the pocket linings to the inside of the jacket. You can use a strand of the knitting yarn for this and work a version of the mattress stitch going back and forth between running threads on the sweater body and the pocket. Or tack it down in any unobtrusive way.

Sewing it all together

Measure down 8½ (9, 9) inches on either side of the shoulder seam and mark the armhole with safety pins or yarn markers. Sew or graft the tops of the sleeves to the front and back between the markers.

Sew up the side and sleeve seams using mattress stitch.

Sew the buttons to left front jacket band opposite the buttonholes.

Use a medium-weight smooth yarn in a similar color to work the seams. It will be much less bulky than a heavier yarn.

Varying your jacket

Try some of the following variations to design a garment all your own:

- ✔ Work the entire sweater in garter stitch or the stitch pattern of your choosing. See Chapter 2 for ideas.
- ✔ Use different buttons: a matching set or five different buttons.
- ✔ Make it shorter for a cropped version or longer for a coat.

- Make it in stockinette stitch, only with "self" edges that roll in a casual fashion, and forget the collar.

- Add patch pockets instead of hidden ones. Work the sweater without pockets. When you've completed it, knit two squares the size you'd like your pockets to be. Sew them onto the fronts unobtrusively with mattress stitch, or use a decorative blanket stitch in a contrasting color.

- Make patch pockets and the collar in a different color. Add 4 or 5 inches to the sleeve in the same color as pockets and collar and turn up the sleeves for contrasting color cuffs.

- Work a little embroidery on the pockets and collar.

Getting to know Elizabeth Zimmerman

There are many ways to knit a sweater (or a hat, or a mitten, or a sock). Elizabeth Zimmerman, one of the knitting greats, has, in her phrase, "unvented" many a technique for knitting garments. Her innovative use of circular knitting, her commonsense approach to knitting garments and accessories, and her incomparable wit have earned her a strong following. Look for these books for knitting ideas and basic patterns that allow ample room for your own creative variations.

- *Knitter's Almanac* (Dover, 1985)

- *Knitting Without Tears* (Simon & Schuster, 1973)

- *Knitting Workshop* (Schoolhouse Press, 1981)

For more titles, contact Schoolhouse Press, 6899 Cary Bluff, Pittsville, WI 54466; call 800-968-5648; or go to www.schoolhousepress.com.

Part V
The Part of Tens

"So how old were you when you realized that metallic yarn didn't come from steel wool?"

In this part . . .

Check out this part for exercises for unkinking your knitting muscles, and a useful list of my favorite knitting books. Check them out for ways to continue to explore the creative possibilities of two needles and a ball of yarn.

Chapter 19
Ten Great Knitting Books

The ten books in this chapter comprise a sampling of books that I consider the classics. Most are currently in print, and where I have been able to, I list the most recent edition. Some are out of print but are still available through libraries, the interlibrary loan service, and used book dealers. (Amazon.com can put you in touch with booksellers who have copies of specific out-of-print books.)

New books on various aspects of knitting are published all the time. You can find them in catalogs, local bookstores, and yarn shops. Knitting magazines regularly publish reviews (see the appendix for information on great knitting magazines), so look through their suggestions for books to seek out.

In addition to the books listed here, check the sidebars on knitting greats Barbara Walker (Chapter 2) and Elizabeth Zimmerman (Chapters 18) for information on their books.

Mary Thomas's Knitting Book and Mary Thomas's Book of Knitting Patterns

These books were originally published in 1938 and are now published inexpensively in their original format by Dover (1972). They're excellent reference books with lots of reference material and discussion on the structure of knitting.

Knitters Handbook

By Montse Stanley, Reader's Digest (1999). Excellent reference with dozens of techniques and their variations.

Alice Starmore's Book of Fair Isle Knitting

By Alice Starmore, Taunton Press (1988). History of Fair Isle knitting, discussion of the use of colorways, charted stitch patterns, and patterns for sweaters.

Patterns for Guernseys, Jerseys and Arans: Fishermen's Sweaters from the British Isles

By Gladys Thompson, Dover Publications (1971). A short history of the classic fisherman sweaters of the Aran Isles with charted patterns.

Knitting in the Nordic Tradition

By Vibeke Lind, Lark Books (1984). Wonderful book with information on specific knitting technique and general construction of hats, mittens, and sweaters.

The Complete Book of Traditional Scandinavian Knitting

By Sheila McGregor, St. Martin's Press (1984). Short histories of the knitting traditions in the various Scandinavian countries with lots of charted patterns.

Folk Socks

By Nancy Bush, Interweave Press (1995). Good basic sock book that explains sock construction, shows ways to vary them, and gives patterns for great-looking socks.

Knitting Lace: A Workshop with Patterns and Projects

By Suzanna Lewis, Taunton Press (1992). An absolutely thorough exploration of the structure of knitted lace and how to make it.

Designing Knitwear

By Deborah Newton, Taunton Press (1992). An inspirational book by a master knitwear designer.

Creative Knitting: A New Art Form

Mary Walker Phillips, Van Nostrand Reinhold Co. (1971). An excellent exploration of the underlying structures of knitted fabric and their creative possibilities.

Chapter 20

Ten Unkinking Exercises for Knitters

*E*specially while you're learning to knit, sitting in one position and concentrating on your knitting for long (or even short) periods of time can make you stiff in your shoulders and neck. And holding onto needles and making small movements with your hands can cramp fingers and wrists. The exercises in this chapter (they're so helpful that I couldn't stop at just ten) will keep your body's knitting parts loose and limber and fatigue-free if you take a break and do them every 20 minutes or so while you're working.

Relaxing Your Neck

Start your unkinking with neck stretches. Sit (or stand) with your arms hanging naturally at your sides. Keeping your shoulders relaxed, do the following moves and remember to breathe. Be sure to keep your shoulders relaxed and down while you stretch.

Tilt your head forward gently to stretch the back of your neck. Hold for 5 seconds. Turn your head to one side and look over your shoulder. Hold for 5 seconds. Slowly turn and look over the other shoulder and hold. Next, tilt your head to one shoulder. Hold for 5 seconds. Finally, tilt your head to the other shoulder and hold.

Sloughing Stress from Your Shoulders and Arms

At the first signs of tightness in your shoulders or arms, take a few minutes to do the stretches that follow:

- Bring your shoulders up to your ears and hold for 3 to 5 seconds. Then relax your shoulders down into their natural position.

- Interlace your fingers and stretch your arms out in front of you, palms facing away from your body. Hold the stretch for 10 seconds.

- Keeping your fingers interlaced and your palms facing out, reach your arms over your head. Stretch your arms up until you can feel the stretch as far down as your upper rib cage. Hold for 10 to 15 seconds and breathe deeply.

- Standing or sitting up straight, interlace your fingers and cup the back of your head. Bring your elbows back and pull your shoulder blades together. Hold for 5 seconds and then relax.

- Place your right hand on your left shoulder. With your left hand, grab your right arm just above the elbow and look over your right shoulder. As you look over your shoulder, use your left hand to gently pull your right arm to the left until you feel a stretch. Hold for 10 to 15 seconds. Change sides and stretch the other shoulder and arm.

Relaxing Your Hands and Wrists

The stretches that follow will uncramp tightened fingers and wrists. Keep breathing as you do them.

- Spread and stretch your fingers as widely as you can. Hold for 10 seconds. Then ball your fingers into fists and hold for another 10 seconds.

- With your arms extended straight out in front of you, bend your wrists back, bringing your fingers straight up. Hold for 10 seconds. Then bend your wrists down and point your fingers to the floor. Hold again.

- With your elbows bent and close together, interlock your fingers. Rotate your hands and wrists clockwise 10 times. Reverse direction and rotate your hands in the other direction 10 times. This feels a little awkward at first.

✔ With your arms extended in front of you, slowly rotate your wrists so that the backs of your hands are together. Hold this position and enjoy the stretch.

✔ Arrange your hands in prayer position palm to palm in front of you. Keeping your palms together, rotate your wrists away from your body, pointing your fingers downward until you feel a mild stretch. Don't let your shoulders tense up or lift while you do this one. Hold for 5 to 8 seconds.

End your stretches with arms hanging loosely at your sides, shake your hands, and wiggle your fingers.

That should do it. Now, back to knitting.

Appendix A

Knitting Resources

· ·

Magazines

Knitting magazines are a great source of technical information, patterns, inspiration, suppliers, knitting news, new products, and happenings. Be sure to subscribe to at least one and check out the others at your favorite magazine rack.

Interweave Knits
201 E. Fourth Street
Loveland, CO 80537-5655
970-669-7672
800-340-7496 (subscriptions)
www.interweave.com
E-mail: knits@interweave.com

Knitters
XRX, Inc.
231 S. Phillips Ave.
Suite 400
Sioux Falls, SD 57104-6326
605-338-2450
www.knittinguniverse.com

Vogue Knitting
233 Spring St., 8th Floor
New York, NY 10013
212-937-1522
www.vogueknitting.com

Knitting Supply Sources

These suppliers of yarn and knitting books and accessories also publish catalogs showcasing their products. You'll find others through the Web sites listed in the Web site section later in this appendix.

Halcyon Yarn
12 School St.
Bath, ME 04530
800-341-0282
www.halcyonyarn.com

Kruh Knits
Gateway Bus Ctr.
1097 Hwy. 101 S.
Suite D5
Greer, SC 29651
800-248-KNIT
Kruh Knits is a supplier for machine knitters, but it has lots to interest hand knitters as well — blocking equipment, for example.

Patternworks
P.O. Box 1690
Poughkeepsie, NY 12601
800-438-5464
www.patternworks.com

Schoolhouse Press
6899 Cary Bluff
Pittsville, WI 54466
800-968-5648
www.schoolhousepress.com

The Wool Connection
34 E. Main St.
Old Avon Village North
Avon, CT 06001
800-933-9665
www.woolconnection.com
E-mail: wool@tiac.net

Wooly West
P.O. Box 58306
Salt Lake City, UT 84158
888-487-9665
www.woolywest.com
Specializes in socks and other small projects

Yarn Barn of Kansas
930 Massachusetts
Lawrence, KS 66044
800-468-0035

Yarn Suppliers

The yarns used for the projects in this book are readily available in most yarn shops. If you can't find them or a reasonable substitute locally, you can contact the company directly to find out where to get them.

Berroco, Inc.
P.O. Box 367
Uxbridge, MA 01569
508-278-2527
E-mail: info@berroco.com

CascadeYarns
2401 Utah Ave. S.
Seattle, WA 98134
800-548-1048

Classic Elite
300 Jackson St.
Lowell, MA 01852
978-453-2837

JCA International, Inc. (Reynolds and Lopi)
35 Scales Lane
Townsend, MA 01469
978-597-8794

Plymouth Yarn Co.
P.O. Box 28
Bristol, PA 19007
www.plymouthyarn.com
E-mail: pyc@plymouthyarn.com

Tahki-Stacy Charles, Inc.
1059 Manhattan Ave.
Brooklyn, NY 11222
718-389-0411
E-mail: tscz@rcn.com

Web Sites

Numerous Web sites provide information on knitting and supplies. Most sites link you to other sites. You could spend days visiting yarn country via cyberspace.

For the beginner looking for more information on the basics, try the following sites:

- ✔ `www.learntoknit.com`, **sponsored by the Craft Yarn Council of America**
- ✔ `www.knittersreview.com/links.aspknittersreview`
- ✔ `www.knitting.about.com`
- ✔ `www.tkga.com`, **site for The Knitting Guild Association**

For more general information and sources, check out these sites:

- ✔ `www.gohotline.com/crafts/knitting.html`
- ✔ `www.debbiebliss.freeserve.co.uk`
- ✔ `http://yarnXpress.com`
- ✔ `www.eknitting.com`
- ✔ `www.forknitters.com`
- ✔ `www.halcyonyarn.com`
- ✔ `www.patternworks.com`
- ✔ `www.knittinggoddess.com`
- ✔ `www.stylesalon.com`
- ✔ `www.woolconnection.com`
- ✔ `www.knitting-and.com`
- ✔ `www.gotyarn.com`

Keep your knitting handy while you wait for sites to download.

Appendix B
Practicing with More Samplers

Sampling Lace: The Basic Unit

The absolute best way to learn how knitted lace is constructed is to try out different ways of combining yarn overs and decreases. This lace sampler (Figure B-1) begins by showing you two ways to make a basic eyelet — the fundamental lace unit. Each of the five eyelet V-shapes (called *chevrons*) that follows uses a different pairing of yarn over and decrease for a different effect. If you make this sampler, you'll gain a working knowledge of the basic lace moves and practical skill at reading lace charts.

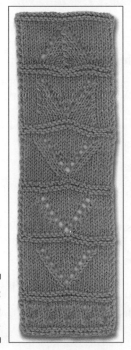

Figure B-1:
Lace
sampler.

Before you start the lace sampler, flip back to Chapter 7 to review how to make a yarn over between 2 knit stitches. And check Chapter 8 for how to work the k2tog and ssk decreases and Chapter 10 for how to follow a lace chart.

It's best to make this sampler with a medium- or sport-weight yarn in a light color. Mercerized cotton is a good choice for lace knitting. Its crispness will help you to read the pattern details.

Knitting the sampler

You'll need the charts in Figure B-2 to complete this sampler. The first row of the sampler is a right-side row. Cast on 21 stitches, then follow these steps:

1. **Work Rows 1–5: Knit (garter stitch for a flat border).**

2. **Work Row 6: Purl.**

   The right side of your sampler should be facing you when you're ready to start the next row.

3. **Reading the chart from right to left and starting at the bottom right-hand corner, work the 8 rows of Chart 1, ending with a wrong-side row.**

4. **Repeat Steps 1 and 2.**

5. **Work Charts 2 through 6 to complete the sampler.**

   Note: Charts 2 through 6 show only the right side of the pattern. After you work Row 1 of each chart, purl the next wrong-side row. Then work Row 3 from the chart, purl the next wrong-side row, and so on. At the end of each chart, work one more purl row followed by the 6 rows of Steps 1 and 2.

Notes on the sampler

In the first row of eyelets in Chart 1, the yarn over is followed by an ssk decrease. In the second row, the yarn over is preceded by a k2tog decrease. In both cases, the decreases slant *away from* the yarn over. Slanting the decease away from the yarn over opens it out a bit.

In Chart 2 (the first chevron pattern), the decreases are worked adjacent to the eyelets and slant in the same direction the eyelets are moving. The eyelets moving to the right are preceded by a k2tog decrease that slants to the right. The eyelets moving to the left are followed by an ssk decrease that slants to the left. Notice the strong diagonal lines made by the stacked decreases and how they frame the eyelet lines.

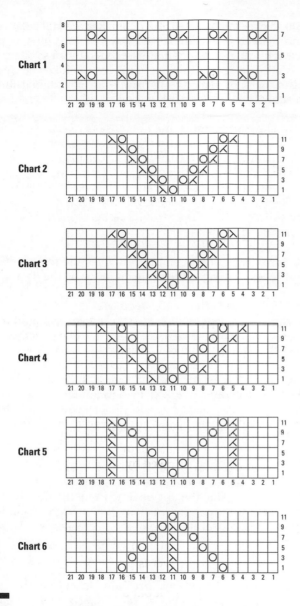

Figure B-2:
Using charts
to make
your lace
sampler.

Key

☐ knit on RS, purl on WS

⊙ yarn over

◪ k2tog

◪ ssk

◪ sl 1, k1, psso

In Chart 3 (the second chevron pattern), the decreases are still adjacent to the eyelets, but they are slanted in the direction *opposite* to the one the eyelets are traveling. The eyelets moving to the right are preceded by an ssk decrease, which slants to the left. The eyelets moving to the left are followed by k2tog decreases slanting to the right. Here, the decreases are almost invisible, and there is no hard diagonal line. The effect is softer.

In Chart 4 (the third chevron pattern), the decreases are slanted in the same direction the eyelets are traveling, but this time they are one stitch away from the yarn over, not right up next to it. In this example, the diagonal line is wider because not only do the decreased stitches form a strong diagonal line, the stitches in between the decreases and the yarn overs slant in the same direction as well. They are, in knitter-speak, biasing. (You may remember from Chapter 8 that stitches slant away from a series of increases toward a corresponding series of decreases.)

If you were to put more stitches between the yarn over and the decrease, you would have more stitches slanting in the same direction as the decrease. Try it!

In Chart 5 (the fourth chevron pattern), the decreases aren't spaced the same distance from the yarn overs. Instead they are stacked vertically. As the eyelets move apart, they get closer to the decreases. There is still one decrease for every yarn over, but the pairing is different in each row. Notice the strong bias of the stitches in the sections between the decreases and the yarn overs. Also, because of the stacked decreases, the bottom edge of the pattern dips down slightly at the column of decreases. Worked inside a knitted fabric for a few rows, this waviness will be absorbed or possibly balanced by other decreases in the pattern. If you work this chevron pattern on a garment border, you can accentuate the scallop by pinning it out and blocking it well.

In Chart 6 (the final chevron pattern), the V is turned upside down and the decreases are worked as a series of double decreases down the center. Notice that this time the biasing is inside the upside-down V, in the direction of the decreases, and the rest of the stitches remain in their straight up-and-down position. This pattern dips, too, at the base of the decreases. Worked side to side and for a single vertical repeat, this little pattern makes a sweet scalloped border for a child's sweater.

Note: This sampler is adapted in a very abbreviated form from the excellent book *Knitting Lace: A Workshop with Patterns and Projects* by Susanna Lewis, Taunton Press, 1992. If you want to find out just about everything there is to know about lace knitting, get a copy of this book.

Sampling Color: Assorted Slip-Stitch Sampler

This Assorted Slip-Stitch Sampler (Figure B-3) introduces you to a number of different ways you can use the simple slip-stitch technique. As you work the sampler, keep checking how each little move changes the look of your knitted piece. A stitch slipped one row looks different than a stitch slipped two rows or four rows.

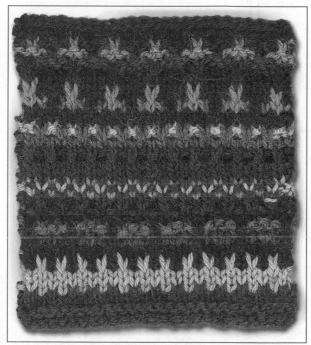

Figure B-3:
Assorted
Slip-Stitch
Sampler.

The chart for the slip-stitch sampler (Figure B-4) works the same as other charts. Each square represents a stitch. Each square has a symbol that tells you how to work the stitch. What the square doesn't tell you is which color to use. Instead, all the color changes are indicated to the right of the row you're working. For example, to the right of Row 1 is "Color A." This tells you to start with color A. Work the first row of the chart in color A and continue in A until you see "Color B" next to the row you are to knit. Drop A and start B. All color changes are made on *right-side* rows.

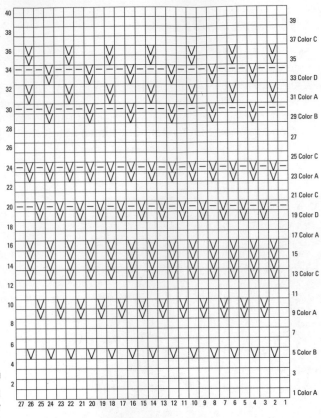

Figure B-4:
Chart for
Assorted
Slip-Stitch
Sampler.

Key

☐ knit on RS, purl on WS

⊟ purl on RS, knit on WS

Ⓥ slip stitch as if to purl on right and wrong side rows

Only use *one* color when you're working a row. It's tempting to try to knit slip-stitch patterns with two colors at a time because you *see* two colors in each row in the final fabric — but don't. The second color you see comes from the row below. The slipped stitch pulls it up into the current row. You create the second color by slipping stitches, not by knitting them.

When changing colors, work the old color and the new color together for the first stitch and then drop the old color. Be sure to knit the two strands together as one stitch on the next row, or you'll find your sampler starting to grow stitches on the right.

You'll need four colors for this sampler: A, B, C, and D.

Begin in the bottom right-hand square of the chart and work from right to left for right-side (odd number) rows. Work from left to right on wrong-side (even number) rows.

Knitting your sampler: Cast on 27 stitches. With A, work 4 rows of garter stitch (knit, knit, knit, knit) to create a border. Then knit your sampler as follows:

1. **Next row (RS): With A, work Row 1 of the chart in Figure B-4.**

2. **Next row (WS): Work Row 2 of the chart.**

3. **Continue working each row of the sampler chart, changing yarn on right-side rows as indicated to the right of the chart.**

   You can carry yarns up the side for a few rows, but when they become too entangled to work with easily, cut them. You can weave them in later.

After you've worked the sampler once, try it again by using yarns of different textures. Throw in a mohair, a tweed, or a yarn with something sparkly in it. The sequence of patterns in this sampler look great worked into the ends of a scarf, as a border on a sweater, or as the fabric for a pillow or bag.

Appendix C

Some Thoughts about Color

When you're in a yarn shop surrounded by colors — luscious colors, soft colors, rich colors, subtle colors — spilling from bins and piled in baskets, you'd think it would be easy to pick a few congenial skeins and create a pleasing color combination in a knitted piece. But several skeins of yarn that make a stunning combination grouped together in a basket may lose their appeal when worked together as neighboring stitches in a knitted fabric.

Knitting successfully with different colors is a matter of trial, error, and "aha" discoveries. There are no rights or wrongs, just what pleases you and what doesn't. Being able to choose and combine colors for your own ends is a matter of experience and a willingness to keep at it. It's a matter of allowing your intuitive response to colors to guide you first and then fine-tuning your choices with some theoretical knowledge that can help you perceive colors better and allow you to think about color, not just respond to it.

Color Theory for Knitters

Becoming familiar with basic color theory and how it applies to knitting in general and your eye in particular will help you arrive at color combinations you like with the least amount of frustration. Far from taking the spontaneity out of color work, a little familiarity with the color wheel and the relationships of colors to each other can often help you to figure out what's wrong when colors aren't working together and suggest ways to fix or improve the grouping.

The first thing to master is the language of color.

The color wheel. The color wheel (see Figure C-1) is a way to arrange colors so you can talk about their properties and compare them. If you aren't familiar with the color wheel, picture a bicycle wheel where connecting colors of the rainbow — red, orange-red, orange, yellow-orange, yellow, green-yellow, green, and so on — are arranged along the tire between the spokes. Your local library is sure to have books on color theory that show the color wheel.

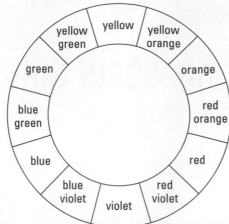

Figure C-1:
The color
wheel.

Color words. Although you may regularly use words like *color* and *shade* in everyday talk about color, these words have very specific meanings in color theory. They describe in detail particular things about colors and how they relate to each other. You probably know most of them already:

- ✔ *Hue.* A hue is a color, for example red, blue, green, yellow, purple, and so on.

- ✔ *Value.* Every hue has a value. It can be light, medium, or dark — and anywhere in between. If you add white to red, you'll get pink. Pink is lighter in value that red. Pink is a *tint.* If you add black to red, you get maroon. Maroon is darker in value than red. Maroon is a *shade.* If you were to take a black-and-white photograph of a red sock next to a green sock of the same value, they would look identical in the picture. On the other hand, if you were to take a black-and-white photo of a red sock and a pink one, you would see a contrast. In color language, *tint* and *shade* refer to the *value* of a *hue.*

- ✔ *Tone.* If you add gray of the same value to a hue, it doesn't change the value of the hue, but it changes the *intensity* or brightness and clarity of the hue. The hue becomes a *tone.*

  Tones play a large part in knitting. A yarn spun from a blend of fibers dyed robin's egg blue, lavender, and natural sheep's gray has a subtle diluted feeling, less dense than single-color yarns. It will read in your knitted piece the way watercolor does in a painting.

Color relationships — complementary and analogous colors. Colors situated next to each other on the color wheel are *analogous* colors, for example, red and purple are analogous. Colors that lie across the wheel from each other are *complements,* such as red and green. You can go around the color wheel and look at the different hues and their neighboring colors. Every hue has analogous colors on either side of it and a complement across from it.

When you combine *analogous* colors, no matter which point on the color scale you take them from, you get color combinations that share certain characteristics. Generally, they are subtler than other combinations and are often moody and quiet in feeling. They tend to suggest temperature. Though it isn't always true, don't you usually think of blues shading to purple as cool colors? And reds shading to orange and yellow as warm?

Color combinations that use *complementary* colors, on the other hand, tend to be bold and strong. Because they don't share any base color, they don't reinforce the temperature or feeling a color may have in company with its neighbors. Instead, complements balance each other and tend to cancel each other out on the mood level. They stimulate your eyes, keeping them moving back and forth.

Contrast. Contrast is the key to a successful color combination. If a color combination lacks contrast, it can lack interest. But don't confuse contrast with clash. Contrast can be mild and subtle or strong and bold. It's easiest to imagine contrast in terms of hue. Red and aqua, for example, make a strong contrast because they're on opposite sides of the color wheel. If you put colors that sit next to or near each other on the color wheel, such as red and purple, you create subtle contrast. You can also make contrast by using the same hue in different values, for example red with pink. The greater the difference in value, the greater the contrast.

Be sure to spend time actually knitting with a variety of colors and experimenting and finding out through trial and error the unique way that color works in knitted fabric. Yarn as a color medium brings special qualities to the project you use it in, just as glazes do to pottery and paint does to canvas. Get to know your medium, and you'll become a color virtuoso.

There's more to color than you think

If "color" makes you think of crayons and paint boxes, remember that before dyes were introduced to the Fair Isles, beautiful color patterns were worked in nothing but the grays, blacks, browns (called moorit), and whites of the native sheep. The lovely Delft tiles from Holland use two colors, blue and white. The blue-on-blue indigo-dyed textiles made by the Yoruba in Nigeria are a testament to the power and potential beauty in subtle contrasts of a single color or simple two-color combinations.

Experimenting with Color

If you find yourself overwhelmed when choosing colors, starting with one of the following exercises can help jump-start your own color sense. Work a small geometric pattern (refer to the triangle chart in Chapter 12) organized around one of the following:

- Make a denim-inspired study: blues on blue.

- Combine an unlikely group of strong colors on a neutral, charcoal, or cream background. The neutrality of the background will help the strong colors to harmonize.

- Pick a group of analogous colors (colors next to each other on the color wheel) and vary them in value, for example purples, magentas, and blues or reds, oranges, and golds.

- Take the group of analogous colors from the study in the preceding exercise and stretch the range to include another hue. If you're working with greens and blues, add purple or stretch a little further and include magenta.

- Take an analogous grouping and combine it with accents of the complement. Take a number of greens of different values and intensities and combine them in a pattern with accents of tomato red and orange for a perky combination, or with accents of maroon and rust for a more subtle one.

- Work with almost equal amounts of two complementary colors in clear hues, such as tomato red and aqua. Your piece will almost vibrate. Then try this with tonal versions of the same colors — a soft brown-red with celadon green, or deep cherry red with sage.

- Work with a variety of hues that all share the same value, such as all pastels or all deep rich shades.

- Take your pastel or dark color swatch and add a touch of a contrasting value, such as a deep magenta on a pastel swatch, a melting lavender on a dark swatch.

- Combine complementary colors of different purity and intensity with each other, for example gray green and emerald with magenta and tomato.

Color "rules" are never the final word. Your eye is. Experiment and see what works. When something doesn't quite appeal to you and you make a change that brings it all together, see whether you can articulate what the change was: hue, value, intensity, or proportion. By asking yourself questions about what you see and what you like, you'll soon be turning out color combinations that bring you untiring pleasure.

Index

• Z •